Worldviews and the American West
The Life of the Place Itself

Worldviews and the American West
The Life of the Place Itself

Edited by

Polly Stewart, Steve Siporin,
C. W. Sullivan III, and Suzi Jones

Utah State University Press
Logan, Utah

Utah State University Press
Logan, Utah 84322–7800

"Faith of Our Fathers" by George Venn is printed by permission of the author. Copyright © 2000 George Venn

"Icons of Immortality: Forest Lawn and the American Way of Death" by Elliott Oring is reprinted by permission of the author. It originally appeared, in slightly different form, as "Forest Lawn and the Iconography of American Death," *Southwest Folklore* 6, no. 1 [1985]. Copyright © 1979 Elliott Oring.

"John Campbell's Adventure, and the Ecology of Story," by Jarold Ramsey is reprinted by permission from *Northwest Review* 29 (1991).

"The Language of Animals" by Barry Lopez is reprinted by permission of Sterling Lord Literistic, Inc. Copyright © 1998 Barry Lopez.

"Local Character" by Kim Stafford is reprinted by permission of the author from *Having Everything Right: Essays of Place* (Seattle: Sasquatch Books, 1997). Copyright © 1997 Kim Stafford.

Manufactured in the United States of America

Library of Congress Cataloging-in-Publication Data

Worldviews and the American West : the life of the place itself / edited by Polly Stewart ... [et al.].
    p. cm.
  Includes bibliographical references.
  ISBN 0-87421-407-6 (pbk. : alk. paper) —ISBN 0-87421-408-4 (hardback : alk. paper)
    1. West (U.S.)—Ethnic relations. 2. Minorities—West (U.S.)—Social life and customs.
3. West (U.S.)—Civilization. 4. Ethnophilosophy—West (U.S.) 5. Folklore—West (U.S.).
6. Group identity—West (U.S.). 7. West (U.S.)—In Literature. I Stewart, Polly, 1943-
    F596.2.W67 2000
    306'.0978—dc21

                                                    00-010268

Contents

Acknowledgments

This anthology started taking shape almost a decade ago, independently and more or less simultaneously, in the minds of two of the volume's editors. We were widely separated geographically but alike in our regard for a teacher and mentor whose impact upon us and upon our field has been immense. Each of us imagined putting together a volume of essays in honor of him, and before long each learned, quietly networking among old schoolmates, that the other had the same bright idea: Say, kids, let's put on a show.

We are deeply grateful now to the people without whom we surely could not have put this show on. Polly Stewart thanks Jennifer Chatfield for early help with the mysteries of scanning, word processing, and file management. We editors wish also to express our gratitude to Simon Bronner, who generously gave us advice early on; to Miiko Toelken, who kept this venture a secret far longer than a spouse ought to have; to Kim Stafford, from whose essay we appropriated a resonant and fleeting line—*the life of the place itself*—for our volume's subtitle; to John Alley and his colleagues Michael Spooner and Anna Furniss of Utah State University Press, who went well beyond the call of duty to make this book a reality; to Randy Williams and Jeannie Thomas, who made the local arrangements for a long-awaited surprise party; and—most of all—to our contributors. They stood by us and were patient.

Introduction

This book, a collection of essays on worldview and the American West, started life some years back as a festschrift honoring Barre Toelken. The four of us who edited this volume are all past students of Barre's. We wanted to assemble essays written by students and colleagues who over the years had, like us, benefitted from Barre's thought and wished to celebrate him as friend, colleague, and mentor. Yet, as we four eagerly began consulting (we hoped clandestinely) with a few trusted colleagues and publishers, we realized that although the traditional potpourri of festschrift-as-testimonial might have its special pleasures, we could honor Barre best by producing an anthology meant to stand on its own merits. We think readers will like the resulting book, which is diverse in approaches and writing styles but harmonious in its venture, variously applying Toelken's path-breaking ideas about worldview to the topic of the American West, a region that is both prominent in his work and a source of endless fascination to the rest of us. In our selections, we have aimed for a range of voices, methods, and visions but have integrated them through the focus of one theme, worldview, in one region, the American West.

What is *worldview*? Toelken gives us an entry point in *The Dynamics of Folklore*: "'Worldview' refers to the manner in which a culture sees and expresses its relation to the world around it" (1996a, 263). A simple claim—with complex implications. As members of the species *Homo sapiens*, we possess five senses for collecting information, but the ways in which we use these physiological structures to do the collecting are dramatically conditioned by the particular culture in which we are raised. The worldview we acquire from those around us becomes as much a part of our perceptual equipment as the physical engineering of our senses.

Worldview is social as well as material, spiritual as well as physical. It refers to the socially agreed upon way in which a group with continuity in time and space shapes and expresses its reality. Thus worldview inevitably permeates all of every group's culture, yet, as members of a specific culture ourselves, it is hard for us to understand that worldview is only our *take* on reality (and our *only* take on reality) since it is the very conceptual tool with which we see and communicate. As Toelken puts it, "each culture has a distinctive way of

1

thinking that it passes on to its young, and this way of thinking is made up of codes so deeply represented in language that they become . . . the primary way in which people of that culture can understand anything" (1996a, 263).

Features of worldview extend beyond folk groups and may be surprisingly consistent at the folk, popular, and elite levels of a nation or even throughout a whole civilization over a long period of time, as Alan Dundes showed so powerfully in a series of pioneering essays (1968, 1969, and 1971). But even when folk and elite culture share the same worldview—as with the reliance on the number three in Euro-American culture for organizing everything from deity to small, medium, and large clothing sizes, to joking formulas—we are likely to acquire such fundamentals initially (as infants and children) at the informal, folk level and then find them reinforced through folklore on a daily basis throughout our lives.

Worldview is also an analytic tool, a holistic concept that we can use to attempt to grasp a culture's way of seeing "from inside the culture rather than outside" (Mendelson 1968, 576). Rather than leading us to regard national, mass, or elite culture as more highly developed or more scientific or more all-encompassing than "primitive," folk, and local culture, the concept assumes that there are legitimate, varied, logical systems of perception and expression flowing out of different, time-tested assumptions. Perhaps no scholarly concept involves so profound a move away from ethnocentrism as does the concept of worldview.[1]

How, then, have we involved worldview in the interpretation of the American West in this collection of essays? A first answer, through analogy, might be this: imagine a huge, powerful, revolving telescope somewhere on the crest of the Rockies, swinging to focus on different places in the West— ethnic places, occupational places, places at a remove in time, gendered places. Do you have that image?

That's exactly what this offering is not. Instead, in these essays we go to those same places and look outward from inside them. What does the world of the nineteenth-century West look like from the vantage points of women isolated on the plains of Texas or Nebraska? For one thoughtful answer, read Margaret Brady's essay, "In Her Own Words: Women's Frontier Friendships in Letters, Diaries, and Reminiscences." What "might have been going on" when George Venn heard local Native Americans in the Skagit Valley of Washington State sing a popular Christian hymn in the 1950s? It took him two decades to recognize what it was, and he lets us in on his discovery in "Faith of Our Fathers."[2] What did, and do, some promoters of different areas of the West want outsiders to think the West represented? Read Steve Siporin's "Tall Tales and Sales." And what particular religious visions exist in the Pimería Alta, a "shared space" (Griffith 1995), a region that straddles an international border? Jim Griffith's "A Diversity of Dead Helpers: Folk Saints of the U.S.-Mexico Borderlands" delivers a wealth of answers.

In other words, in taking our inspiration from Toelken's writings, we sought to see with the many "native eyes" that look outward into the western landscape and make different senses of it (Toelken 1971, 1982a, 1982b, 1983, 1996a). One goal for the writers of this anthology was to illuminate that coherent thread of human reasoning that someone else, usually someone representing another group, had created from within a historically derived cultural tradition, often in contact with a changing social environment. Thus Jarold Ramsey, in "John Campbell's Adventure, and the Ecology of Story," suggests that there is "an ecology of memory, imagination, and story, just as there is an ecology of land, water, and air"; then, reconstructing John Campbell's story from the fragments available to him, Ramsey provides a cogent example of the value, for nature and for the intellect, of preserving and handing down a story in a particularly western context. Barry Lopez's wanderings in the uplands near his home on the western slope of the Oregon Cascades these past thirty years have yielded subtle clues about how the Tsanchifin Kalapuya Indians listened to "The Language of Animals" and how we might also. Twilo Scofield's reminiscence, "'Two Moonlight Rides and a Picnic Lunch': Memories of Childhood in a Logging Community," recalls the inside of a complete universe that, like George Wasson's Oregon Coast Native culture of the Coquelle Indians, has all but disappeared ("The Coquelle Indians and the Cultural 'Black Hole' of the Southern Oregon Coast"). Even Native Americans whose narrative repertoires have been well collected offer us stories that make little sense without a context grounded in worldview. As Nora and Richard Dauenhauer write,

> the expression of comedy is somehow more culture specific and more enigmatic to outsiders than tragedy. During the summer of 1984 field test with Raven we ourselves were laughing until the tears came, but many of our students just sat, finding the stories more puzzling than amusing. (p. 136)

The Dauenhauers go on to explicate the Tlingit story, "Raven and the Tide," through a line-by-line commentary that does let us in on the joke.

Some of the authors have taken us into worldviews we usually do our best to avoid—because they come from people who scare us, who force us to look at ourselves and our assumptions, whose view of the world might be philosophically threatening: the lonely "crazies" like Gypsy Slim, Kid Gilnap, Pro Human, Bottle Mary (who lived on the income from returnable bottles), Acy Deucy, and Tubby Beers (who logged with a World War II tank). Kim Stafford calls these eccentrics "local saints"—saints of small western places like Wallowa County, Junction City, Redmond, Florence, Celilo, Otis, Swisshome, all in Oregon. He seeks them out in "Local Character," giving us their stories and their idiosyncratic ideas and lives. We learn from Stafford and his saints what our own worldviews exclude.

Robert McCarl, in "Visible Landscapes/Invisible People," also unearths silent (and sometimes silenced) worldviews—this time the heritage of miners and mining families in North Idaho:

> the cultural and historical contributions of miners and their families also lie, for the most part, beneath the surface: miles of hand-dug drifts and stopes, row upon row of miners' headstones in the grave-yards, and page upon page of family pictures commemorating the cradle-to-grave passage of thousands of lives. This material is invisible to outsiders (page 225).

Such diversity typifies the West, and that in itself may still surprise some outsiders, to whom much is invisible in a deceptively transparent landscape. This is, after all, the region that contains the oldest European "core cultural area" in the United States—the Hispanic "hearth" in the Upper Rio Grande Valley of New Mexico (Zelinsky 1992, 119). It also holds the historical heartland (most of Utah and parts of Idaho, Arizona, Nevada, Colorado, and Wyoming) of one of the newest major religions in the world—the Church of Jesus Christ of Latter-day Saints.[3] Further, the intermountain section of the region is at once the most urbanized *and* most sparsely populated part of the nation. With such extremes, perhaps the range of worldviews should not be such a surprise after all.

Our goal has not been to reconcile these sometimes inharmonious worldviews, but to try to get inside them through their outward expressions and to represent them accurately and fairly. Indeed, our shared assumption is that they are not reconcilable, for "reconciliation" would take us back to the crest of the Rockies—or to some academic high place—that supposedly would transcend (and be superior to) any given worldview. In this land of mountains and valleys, we know that each vantage point has its own integrity, value, and particular truth. We have tried to see with others' eyes, and touch the thread of another's reasoning, if only for a moment.

Our own worldview is, of course, the most difficult to see. Thus Elliott Oring, in "Icons of Immortality: Forest Lawn and the American Way of Death," makes the case that it is a mistake to attribute the aesthetic ideas of Forest Lawn Cemetery (in the Los Angeles area) to nearby Hollywood. Evelyn Waugh's *The Loved One* satirized the cemetery in both novel and film. How convenient it was to assign Forest Lawn's "artificiality, superficiality, and sentimentality" (p. 54) to Southern California! Oring argues, however, that Forest Lawn cannot be cordoned off or assigned to the fringe, because it is part of the inheritance of Victorian America, an enduring piece of Anglo-American worldview. Jeannie Thomas's "Ride 'Em, Barbie Girl: Commodifying Folklore, Place, and the Exotic," reads well as a companion to Oring's piece, for Barbie also attracts and repels, with her "artificiality, superficiality, and sentimentality," marketed as authenticity.

Jesse James could be included in that nineteenth-century inheritance Oring describes as well, but as Chip Sullivan shows in "Jesse James: An American Outlaw," the James story began long before James was born, in British legends about outlaws like Robin Hood. With Jesse James, the outlaw narrative takes an American turn, never quite resolving "the tension between hero and outlaw" (p. 116). Jesse James stands for an American outlaw hero who continues to be recreated anew in the West, even today.

One author, William A. Wilson, turns our regional focus on end by bringing outsider (exoteric) views of Mormon culture into the discussion in his "The Concept of the West and Other Hindrances to the Study of Mormon Folklore." The facts *are* startling: though "the public perception of Mormons places them squarely in the center of the West," and folklorists like Dorson identified Mormons as a regional group, "only ten percent live in Utah, and over half of all Mormons live outside the United States and Canada" (p. 189). Wilson shows us how Mormon stories that outsiders take to mean one thing have an additional (and sometimes contradictory) set of associations and meanings for Mormons, regardless of where they live. There is no secret code operating among Mormons any more than there is among Tlingits who tell Raven trickster tales or among miners who have shared working lives underground. What Wilson brings to bear on his interpretation of these stories— besides an unceasing effort to "discover what it means to be human"—is Mormon worldview, carried forward in religious folklore that arises out of "the circumstance of being Mormon."

Perhaps the consecutive presentation of all these diverse worldviews will jar the reader. Perhaps even more jarring will be the range of writing styles (from literary to technical), writing genres (from personal essay and reminiscence to exposition), and the idiosyncratic perspectives (the functional individual equivalent of worldview). We wondered, in fact, if we could honestly extol the virtues of studying a variety of worldviews without encouraging such variety in our own work. Should all attempts to get at others' worldviews adapt the same methodology and style? Isn't there in fact a *necessity* for a range of approaches to reveal what worldview consists of? And if worldview is as real as we say it is, aren't the worldviews of our own authors inevitably entwined in their research and writing? Do we want to deny this? We may, as scholars and writers, be able to identify with another person, including his/her worldview, but we never completely stop being ourselves. Thus, these essays, by virtue of their many contrasts with each other, make us aware of who is doing the seeing, the feeling, and the writing; and we become aware that the various ways the authors see and feel and write are due also to the multiplicity of *their* worldviews. Different styles and methods, then, may be the most appropriate way to do justice to the subject of worldviews in the American West.

Barre Toelken once wrote that walking in someone else's moccasins is not just a cliché or an item of pseudo Indian lore (1976). For traditional

Navajos this idea conveys a deep meaning partly because the word for "moccasin" and the word for "foot" are the same word, and one's moccasin is
shaped by one's foot. So to walk in someone else's moccasins is not only to
experience the world as someone else does, but to adopt part of that person
as yourself for a while, and perhaps to let go of part of yourself for a while,
too. Clearly that goal has been the intention of many of our essays, reflecting, we believe, a recurrent theme in Toelken's work.

It is also interesting that this Navajo metaphor is one of *touch* and
motion. Walking in someone else's moccasins/feet suggests feeling what they
feel as they move across a landscape rather than seeing what they see from
a static position. Yet the language we Euro-American editors employ to
describe the cultural relativity of experience depends on metaphors of vision
and seeing (world*view*, *perspective*, *view*point, out*look*, etc.) In other words,
the very language and metaphors we use for trying to understand another
culture's worldview inevitably recode it to fit our own. Even our word *worldview*, an intellectual attempt to get outside it, reproduces it once again. And
again we run smack into the wall: we can't escape our own wiring, our own
culture, or our own worldview. But we can hope that the effort to do so
improves our awareness and understanding.

To appreciate, acknowledge, and value the multiplicity of worldviews,
then, is one of the highest goals we can ethically aspire to in the world of
scholarship. Many may regard this goal as too simple, bald, or naive, but we
believe it still underlies significant efforts in the discipline of folklore. We are
not talking about pro forma bowing at the temple of political correctness, or
polite (but ultimately indifferent) acceptance of all ideas as equally valid. To
try to get inside another worldview is not as easy as that. It takes more than
reading. Walking in someone else's moccasins isn't a bad way to put it.

Notes

1. For a rich bibliography on worldview, especially in reference to cultures found in
    North America, see Toelken 1996a, 308–313.
2. The time-lapse Venn reports in coming to understand a cross-cultural performance is
    reminiscent of the one reported by Toelken in *Dynamics of Folklore* (1996, 246) and
    cited herein by Dauenhauer and Dauenhauer (p. 136): "What my Indian friends
    understood and relished in a few moments took me over four years to understand. Yet
    it was only one joke."
3. Yet William A. Wilson's "The Concept of the West and Other Hindrances to the Study
    of Mormon Folklore" (in this volume) unearths entrenched assumptions and gives us
    new perspective on the purported impact of geography on religion and vice-versa.

Personal Essay

The Language of Animals
Barry Lopez

The steep riverine valley I live within, on the west slope of the Cascades in Oregon, has a particular human and natural history. Though I've been here for thirty years, I am able to convey almost none of it. It is not out of inattentiveness. I've wandered widely within the drainages of its eponymous river, the McKenzie; and I could offer you a reasonably complete sketch of its immigrant history, going back to the 1840s. Before then, Tsanchifin Kalapuya, a Penutian-speaking people, camped in these mountains, but they came up the sixty-mile long valley apparently only in summer, to pick berries and to trade with a people living on the far side of the Cascades, the Mollala. In the fall the Tsanchifin returned down valley to winter near present-day Eugene, Oregon, where the McKenzie joins the Willamette River. The Willamette flows a hundred miles north to the Columbia, the Columbia another hundred miles to the Pacific.

The history that occupies me, however, in this temperate rain forest is not human history, not even that of the highly integrated Tsanchifin. Native peoples seem to have left scant trace of their comings and goings in the McKenzie Valley. Only rarely, as I hear it, does someone stumble upon an old, or very old, campsite, where glistening black flakes of a volcanic glass called obsidian, the debitage from tool-making work, turn up in soil scuffed by a boot heel.

I've lingered in such camps, in a respectful and deferential mood, as though the sites were shrines, but I'm drawn more to the woods in which they're found. These landscapes are occupied, still, by the wild animals who were these people's companions. These are the descendants of animals who coursed these woods during the era of the Tsanchifin.

When I travel the McKenzie basin with visiting friends, my frame of mind is not that of the interpreter, of the cognoscente; I amble with an explorer's temperament. I am alert for the numinous event, for evidence of a world beyond the rational. Though it is presumptuous to say so, I seek a Tsanchifin grasp, the view of an indigene. And what draws me ahead is the possibility of revelation from other indigenes—the testimonies of wild animals.

The idea that animals can convey meaning, and thereby offer an atten-tive human being illumination, is a commonly held belief the world over. The view is disparaged and disputed only by modern cultures with an alle-giance to science as the sole arbiter of truth. The price of this conceit, to my way of thinking, is enormous.

I grew up in a farming valley in southern California in the 1950s, around sheep, dogs, horses, and chickens. The first wild animals I encoun-tered—coyotes, rattlesnakes, mountain lion, deer, and bear—I came upon in the surrounding mountains and deserts. These creatures seemed more vital than domestic animals. They seemed to tremble in the aura of their own light. (I caught a shadow of that magic occasionally in a certain dog, a par-ticular horse, like a residue.) From such a distance it's impossible to recall precisely what riveted my imagination in these encounters, though I might guess. Wild animals are lean. They have no burden of possessions, no need for extra clothing, eating utensils, cars, elaborate dwellings. They are so much more integrated into the landscape than human beings are, swooping its contours and bolting down its pathways with bewildering speed. They travel unerringly through the dark. Holding their gaze, I saw the intensity and clarity I associated with the presence of a soul.

In later years I benefitted from a formal education at a Jesuit prep school in New York City, then at New York University and the universities of Notre Dame and Oregon. I encountered the full range of Western philosophy, including the philosophy of science, in those classrooms, and studied the theological foundations of Christianity. I don't feel compelled now to repu-diate that instruction. I regard it, though, as incomplete, and would say that nothing I read in those years fundamentally changed what I thought about animals. The more steeped I became in the biology and ecology of animals, the more I understood about migration, the more I comprehended about the intricacy of their neural impulses and the subtlety of their endocrine sys-tems, the deeper their other unexplored capacities appeared to me. Biochemistry and field studies enhanced rather than diminished my sense that, in Henry Beston's phrase, animals were other nations.

If formal education taught me how to learn something, if it provided me with reliable structures (e.g., *Moby-Dick*, approaching the limit in calculus, von Clausewitz's tactics) within which I could employ a metaphorical imagi-nation, if the Jesuits inculcated in me a respectful skepticism about authori-ty, then that education gave me the sort of tools most necessary to an exam-ination of the history of Western ideas, a concept fatally flawed by an assumption of progress. I could move on from Gilbert White's Selbourne to Thoreau's Walden. I could trace a thread from Aristotle through Newton to Schrödinger. Or grasp that in the development of symphonic expression, Bach gives way to Mozart who gives way to Beethoven. But this isn't progress. It's change, in a set of ideas that incubate well in our culture.

I left the university with two ideas in my mind. One was the belief that a person had to enter the world to know it, that it couldn't be got from a book. The other was that there were epistemologies as rigorous out there, as rigorous and valid, as the ones I learned in school. Not convinced of the superiority of the latter, I felt ready to consider these epistemologies, no matter how at odds.

When I moved into the McKenzie Valley I saw myself beginning a kind of apprenticeship. Slowly I learned to identify indigenous plants and animals and birds migrating through. Slowly I began to expand the basis of my observations of their lives, to alter the nature of my assumptions. Slowly I began to recognize clusters of life in the valley as opposed to individual, isolated species. I was lucky to live in a place too steep for agriculture to have developed, too heavily wooded to be good for grazing, and too poor in commercial quantities of minerals for mining (though the evidence that all three occurred on a small scale is present.) The only industrial-scale impact here has come from commercial logging—and the devastation in parts of the valley is as breathtaking a sight as the napalmed forests of the Vietnam highlands in the 1960s. Pressure is building locally now to develop retirement real estate—trailer parks, RV parks, condominiums; but, for the moment, it's still relatively easy to walk for hours across stretches of land that have never been farmed, logged, mined, grazed, or homesteaded. From where my house sits on a wooded bench above the McKenzie River, I can look across the water into a four- or five-hundred-year-old forest in which some of the Douglas firs are more than twenty feet around.

Two ways to learn this land are obvious: enter it repeatedly and attentively on your own, or give your attention instead—or alternately—to its occupants. The most trustworthy occupants, to my mind, are those with no commercial ties, beings whose sense of ownership is guided not by profit but by responsible occupancy. For the valley in which I live, these occupants would theoretically be remnant Tsanchifin people and indigenous animals. To my knowledge, the Tsanchifin are no longer a presence; and the rational mind (to which many of us acquiesce) posits there is little to be learned from animals unless we discover a common language and can converse. This puts the emphasis, I think, in the wrong place. The idea shouldn't be for us to converse, to enter into some sort of Socratic dialogue with animals. It would be to listen to what is already being communicated. To insist on a conversation with the unknown is to demonstrate impatience and to imply that any such encounter must include your being heard.

To know a physical place you must become intimate with it. You must open yourself to its textures, its colors in varying day and night lights, its sonic dimensions. You must in some way become vulnerable to it. In the end, there's little difference between growing into the love of a place and growing into the love of a person. Love matures through intimacy and vulnerability, and it grows most vigorously in an atmosphere of trust. You learn, with regard to the land, the ways in which it is dependable. Where it has no strength to offer you, you do not insist on its support. When you yourself do not understand something, you trust the land might, and you defer.

When I walk in the woods or along the creeks, I'm looking for integration, not conversation. I want to be bound more deeply into the place, to be included, even if only as a witness, in events that animate the landscape. In tracking a mink, in picking a black bear scat apart, in examining red alder trunks deer have scraped with their antlers, I get certain measures of the place where I live. In listening to the songs and tones of Swainson's thrushes and to winter wrens, to the bellows of elk, I get a dimension of the valley I couldn't get on my own. In eating spring chinook, in burning big-leaf maple in the stove, in bathing in ground water from the well, in collecting sorrel and miner's lettuce for a summer salad, I put my life more deeply into the life around me.

The eloquence of animals is in their behavior, not their speech. To see a mule deer stot across a river bar, a sharp-shinned hawk maneuver in heavy timber, to watch a female chinook build her nest on clean gravel, to see a rufous hummingbird extracting nectar from foxglove blossoms, to come upon a rubber boa constricting a shrew is to meet the world outside the self. It is to hear the indigenes.

We regard wild creatures as the most animated part of the landscape. We've believed for eons that we share a specific nature with them, different from the nature of wild berries or lightning or water. Our routine interchanges with them are most often simply a verification of this, reaffirmations that we're alive in a particular place together at a particular time.

Wild animals are like us, too, in that they have ancestors. When I see river otter sprawled mid-stream on a boulder in the noon sun, I know their ancestors were here before the fur trappers, before the Tsanchifin, before *Homo*. The same for the cormorant, the woolly bear caterpillar, the cutthroat. In all these histories, in the string of events in each life, the land is revealed. The tensile strength of the orb weaver's silk, the location of the salmon's redd, the shrew-moles' bones bound in a spotted owl's cast, each makes a concise statement.

Over the years and on several continents I've seen indigenous people enter their landscapes. (I say enter because the landscape of a semi-permanent camp or village, as I have come to understand it, is less intense, less numinous.) Certain aspects of this entry experience seem always to be in evidence. Human conversation usually trails off. People become more alert to what is around them, less intent on any goal—where to camp that night, say. People become more curious about animal life, looking at the evidence of what animals have been up to. People begin to look all around, especially behind them, instead of staring straight ahead with only an occasional look to the side.

People halt to examine closely things that at first glance seemed innocuous. People hold up simply to put things together—the sky with a certain type of forest, a kind of rock outcropping, the sound of a creek, and, last, the droppings of a blue grouse under a thimbleberry bush. People heft rocks and put them back. They put their hands into river mud and perhaps leave patches of it on their skin. It's an ongoing intercourse with the place.

Learning one's environment through attention to animals is not solely a matter of being attentive to "statements" they make about the physical, chemical, and biological realms we share. A more profound communication can take place. In this second sphere, animals have volition; they have intention and the power of influence; and they have the capacity to intervene in our lives. I've never known people who are comfortable addressing such things. However we may define "consciousness" in the West, we regard it as a line of demarcation that separates human nature from animal nature. A shaman might cross back and forth, but animals, no.

In my experience indigenous people are most comfortable in asserting a spiritual nature for animals (including aspects of consciousness) only when the purpose of the conversation is to affirm a spirituality shared by both humans and animals. (They're more at ease talking about animals as exemplars of abstract ideals, as oracles and companions, and as metaphorical relations.) When someone relates something previously unheard of that they saw an animal do, something that demonstrates the degree of awareness we call consciousness, the person is saying the world still turns on the miraculous, it's still inventing itself, and that we're a part of this. These observations keep the idea alive that animals are engaged in the world at a deep level.

The fundamental reenforcement of a belief in the spiritual dimension of animals' lives (i.e., in the spiritual nature of the landscape itself) comes from a numinous encounter with a wild creature. For many indigenous people (again, in my experience) such events make one feel more secure in the "real" world because their unfolding takes the event beyond the more readily apparent boundaries of existence. In a numinous encounter one's suspicion–profound, persistent, and ineluctable, that there is more to the world than appearances–is confirmed. For someone reared in the tradition of the cultural West, it is also a confirmation that Rationalism and the Enlightenment are not points on a continuum of progress but simply two species of wisdom.

Whenever I think of the numinous event, and of how vulnerable it is to the pincers of the analytic mind, I recall a scene in a native village in Alaska. A well-meaning but rude young man, a graduate student in anthropology, had come to this village to study hunting. His ethnocentric interviewing technique was aggressive, his vocabulary academic, his manner to pester and interfere. Day after day he went after people, especially one older man he took to be the best hunter in the village. He hounded him relentlessly, asking him why he was the best hunter. The only way the man could be rid of the interviewer was to answer his question. He ended the assault by saying, "My ability to hunt is like a small bird in my mind. I don't think anyone should disturb it."

A central task facing modern Western culture is to redefine human community in the wake of industrialization, colonialism, and, more recently, the forcing power of capitalism. In trying to solve some of the constellation of attendant problems here—keeping corporations out of secondary education, restoring the physical and spiritual shelter of the family group, preserving non-Western ways of knowing—it seems clear that by cutting ourselves off from Nature, by turning Nature into scenery and commodities, we may have cut ourselves off from something vital. To repair this damage we can't any longer take what we call Nature for an object. We must merge it again with our nature. We must reintegrate ourselves in specific geographic places, and to do that we need to learn those places at a greater depth than any science, Western or Eastern, can take us. We have to incorporate them again in the moral universe we inhabit. We have to develop good relations with them, ones that will replace the exploitative relations that have become a defining characteristic of twentieth-century Western life, with its gargantuan oil spills and chemical accidents, its megalithic hydroelectric developments, its hideous weapons of war, and its conception of wealth that would lead a corporation to cut down a forest to pay the interest on a loan.

In daily conversation in many parts of the American West today, wild animals are given credit for conveying ideas to people, for "speaking." To some degree this is a result of the pervasive influence of Native American culture in certain parts of the West. It doesn't contradict the notion of human intelligence to believe, in these quarters, that wild animals represent repositories of knowledge we've abandoned in our efforts to build civilizations and to support ideals like progress and improvement. To "hear" wild animals is not to leave the realm of the human; it's to expand that realm to include voices other than our own. It's a technique for the accomplishment of wisdom. To attend to the language of animals means to give yourself over to a more complicated, less analytic awareness of a place. It's to realize that some of the so-called equations of life are not meant to be solved, that it takes as much intelligence not to solve them as it does to find the putative answers.

A fundamental difference between early and late twentieth-century science in the cultural West has become apparent with the emergence of the phrase "I don't know" in scientific discourse. This admission is the heritage of quantum mechanics. It is heard eloquently today in the talk of cosmologists, plasma physicists, and, increasingly, among field biologists now working beyond the baleful and condescending stare of molecular biologists.

The Enlightenment ideals of an educated mind and just relations among people have become problematic in our era because the process of formal education in the West has consistently abjured or condemned non-Western ways of knowing and because the quest for just relations still strains at the barriers of race, gender, and class. If we truly believe in the wisdom of Enlightenment thinking—and certainly, like Bach's B-Minor Mass, Goethe's theory of light, or Darwin's voyage, that philosophy is among the best we have to offer—then we should consider encouraging the educated mind to wander beyond the comfort of its own solipsisms, and we should extend the principle of justice to include everything that touches our lives.

I do not know how to achieve these things in the small valley where I live except through apprenticeship and the dismantling of assumptions I grew up with. The change, to a more gracious and courteous and wondrous awareness of the world, will not come in my lifetime, and knowing what I know of the modern plagues—loss of biodiversity, global warming, and the individual quest for material wealth—I am fearful. But I believe I have come to whatever I understand by listening to companions and by trying to erase the lines that establish hierarchies of knowledge among them. My sense is that the divine knowledge we yearn for is social, it is not in the province of a genius any more than it is in the province of a particular culture. It lies within our definition of community.

Our blessing, it seems to me, is not what we know, but that we know each other.

Song

Faith of Our Fathers

George Venn

To a boy entering Theodore Roosevelt Grade School in 1949, there was no history, racism, justice, or culture in Burlington, Washington. For first graders, the town seemed to be magically defined by Burlington Hill, which rose above the flat Skagit Valley like a wooded turtle shell—just across the railroad tracks, just north of the school, just north of our home in the Presbyterian manse. No one lived on Burlington Hill. After school, my brother and I and our grade school friends would scrabble up the rocky trails and play for hours. Under the green and shadowy canopy of alder, fir, maple, moss, cedar, snag, and fern, we explored mysterious crisscross trails. One switchback led to the Burlington "B," a yellow, thirty-foot concrete letter embedded in the south slope. For children learning the alphabet, this huge capital letter was a mystery of mysteries. We would walk the B, study the peeling yellow paint, and wonder and wonder. Hidden in the hilltop underbrush and trees we found rusting antennae, abandoned concrete foundations. Another switchback led to a dry concrete water reservoir, a hundred-by-two-hundred-foot rectangle. Wide jagged cracks faulted its walls and floor, as though it had been fractured by some beanstalk giant. To us, that hill seemed like another civilization, a private children's wilderness. Deer, squirrels, weasels, hawks, wrens—so many wild things we never could see for long. Adults did not ascend.

Sitting on Burlington Hill, we could see the flat Skagit Valley connecting the Cascade Mountains to the Pacific: the Skagit River shining gray through the cottonwood trees; the serpentine curve of dikes; fields of berries, peas, and hay; green blocks of pasture; black and white herds of dairy cows; stores along Fairhaven Avenue. From the hill, we could also see our other escapes from adults: the brown Presbyterian Church with its crawlspace where we played doctor with neighbor girls, the English walnut tree where my brother and I had built a treehouse so we could read comic books that were always taboo in our Presbyterian manse. Immediately below, there was the cream-color-painted rectangle refuge of Roosevelt Grade School, where twice a day sweet cold milk came in half-pint glass bottles sealed with paper

19

lids. Lifting the paper tab, we licked fresh cream from the backside of the lids, then drank through paper straws. There, Mrs. Strong and Mrs. Nattress and Mrs. Bumgardner and Mrs. Norris taught us all to read and write with thick green pencils and black and white cursive charts arrayed around the room. We could see the evergreen grove at Burlington Park where big kids picked on Alfred Weymouth during baseball season, shouting "Burn Weymouth out, burn Weymouth out" as they threw baseballs to him, trying to hurt his hand inside his thin leather mitt. Why they were trying to hurt Alfred Weymouth, I didn't know. There was the playground where marbles became our dirt-knuckled, dirt-kneed passion, where flying balsa-and-paper kites became a compelling art in the always afternoon sea breeze. From Burlington Hill, we could also see the boxy buildings of the Darigold Creamery and its high, black-stained smoking stack. Every afternoon at five o'clock, the Darigold horn blatted so loudly from that gigantic column that it sounded like an industrial muzzein calling to everyone in town, "Time to quit, time to go home, time to eat."

In this world where innocent play was our delight and retreat from adults seemed possible and desirable, my stepfather, the new minister at the Presbyterian Church, first introduced me to the word *Indians*. After dinner one evening, he announced that he was going out to "preach to the Indians." As a child, I had no idea what that sentence might mean. In the fall or spring, I sometimes heard my parents say they were going "to buy salmon from the Indians" on Lummi Island, or they would report that someone brought us a salmon they got "from the Indians." In those years, so much fresh salmon was available "from the Indians" that my parents bought a Burpee processing system, and my mother canned many king salmon to eat all winter. (I can still see the white bones of those pressure-cooked salmon and taste how their dangerous ribs and jointed spines had been turned to soft white paste in the metal can.) The only other adult use I heard of the word *Indians* was in reference to a miniature Kwakiutl totem pole, a typical tourist curio which stood on a living room bookcase. It was referred to as "from the Indians." No one said more about it.

So like most Whites who've grown up in the Pacific Northwest, I was taught almost nothing by my family about the Indian people who lived the Skagit River valley with us. The people who Vi Hilbert calls the "Looshootseed" in *Haboo*; the people who June Collins names the "Upper Skagit" in *Valley of the Spirits*; the people who called themselves *bastùlk*, "people of the river"; the people who Martin Sampson in *Indians of Skagit County* divides into eleven historic tribes of more than a thousand individuals; the people who had lived for centuries in the Skagit River watershed; the people whose ancient Noo-qua-cha-mish village site lay just outside Burlington; the people who had signed the Point Elliott Treaty in 1855 but whose land was taken without treaty for twenty years; the people who enjoyed their own history, religion, and culture; the people whose language and mythology is so complex that most Whites still have trouble learning and understanding it—these people were barely visible from Burlington Hill, or anywhere else, as far as my family taught me. Our neighbors, whose king salmon my parents relished for their larder, were implicitly presented to me as "heathen savages" to be converted to Christianity.

Only once in the early 1950s did Burlington schools have anything formal or memorable to say about Native Americans. In the fourth grade, we were asked to perform in a pageant at Burlington High School. With my classmates, I had to memorize words, music, and dance steps to what may have been part of a Navajo ceremony: *"No eh hi-yo / hi-yo wich-e nigh-yo / hi-yo, hi-yo wich-e nigh-yo."* We practiced and practiced dancing to that unforgettable song for my fourth-grade music teacher, and I can still see the red-dyed turkey feather headdress which my reluctant parents bought at Younger's Drugstore and which I wore for the performance—with some red face paint, no less. While it is tempting to believe that this school pageant was, at least, a start on authentic knowledge of Native Americans, the pageant was teaching one more dubious lesson: "all those Indians in war bonnets are the same." In fact, the feather headdress is Plains Indians regalia that had been spread everywhere, including the Washington coast, by popular media and the Pan-Indian movement. As Collins and others make clear, no traditional Upper Skagit, or any Northwest coast peoples, ever wore a headdress of eagle feathers formed into a war bonnet.

Had traditional Upper Skagit dress disappeared from Skagit County in the 1950s? No. Had traditional Noo-qua-cha-mish singing and dancing disappeared from Skagit Valley? No. Was it possible to find Upper Skagit people who would share traditional stories? Yes. One woman, Emma Conrad, was living just outside Burlington. Were the Upper Skagit willing to talk with Anglo-Americans? Yes. During the 1940s and 50s, Thom Hess, June Collins, and Sally Snyder, among others, were recording Upper Skagit oral literature up and down the river. Were any Noo-qua-cha-mish individuals ever invited to my classrooms at Roosevelt Grade School? No.

So what was a boy to conclude from that void of information: Indians in Skagit County, who actually numbered about a thousand people, who were selling fresh abundant salmon to my parents, who were listening politely to my stepfather's Protestant sales talks—these people had apparently vanished.

With neither school nor family providing any accurate images of native people, a boy was left to make his own discoveries in popular culture—which usually markets juicy stereotypes for profit. Throughout grade school, my brother and I listened faithfully to *Straight Arrow* on the radio. Though I cannot remember now any of this noble red man's adventures, his magic gold ring, which opened a secret cave whenever he needed to be rescued, enchanted me so much that, in first grade, I sent away for a Straight Arrow ring. As an adopted stepson, I needed that power. When my ring came in the mail, I took my golden amulet to school, where I lost it immediately.

Was there authentic magic among the Upper Skagit? Yes. Traditionally the Squa-de-lich, as Collins explains, was believed to be a spirit that animated objects: cedar boards, vine maple boughs, painted ducks, and goat hair. In one story, Martin Sampson tells how the cedar-boards Squa-de-lich came from the bottom of Big Lake. A young Noo-qua-cha-mish man was seeking knowledge by fasting and diving in the lake. In deep water, he contacted powerful spirits who rewarded him for his quest by giving him magic cedar boards to help his people—healing, finding lost objects, divining. Doesn't any boy or girl need to know such a story?

My brother and I also listened faithfully to *The Lone Ranger* and his Native American partner, Tonto. Every night for four or five years, we huddled together in front of the glowing Admiral radio to listen to these programs, not knowing that we were absorbing the notion of the Indian as the faithful but ignorant, illiterate, inarticulate companion of the White man. Tonto, "stupid" in Spanish, had a three-word vocabulary, at best, and couldn't form English sentences.

One night, I found a hardbound copy of *The Last of the Mohicans* packed away in Coke boxes of old books belonging to my parents. Chingachgook was painted on the cover of Cooper's novel—red, muscular, ferocious. I remember staying up after midnight to read Cooper and shocking my parents when they found me, a fourth grader, wide-eyed and reading a novel when they thought I was asleep. However, Cooper's impact on me had nothing to do with understanding the Upper Skagit. At that time, I had a child's passion for making boats, so instead of considering Cooper's noble savages or the friendship and equality between Leatherstocking and Chingachgook, I only took from Cooper every detail about making birchbark canoes. During hikes on Burlington Hill or in the woods, I began to cut rectangles of bark from white birch trees for my miniature Delaware canoes.

Were there canoe builders among the Upper Skagit at this time? Yes. While river canoes were disappearing, there were still people living within twenty miles of our Presbyterian manse who knew the ancient, complex skills for carving cedar. And were there friendships I might have learned about between the Upper Skagit and Anglo-Americans? Yes. Sampson, Collins, and Hilbert give many great stories: Upper Skagit befriending settlers, settlers befriending Upper Skagit. Sampson confirms that early relations were amicable, with lives saved in childbirth, sickness, and starvation. One Noo-qua-cha-mish man piggybacked a sick Anglo schoolteacher sixteen miles to a doctor.

There is only one exception to this picture of my growing up learning that everyone had melted into White American stew. Someone in my family, probably my mother, must have become curious about local tribal life (perhaps her conscience began to move her toward the need for some authentic understanding). From somewhere, a blue, hardback book with spectacular whale-hunting drawings appeared. The story told about a Haida or Tlingit boy who is initially too young to go whale hunting on the saltchuck, but who finally grows old enough to participate. I was captured by the coming-of-age story: men paddling a great cedar canoe, the whale harpooned, inflated sealskin floats flying out, the canoe tied to the harpooned monster, the whale sounding, the canoe cut loose, the row of floats marking the surface, the whale's death, the gift of food for everyone again. That narrative was my only source of knowledge of traditional Indian life on the Northwest Coast. However, that story had almost nothing to do with the Skagit peoples immediately around me, who tended not to hunt whales but were better known for salmon fishing and deer and mountain goat hunting.

So, like most northwest children around the age of ten, I had been unwittingly invited into the fortress of racist stereotypes that Whites had created about Indians. This formidable structure was not visible from Burlington Hill. Those stereotypes had perfectly obscured the authentic lives of every Indian around me in the Skagit Valley—racism at its best. This leaves out the playing of cowboys and Indians, that traditional-enemy ritual that, as children, we perpetuated without any adult assistance.

How could this happen? In a "good Christian home"? In a "good public school"? In a "nice little town"? In the 1950s?

Such an education is easy to acquire because, from the outside, the fortress looks like a normal candy castle. It's fun, free, quick, common, electric, and, most of all, easy. Inside, however, anyone can see that the rooms are all locked and guarded with adult ignorance; unexamined stereotypes; popular culture's anesthesia; adult failure to provide any accurate, humane, or concrete information to children; and no significant cross-cultural or peer experience.

Racist education is also a traditional blind spot. Both my parents had graduated from Washington universities and my stepfather held a graduate degree in theology, but neither had an interest in or awareness of culture. Both had grown up in coastal Washington where Native American tribes were and still are numerous, influential, visible. Like my grade school teachers, both would have considered themselves well informed, civilized, polite, religious, and thoughtful. Every Sunday morning, they taught me about Biblical tribes. Many Sunday evenings, visiting missionaries gave slide shows on saving the tribes in Latin America and Africa. They taught me to love God and to love my neighbors, but "neighbors" did not include the Upper Skagit—who only existed as "heathens" who sold king salmon.

Of course, my devout parents would have never called such a vacuum racism. Not being students of culture, they would not have even called their de facto racism ethnocentricism. They would have called it righteousness.

The spiritual exclusivity of their Christianity, its imperial absolutist rhetoric, its "one true God," would have walled out any doubt. My stepfather would probably not have ever read what Vi Hilbert makes plain in *Haboo*, that there were immense similarities between traditional Anglo-American and Upper Skagit values—including the work ethic. He would not have known that the Indian Shaker Church— incorporated at Mud Bay, Washington, in 1910, and the church to which many Upper Skagit belonged—had blended Catholic doctrine, Protestant organization and singing, and Native American rituals and traditions into a single sacred service in much the same way that historical Christianity had been blended from Judaism, the Oriental mystery cults, and late Greek philosophy. While a common love for fresh salmon could be accepted, a common love for religious ideas could not.

All of these images constructed for me by sincere, literate, and devout people were forever fractured, like that dry and broken reservoir on Burlington Hill, by an event that occurred when I was ten, the year before we left the Skagit Valley. To arrive at that event, however, it takes a strawberry picking detour.

The summer of 1953 my parents decided that my brother and I should not spend our school vacation with our maternal grandparents, as we usually did. My parents were going to try—once—to keep us two adopted boys from my mother's first marriage together with the two younger children from her second marriage. This, of course, presented the problem of "keeping the big boys busy." By checking with Burlington church members who owned berry farms, my parents discovered that my brother and I were old enough, at ages eleven and ten, respectively, to become real strawberry pickers, as long as we only picked for half days. My parents were delighted.

So one bright June morning, my brother and I, a fifth grader and a fourth grader, were sent forth to work. The strawberry fields lay below the high dikes along the Skagit River, and they were ripe for harvest. Like good feisty brothers, we quarreled and teased and played the mile to the fields, where we had to start picking by eight o'clock. The field boss, an ogre under our bridge, demanded that we pick "two carriers by ten o'clock A.M."—if we wanted to keep our jobs. Crawling on hands and knees, pushing along a carrier of empty strawberry baskets, picking only the ripe berries, hoping for clusters of plump ones, soaking hands and knees, getting jeans muddy, staining fingers brown with berry juice, learning back pain, dangling a manila ticket from a sunburning neck, watching for the field boss, and feeling like a slave—those berry boxes just never seemed to fill up. At noon, twenty-five cents richer, my brother and I quarreled and teased and played all the way home again.

About half past nine the third morning, a rotten strawberry hit me in the ear. I stopped and looked up from my row, but, of course, no obvious attacker was in sight. Close to me, Burlington high-school girls in wide, straw sunhats were picking berries to earn money for new saddle shoes and pleated skirts. Farther away, a few dedicated White women from town bent among the green rows in order to buy that new refrigerator or stove. These women seemed to enjoy visiting with each other as much as picking. Still farther away, a group of lank, tanned, tough migrant women picked, shouted, cursed. Following the harvest, these families camped in the trees along the river dike and around the fields. Smoke from their cooking fires rose into the cottonwoods. Sometimes their husbands were drunk.

Across the acres of green strawberry rows, way over by the dike, I could see a group of women and girls with colorful handkerchiefs wrapped around their heads. There were always a lot of little kids with them. That group would always be picking together, and the field boss never assigned me to rows where they were working. As I learned later from June Collins, the Upper Skagit picked berries and hops for Whites during those summers. Such seasonal moves fit their oldest pattern: in summer, Indian families followed the ripening wild berries to the Cascade mountain burns and followed the spawning salmon upriver to creeks, falls, and pools. After Whites planted acres of domestic berries, Upper Skagit would come each summer, camp on the farms, visit with relatives, meet friends from distant villages. And the growers paid them to pick these strange new fruits and eventually built cabins for them. I never saw men picking there. I imagined the women and girls would go through the fields first, since they were the best pickers. All the rest of us came along a week or so after they had been through. We got the seconds off the vines.

The rotten strawberry juice ran down my cheek and neck, and as I dug the strawberry out of my ringing ear, the sun began to dry the juice. Who had heaved this rot at me? It had to be my brother, Doug. He usually picked berries just a few rows away, and his smug prankster grin was now buried deep in the green screen of strawberry leaves. I cleaned myself off as best I could and started picking again, looking for a rain-rotted berry of my own so I could return the favor. We called this entertainment "brotherly love."

Over the next few days, berry-fighting became more compelling than obeying that immortal commandment—"two carriers by ten o'clock or you're fired." To quell his own boredom, my brother started throwing rotten berries at the son of the owner, at several kids at once, at anyone he could hit from his row, and eventually the air was a strawberry crossfire. This riot brought the field boss shouting, red-faced, glowering, and warning us all that someone would be asked not to come back the next day and who started this anyway.

On Friday, my brother got fired for berry-fighting with the boss's son. I thought it was funny and carved birch bark off a tree for another miniature Delaware canoe. If my big brother wasn't going back, I wasn't either and who wanted to pick strawberries anyway? After a last wrestling match with the owner's son, my brother started walking toward Burlington. I had gone ahead. He tried to catch me, but I ran and climbed a tree and got away from him, then I walked back to Burlington alone. The hot tar from that Skagit Valley road stuck to the soles of my shoes, and gravel stuck to the tar. I sounded like a giant coming down the road—all my swift Delaware subtlety gone.

After my brother was fired, our stepfather had to think of work for us to do. So, after dinner one June evening, my stepfather announced he was going to "preach to the Indians," and he told me to go to the church and get about thirty spiral-bound songbooks. I was to assist him. Picking up his Bible and accordion, he started for the new gray Chevrolet.

The Skagit Valley evening was palpable, a bowl of soft gold light. From the North Cascades a cooling land breeze flowed easy down river. The air smelled of cream, ripe peas, dairy cows, new-mown lawn. Everything seemed muted and quiet—the log train chuffing toward Sedro Woolley, the dog sleeping in the street, our neighbor Grant washing his boat, Johnny Martin's logging truck rattling home empty, one cheeseblock missing. Chunks of orange fir bark fell quietly before our manse at 316 North Regent Street. In the alley, kids played hide-and-seek or kick-the-can. Bats, nighthawks, herons, ducks, geese—toward Burlington Hill, the whole sky seemed to be flying.

My stepfather crossed the dike and drove south from Burlington on almost the same tarbaby road that my brother and I had walked during our infamous strawberry picking week. At a large white farmhouse, he slowed down, and I saw—for the first time—a group of real Upper Skagit people sitting in rows on the green lawn. My stepfather turned in the gravel driveway and parked in the shade of some cottonwoods. Out my window, I saw children running and playing on the lawn, and behind them, quiet adults seemed to be waiting for us. There must have been a group of about thirty people there. In front, women and older children—washed, dressed, quiet— sat on the grass in several rows, and behind them stood a row of men of all ages: black hair recently washed, combed, gleaming. I could see the stained fingers of the women and girls. Strawberry pickers. I identified with them. I had been one of them in the fields, however briefly. They were going to listen to my stepfather preach, which I always pretended to do but never did. Except for his music, he was boring and he could be dangerous, especially at meals. Still, there was a formal feeling in that yard—like getting ready for a school picture. The Upper Skagit were all poised, quiet, ready for something. I didn't know what. They were expecting us. They seemed organized. One or two men in the back row seemed to be watching us intently.

"Come along now, George, and pass out the songbooks," my stepfather ordered. I sat still. Reverend Venn went to the trunk of his polished gray Chevrolet and took his accordion out of its black patent leather case. I thought that instrument was like him somehow. Heavy, awkward, strapped, difficult—he seemed to slip it on as though an accordion were breastplate armor. Peering over the door of the car, I could see everyone watching him now. Some women were whispering to each other. One man pushed his hands back and forth to signal accordion. Behind the car, my stepfather adjusted the leather straps on his instrument, then summoned me again. "Get to it now, like I asked you. Pass out the songbooks, George."

Carrying the stack of spiral-bound, yellow-red-white songbooks with smiling White children's faces on the cover and "He Owns the Cattle on a Thousand Hills" all over the back, I walked down the front row and gave one to each child. They all took them very carefully, more carefully than I ever did. They stared at them as though they might have been gifts, and, in their culture, they might well have been gifts. At the end of the second row, I gave the woman a stack and did the same for the men's row. They all seemed eager to get a songbook. When I finished, I didn't know where to go, whether to stand or sit or get back in the car. I knew I didn't want to be up front with my stepfather.

So as Reverend Frank A. Venn introduced himself and said, "Let us turn to 'Heavenly Sunshine,'" I sat down on the grass by a girl my size. She seemed beautiful to me—quiet, serene, alert—and I realized that I had seen her briefly one morning when my brother and I were walking by this house. She'd been drinking out of the water standpipe in the yard. I looked down at her hands and saw her fingers were berry-stained—that reddish brown which will not wash out. I held mine up to show her, and she laughed quietly.

My stepfather started playing his accordion. It sounded whining, thin, out of place, but he started singing in his usual drone, and a few Upper Skagit attempted to sing along, but it was obvious that "Heavenly Sunshine" was not their song or even in their repertoire. Distance between my stepfather and his audience was not new to me, but here was a group of people who were just not singing with him at all. That was a surprise.

Reverend Venn chose another song and sang it largely by himself again, though he nodded his head at me vigorously, by which he intended to encourage me to sing loudly with him, so the Upper Skagit could hear me singing too. Something was happening. I didn't know what it was. People were looking at me. I was embarrassed now, and I did not want to identify with this stepfather of mine. I sensed something strange was happening, something I did not understand, something that had never happened to me before. There was silence, there was waiting. There was polite but explicit non-participation.

I did not sing loudly enough for anyone to hear me. I pulled up grass, stared at the sky, watched the cottonwood leaves clittering in the late gold light across the road. When a brown dog came from the cabins behind the house and began to sniff and amble around the way dogs do, I was extremely grateful. When the dog lifted his leg and peed on the mailbox post behind my stepfather, I saw several women put their hands over their smiles. One of the men, however, called the dog with a word I had never heard before; the dog came to him, and he led him away behind the main house again.

After three or four attempts to get the Upper Skagit to sing his hymns, my stepfather stopped, snapped his accordion shut, slipped it back in its stiff patent leather case, and picked up his black, leather-bound, gold-lettered, gilt-edged Bible. "Let us pray," he said, and then there was the usual flurry of "thees" and "thous" and "Our Fathers" and "look downs." After the prayer he read some Biblical passage to these polite and quiet people, who were obviously being respectful toward him. His strategy was about the same as St. Paul's: there's this perfect God and just when you think you're good, you're really evil, and there's nothing you can do about it; your lower nature will always win out, and, no matter what you do, you're helpless in your own destruction unless, well, there is one way—outside help, from Jesus the son of this perfect God. My stepfather just happened to know personally this Jesus and this God. He would explain what God wanted, quote some supporting texts, read some more, explain some more of why God killed his son, and so on. I was always terrified when he told why God killed his son, but my stepfather's story never changed. As the sunset light came down, the scattering clouds over us became brilliant orange fish scales, and I knew that we were now headed toward the last song and final prayer of the service.

My stepfather once more strapped on his accordion and asked again if anyone would like to choose a song. It was obvious now that the Upper Skagit were not on his side. Some huge differences charged the silence now, differences not bridged at all. By this time, I was wanting to leave or hide or become invisible. However, a preacher's stepson has only the right to move around, so I had taken up a new seat—away from everyone by a stack of new empty strawberry crates. So, when my stepfather made this last invitation, I was astounded to see a younger Upper Skagit man in the back row put up his hand and say, "Yes, please. Page seventeen, please." My stepfather seemed visibly shocked and surprised, then I thought he looked relieved. He turned the pages in his hymn book and began to play an introduction to "Faith of our Fathers." He knew all the music from memory.

As my stepfather began to sing, so did all of the Upper Skagit. They *knew* this music, these words, and they knew them well. Men, women, and children all sang and their unison voices drowned my stepfather out completely from the very first words. "Faith of our fathers living still, in spite of dungeon, fire and sword."

The men's voices were rich and deep, the women's tremulous and strong. My face flushed and my heart started to beat faster. Something was happening. I didn't know what. Was there something wrong? Had they been fooling him all along? "Oh how our hearts beat high with joy, when e'er we hear that glorious word."

Was this their joke? I studied the Upper Skagit faces and they were all happily singing and seemed to be singing at my stepfather whose eel-like face never flinched from its usual stolid self. "Faith of our fathers, holy faith. We will be true to thee 'til death."

And the rest of the stanzas followed, as they must, since my stepfather always believed in singing the entire song:

> Our fathers chained in prisons dark
> Were still in heart and conscience free;
> How sweet would be their children's fate
> If they, like them, could die for thee!
>
> Faith of our fathers we will love
> Both friend and foe in all our strife:
> And preach thee, too, as love knows how
> By kindly words and virtuous life.

When the Upper Skagit stopped singing, I saw all the men in the back row looking at my stepfather, waiting for him to say something more, but he said nothing now. In silence, he shut the golden bellows of his wheezing accordion and snapped the latches. Silence. Everywhere. No one moved. Greater silence. Then, far away in one of the cabins where the pickers stayed, I could hear a baby crying. There was something more going on. When I picked up the songbooks, everyone was still silent. I didn't know what had happened. A huge question mark formed over this moment.

On the way home, my stepfather said nothing to me about it.

I have never forgotten this evening the Upper Skagit sang "Faith of our Fathers." Their singing created some powerful unspoken feeling, but it took me twenty years to recognize what might have been going on. They were a captive audience. They'd been forced to accept this meeting because they were picking berries for a member of the Presbyterian Church and they were Indians. But, at least one Upper Skagit man in that captive audience wanted to enlighten my stepfather. After all, the Noo-qua-cha-mish had their fathers, Ch-la-ben, Spik-cum, Be-bash-chad, Scha-ha-lab-ki, and their fathers had their own faith—the guardian spirit tradition—and their own mythic texts, including the beautiful Star Child myth, their creation narrative. Maybe that Upper Skagit man had seen how "Faith of Our Fathers" protested—for everyone everywhere—religious persecution. Maybe he'd learned how American persecution of the Upper Skagit during the invasion of western Washington was similar to papist persecution of Protestants in seventeenth-century Europe. Could Reverend Venn see that shared heritage? Could he recognize who the Upper Skagit were? Their history, beliefs, customs, culture? It is impossible to know how much that man intended that night. One thing, however, is clear: the Protestant hymn had lost its sectarian content. Someone among the Upper Skagit had recognized the universality within Frederick Faber's lyrics and the song had crossed from one religious and cultural tradition to another—without changing a word.

I still see that Upper Skagit man in the back row raising his hand. With a gesture, he opened the fortress of racism that night, with a song, and I walked out a lucky boy. Here, I finally can thank him. I hope that somewhere, his heart and the hearts of his people are still high with their own kind of joy.

Blue Shadows on Human Drama: The Western Songscape
Hal Cannon

> There's a place I know where no man can go,
> Where the shadows have all the room
> I was riding free on the old SP,
> Humming a southern tune
> When a man came along, made me hush my song,
> Put me out a-way out there. . . . (Boyd 1936)

I grew up with one foot in Salt Lake City and one foot in a western agricultural community, Bluffdale, Utah. As a boy I remember visiting our doctor's office. I can picture the waiting room vividly. Cheap prints hung on the wall. One was a picture of a marsh, duck hunters waiting behind a blind as a V of ducks flew overhead. The other was of a Conestoga wagon, with pioneer family, rolling across a desert landscape. As an adult I came back to that same office. The old prints had come down. The wall color had changed, the furniture was modern, and new prints were in place of the old: now there was a print of mallards swimming peacefully in the water—no hunters in sight—and, replacing the pioneers, a photograph of a red-rock landscape. In both cases the human beings were taken out of the landscape.

Recently, during a layover while traveling, I stopped to eat a hot dog at the airport. A poster hung on the wall which advertised a fund-raising campaign for something called "Share the Earth," a joint campaign of forty-nine environmental organizations. Encircling the poster were illustrations of those who would benefit from this sharing—whales, birds, foxes, trees, leaves, and others. Nothing on the poster included people, even those who really could benefit from some sharing of the riches of the earth. The implicit message was that humans are separate from nature. And by contributing to the fund you would assuage your guilt by giving your fair share back to the natural world.

I'm part of the generation of environmental activism which helped form this aesthetic. Two decades ago, when I began searching and researching cowboy music and poetry, I was anxious to find songs and verse which, like the new prints in the doctor's office, had divested themselves of the human element. Focusing on the natural western environment, I hoped I would find works from the folk perspective that would illuminate and give a new vantage to the natural landscape. What I found instead, in this occupational repertoire, were poems and songs full of human drama, with the natural world as a mere backdrop. I asked myself, where are the works from the folk repertoire which explore the pure natural world, the world without Conestogas and duck hunters? Naively, I hoped that if I could find traditional songs and stories that were environmentally sensitive—i.e., not so damn full of people—then I could prove to myself that at least at one time folk culture was more environmentally sensitive. Though I found some western poetry which dealt entirely with the natural world, these works—the works without people—didn't seem to resonate with the same meaning as those focusing on people. I was crestfallen not to find that place where, as in Bill Boyd's "Way Out There," "the shadows have all the room."

> I sat up on a pinnacle and took off my slouch hat
> But all that I could see was the farm shacks on the flat
> Said the Indian to the cowboy, You had better look around,
> Or you're liable to be camping on some other fellow's ground.
> Oh, the Indian and the cowboy, they used to live in peace,
> Till the damned old dry-land farmer come a-creeping from the East.
>
> (Atwood 1976)

My heritage is of people who comprise a mere layer in a myriad of layers of western conquest and displacement. My people are those dry-land farmers who came "a-creeping from the East." I remember asking my father why we called our place a farm, not a ranch. I wanted my dad to be Sky King, flying over some vast kingdom that was all ours. Unfortunately he loved the idea of being a farmer—no show, just agricultural production. This may have been Mormon modesty or it may have been an older family tradition which did not include the potent horse-and-cattle culture that defines ranching. There is a western saying that a man might have a thousand sheep and twenty cows and he will proclaim himself a cattle rancher. I can see how that would go against my father's grain. Though I loved *Sky King*, I had little use for most cowboy movies. I just didn't find the movie cowboys and their stories interesting or believable. I found our farming and ranching neighbors and their stories different from the popular image and, frankly, much more subtle and evocative. Interestingly, though the stories from the cowboy movies and the story of our family and our Utah neighbors contained similar underlying themes, I could not conceive of my family or our neighbors being part of a heroic human drama that marks the West. Our heroism was not monumental. It was a heroism of ordinary life. And now I see drama, both subtle and embellished, in each folk song, poem and story of our region. The relation of environment to these works may not be thematically central, but references to a place, "way out there," contribute in a powerful way to much folk expression from the old West. There is almost a sense of fresh reaction to the place. After all, the people who made these works up and used them were newcomers to the West, and though they may have seen themselves at odds with the environment, they also came to the region with hopes and dreams and a fresh perspective on the landscape. That may be one reason why cowboy songs and poems have persisted, have become emblematic of a common experience.

The cowboy is the symbolic recipient of an enchanted melding of western landscape and human drama. As symbol, his story is universal. But why has the cowboy defined the West so directly? Part of understanding the power of the cowboy is knowing where his song and story come from. Every artistic tradition has a murky past marked by high creativity, low self-consciousness, and marginal popularity to outsiders. For the cowboy it was in those trail-drive days of the eighteen-seventies and -eighties, when the American West still seemed a frontier, that the expressive life of the cowboy became legendary. There are no historic narratives from the trail drives following the Civil War which fully explain the chemistry of an incredibly diverse lot of men brought together, in the wilderness, relying on each other and animals for long and trying odysseys. From this experience came an amazing amalgam of life that forever would identify Americans. It was a jazz of Irish storytelling and lore, Scottish seafaring and cattle tending, Moorish and Spanish horsemanship, European cavalry, African improvisation, and practical Native American survival techniques. All this history makes up what the cowboy is, even today.

> They had not been gone for an hour or two
> When out of his budget a fiddle he drew
> He played her a tune caused the valleys to ring
> Hark hark, cried the maiden, hear the whippoorwill sing.
>
> Oh ho, cried the cowboy, It's time to give o'er
> Oh no, cried the maiden, just play one tune more
> So he played her a tune caused the valley to ring
> Hark hark, cried the maiden, hear the whippoorwill sing
>
> Oh now, cried the maiden, won't you marry me
> Oh no, cried the cowboy, that never can be,
> I've a wife in New Mexico and children twice three
> Two wives on a cow ranch, too many for me.[1]

The beauty of songs that endure through time is that they convey worlds of information. The words (the poetry) both paint the place and chronicle the action. There are also subtle elements that define folk songs, conventions of tradition that build trust in the song by representing the period, the class and ethnicity of the singer and, most importantly, the veracity of the message. Built of word and tune, songs must stay true to specific traditions or they will not be learned and passed on. The critical process of natural selection for songs that last through time is much more stringent than one might think. Therefore, if a song, story, or poem survives, the very fact that it lives on makes it worth examination. In the old British ballad, "The Soldier and the Lady," adapted to the West as "One Morning in May" or "The Cowboy and the Lady," the lusty cowboy and the impressionable young lady cry to each other like ravens cawing: "Hark hark." In this song, the cautionary message of choosing mates carefully is as economically contained in the song as raven DNA containing a road map for mating habits. "Hark hark, cried the maiden."

I've been told that tone-deafness is caused by music teachers who hate their students. In many cultures there is nothing, save deafness, which defines tone-deafness. Otherwise how could we recognize specific voices or muster tone in our own discourse? I've come to mourn, even more than tone-deafness, what Bertrand Russell calls "immunity to eloquence" (Postman 1985, 26). I referred earlier to an impression that some poems carry resonance, others do not. Perceived meaning, the impressionistic appraisal of truth, the relation between the subconscious and improvisational oral discourse, the unconscious gesture—these are potent and real parts of life that might seem ludicrous as the stuff of hard study. Yet that is why some of the finest ethnographic work comes in novels and paintings rather than in analytic observation. You can't always capture the subtlety of cultural expression in didactic ways. The late cowboy singer and poet Buck Ramsey, testifying to the National Endowment for the Arts in 1995, spoke directly to the value of folk eloquence in his folk community, what he calls his tribe, the cowboy tribe:

> I think our nation, and our species has common memory that keeps us, through tradition, connected; reminded of the precious things our minds and hearts and souls have sifted and sanctified from our long and common experience. But, as regards to songs, stories and poems, which are much of the traditional foundation of my tribe, I learned early a curious fact: The older the cowboy, the more likely he was to be plugged into that common memory of the tribe. That is he knew more songs, stories and poems than the younger ones and seemed to be in some way purer in his tribal etiquette.
>
> When it came to my generation, we know only snatches of what the old ones knew. Clearly radio, movies, television began drowning out the resonance of the tradition, acted as something of an Alzheimer's disease on the common memory.[2]

Neil Postman observes in his epistemology of media in *Amusing Ourselves to Death* that "Since intelligence is primarily defined as one's capacity to grasp the truth of things, it follows that what a culture means by intelligence is derived from the character of its important forms of communication. In a purely oral culture, intelligence is often associated with aphoristic ingenuity, that is, the power to invent compact sayings of wide applicability" (Postman 1985, 24–25).

The story of the cowboy and the lady is gloriously compact in its meaning, combining the power of nature, the whippoorwill's song, the beguiling fiddle, the lustiness of the flowing spring in the dry wilderness. And yet the seduction is followed by the rebuke. How's that for landscape and human drama. Folk songs weave landscape and human drama into a single fabric. It's always there. It seems ironic that as my appreciation for folk expression has refined, so has my fervor as an activist for both nature and culture. Thinking that we can divorce human history from natural history now seems ridiculous to me. Many continue to believe that if only we humans were not part of the equation, the world could once again be pristine. The world has never been pristine and it is only pristine because we, as humans, give it that value.

> Blue Mountain, you're azure deep, Blue Mountain with sides so steep
> Blue Mountain with horse head on your side, you have won my heart for to keep
> I chum with Latigo Gordon, I drink at the Blue Goose Saloon
> I dance at night with the Mormon girls and I ride home beneath the moon.
>
> (Keller 1947)

Wallace Stegner's words have always stuck with me: "A place is not a place until a poet has been there" (Stegner 1989). I've come to wonder if it took a poet to tell us the Grand Canyon was majestically beautiful rather than a majestic inconvenience for travelers. Indeed, Ernst Cassirer contends that "Physical reality seems to recede in proportion as man's symbolic activity advances. Instead of dealing with things themselves man is in a sense constantly conversing with himself. He has so enveloped himself in linguistic forms, in artistic images, in mythical symbols or religious rites that he cannot see or know anything except by the interposition of artificial medium" (quoted in Postman 1985, 10).

When I spoke with Judge Fred Keller, the man who made up the song, "Blue Mountain," he told me quite simply that he wrote the song to remember a place and a time in this life. He knew his cowboying days were over. He was going off to school and he was at a loss for ways to keep those memories alive, so he wrote a song. Now it lives on.

Bob Nolan, of the Sons of the Pioneers, wrote a song one day in 1932 as he looked out his apartment window in West Los Angeles, deciding it was too rainy and windy for him to go to his regular job as a caddie at the Bel Air Country Club. He watched as leaves blew past him along the street. His song has survived in popular culture as a symbol of freedom and open spaces in the west:

> See them tumbling down
> Pledging their love to the ground
> Lonely but free I'll be found.
> Drifting along with the tumbling tumbleweeds.
>
> (Nolan 1934)

Across town, Bruce Kiskaddon sat in the lobby of the Mayflower Hotel, where he worked as a bellhop, and measured once again how we are tied to place and how we can find independence to move on:

> My spurs they ring and the song I sing
> Is set to my horse's stride
> We gallop along to an old time song
> As out on the trail we ride.
> CHORUS.
> Oh I'm hittin' the trail tonite tonite
> I'm hittin' the trail tonite
> My horse is pullin' the bridle reins
> I'm hittin' the trail tonite.
>
> (Kiskaddon 1987, 62)

I grew up on radio-format songs, songs lasting rarely more than two or three minutes, songs picked for airplay for very specific commercial reasons. Growing up, I don't believe I quite understood what a song could do, what a song could be, until I traveled to the outback of Australia and spent time with Aboriginal people who talked about their songs being tied directly to the experience of the Walkabout. Quite literally, stanzas of songs are prompted by the passing of certain places. The song is integral to time and place. Later, halfway around the world, interviewing Paul Ethalbah, a White Mountain Apache medicine man and rancher, I got that same sense about his songs and prayers. His blessings for horses and ropes are a part of daily life. He relies on the power of his songs. He believes that his horses and tools are enhanced through the singing.

We have come to underestimate the power of songs, prayers, poems, and stories. Those that resound with truth have great power. They define the eloquence of western experience.

Notes

1. "The Cowboy and the Lady," I. D. Jones's version of the traditional English song, "The Soldier and the Lady," was field-recorded by James Griffith.
2. Buck Ramsey, testimony before the National Endowment for the Arts, Washington, D. C., February 1995.

Objects

A Diversity of Dead Helpers:
Folk Saints of the
U.S.-Mexico Borderlands
James S. Griffith

S ince about 1991, I have been building an archival collection of commer-
cially printed Catholic devotional ephemera—holy pictures, prayers,
novenas, and other aids to prayer and meditation that are produced in vast
quantities for the use of Catholics around the world. The main collection,
obtained in the Southwestern United States and Mexico, now numbers over
fifteen hundred items. (Smaller collections have been made in Bavaria,
Spain, Portugal, Goa, and Sri Lanka.) All the material is housed in the
Southwest Folklore Center (SWFC) of the University of Arizona Library.
These devotional aids are used in several ways by traditional Roman
Catholics. The pictures (which may or may not have prayers printed on the
reverse) may go on home altars, where they focus the attention of the petitioner onto a particular saint or member of the Holy Family. The printed
prayers and novenas (which may or may not have a picture of the sacred
personage addressed) are often kept between the leaves of prayer books.
Such prayers may be used in request of aid from a particular saint in
response to a specific occasional need, or they may be used recurrently, as
on a saint's day.

As I have gone over the Mexican and Mexican-American portions of
this collection, I have been impressed by the many kinds of personages
called upon for supernatural help. Jesus and the Blessed Virgin Mary head
the list in sheer quantity. While these figures are certainly part of mainstream Catholic belief, one begins to enter the realms of folk tradition with
devotional material that addresses specific aspects of Christ and the Virgin
represented by specific statues. Language choice gets tricky in the case of
these popular devotions. Are the prayers addressed to the statues or to the
personages the statues represent—and, if the latter be the case, in what sense
is the Holy Child of Atocha, venerated in Plateros, Zacatecas (Lange 1978;

Frankfurter 1988; Thompson 1994), different from the Santo Niño Doctor de los Enfermos, venerated in Tepeyaca, Puebla (Rodriguez 1994)? What is the relationship between, say, Our Lord of Chalma (Rodriguez 1994, 107–110) and El Señor del Veneno in Mexico City (Griffith 1995, 91–97)? Between the Virgin of Guadalupe (Toor 1947, 171) and the Virgin of San Juan de los Lagos (Rodriguez 1994, 98–100)? I suspect that answers to these and other questions are not simple and would reveal a continuum of Mexican folk Catholic belief, stretching from recognizable—and rationalized—mainstream Catholic Christianity to something that might resemble polytheism to outsiders. William Wroth writes of a Platonic attitude he finds in Mexican Indian thinking that "clearly sees the archetypes [of any given statue] as such, but also just as clearly sees that the archetype is truly present in the 'piece of wood'" (Wroth n.d.).

In addition to Jesus and Mary, the saints are also petitioned. Some of these saints are well known within the Catholic Church, and their concerns are those understood by Catholics the world around. In other cases, mainstream saints are asked to perform unusual tasks. I use the term *folk devotions* to describe these situations. In still other cases, individuals are petitioned for help who are not, and probably never will be, saints in the official Roman Catholic Church. It is these individuals to whom I refer as *folk saints*. In the present study I will describe briefly some of the folk devotions and folk saints which seem to be important in the U.S.-Mexican borderlands. I shall also discuss the advantages and limitations of a collection-based study such as this and suggest further directions a study might take.

It might be wise to begin with a discussion of sainthood as it is understood by the Roman Catholic Church. Saints, according to the *New Catholic Encyclopedia*, are "those members of the mystical body of Christ who have lived and died, whose lives were notable for holiness and virtues practiced, and who have been officially declared saints by the church through the process of beatification and canonization." They are also considered to be spending eternity in the presence of God, and for that reason are approachable through prayer as intercessors for humans, whose trials and difficulties they understand through personal experience. The individual saint does not work miracles; he or she intercedes on the petitioner's behalf with God, who performs or does not perform the desired action (1967).

Saints recognized by the Catholic Church may be asked for non-mainstream favors. For instance, in one printed prayer on file at the SWFC, San Alejo (St. Alexis) is approached to help the petitioner get rid of bad neighbors, possibly as a result of the similarity between the name *Alejo* and the Spanish verb *alejarse*, "to move away." (This kind of searching within names for clues to assist in understanding the meaning of things is reminiscent of the *Golden Legend* and other products of medieval Christian thought [Jacobus de Voragine 1969]).

Another card on file at the SWFC entreats San Martin Caballero—St. Martin of Tours—to visit good fortune upon the petitioner, even at the hands of his enemies: "[G]rant me the favor that my enemies remain enchanted by me and that they hear my voice that calls them and that they come to an accord with me. If I need to see them, may they come to me quickly, in the name of St. Martin of Tours I call them to come quickly to me, and to come to an accord with me. May St. Martin of Tours make them return to me my lost vigor and I desire that they come looking for me at the doors of my house to give me work or money and that they look for me desperately so that until they speak to me or see me they will not be in peace."

These cards to Saints Alexis and Martin were purchased, not in a religious articles store, but at an herb-seller's booth at the annual pilgrimage fiesta of San Francisco at Magdalena, Sonora (Griffith 1992, 59–65). Booths at fiestas and in markets, as well as *yerberías* and *botánicas* (stores specializing in traditional herbal remedies), are rich sources for this sort of folk material, which verges on charms and spells rather than prayers. Who uses these cards, these unorthodox prayers? It is probable that at least some of the users are involved in the most important industry of the borderlands—the drug trade (Strong 1990 and personal communication). This assumption is given some validity by the existence of a huge private shrine to St. Martin about one hundred miles south of the border, placed in a field in an unpopulated area. Local rumor has it that the shrine was erected by an unnamed regional *narcotraficante* or drug dealer.

Another sort of folk devotion, almost impossible to detect through an examination of printed material, is exemplified in the fusing in Magdalena, Sonora, of three holy personages—St. Francis Xavier, St. Francis of Assisi, and Father Eusebio Francisco Kino, S.J. (a local historical figure)—into one composite saint who is represented by a reclining statue of Xavier dressed in brown Franciscan robes but whose day is celebrated on October 4, the saint's day of St. Francis of Assisi (Griffith 1992, 31–57). This composite saint is believed to effect miracles himself, rather than petitioning God for them, and, further, to exact his often fatal revenge on those who show no intention of keeping their sides of any bargain they might make with him. San Francisco, as he exists in popular regional thought, is indeed a folk creation, halfway between my categories of folk devotion and folk saint.

And now to the folk saints themselves. There appear to be three sorts of deceased people in borderlands belief who, although they are not saints, seem to be treated by many as though they were. These can be categorized as *victim intercessors, social bandits,* and *faith healers.* I have described victim intercessors at length elsewhere (Griffith 1995, 67–86), but shall discuss briefly here the main victim intercessor known to me: Juan Castillo Morales, or "Juan Soldado," as he is popularly known. Juan Castillo (in Mexican custom, the matronymic comes last) was a young recruit in Tijuana in 1938.

According to legend, he was accused of a sexual crime which in fact had
been committed by his commanding officer. Juan was executed but
appeared after death to the guilty officer (who immediately confessed and
died) as well as to his mother and other women who were keeping vigil at
his execution site. He began answering petitions and achieved a considerable
local following. He is considered by some an *alma* (soul) rather than a *santo*
(saint), although he seems to behave like a saint, interceding with God on
behalf of petitioners. A chapel has been erected next to his grave. Printed
photographs of and prayers to him are sold at the cemetery where he is
buried and elsewhere in the borderlands. His devotion has spread along
Mexican Highway 2 as far southeast as Hermosillo, the capital of Sonora,
and back up Highway 15 to Magdalena, some sixty miles south of the border

Juan Soldado's death site, Panteón No. 1, Tijuana, Baja California, 1983. The pile
of stones figures in the legendary narratives concerning Juan Soldado's death and
subsequent appearances. In addition to an openwork metal cross marked with
Juan Soldado's name, four ex-voto statements are visible. The only legible one, to
the left of the photograph, reads in translation: "1950. Salvador Gonzales. I give
you infinite thanks, Juan Soldado, for having granted me such a great miracle of
saving me from prison that I hope God has you in His holy kingdom for having
granted me this miracle." The picture on the rear wall is of el Santo Niño de
Atocha (the Holy Child of Atocha), a Mexican manifestation of the Christ Child.
(J. Griffith photo)

El Tiradito, Tucson, Arizona, late 1980s. The stones at the site are occasionally reorganized, and candles, statues, and wreaths appear and disappear, but the general outline of the shrine has remained the same since at least the mid-1950s. (J. Griffith photo)

at Nogales. It is possible to purchase prayer cards to him in Tucson and Magdalena, as well as at his gravesite in Tijuana.

Juan Soldado is not the only figure of this type to have been venerated in the border country. *El Tiradito*, "The Little Cast-away One," has had an important shrine in Tucson, Arizona, since at least 1891. While legend does not agree on who el Tiradito was, or on the circumstances of his death, the shrine commemorates the place where someone is believed to have been killed and buried on the spot without the benefit of last rites. The shrine has changed in character (and at least once in location) over the century of its existence, but it remains an active place of petitions, and candles burn there day and night.

Other victim intercessors have come and gone along the Arizona-Sonora border. A soldier named Pedro Blanco was robbed and killed in Nogales, Sonora, on his way home from winning at cards. He was buried where he fell, a small chapel was erected at his death site, and a devotion to him flourished for several years until he was moved to a cemetery. Now nobody seems to visit his grave. Other victim intercessors whose devotions were important earlier in the century have now sunk into oblivion. Still

A photograph of part of Jesús Malverde's shrine in Culiacán,
Sinaloa. This photo, originally in color, was sold at the shrine.
The bust in the right foreground is Jesús Malverde; the figure in
the left background is the Virgin of Guadalupe. Purchased in
Culiacàn, Sinaloa, by Arturo Carrillo Strong, May, 1975. (David
Burkhalter photo)

DI TU VOLUNTAD

Ayudar
a mi gente
en el
nombre de
DIOS

JESUS MALVERDE

A prayer card to Jesús Malverde, showing him at the moment of his execution. The text reads in translation: "Do Your will. Help my people in the name of God." Purchased at a Tucson *yerbería*, June, 1996. (David Burkhalter photo)

ORACION A PANCHO VILLA

En nombre de Dios Nuestro Señor invoco a los espíritus que te protejan para que me ayudes.

Así como ayudaste en el mundo terrenal a los necesitados.

Así como venciste a los poderosos.

Así como hiciste retroceder a tus enemigos.

Así te pido tu protección espiritual, para que me libres de todo mal y me des el ánimo necesario y el valor suficiente para enfrentarme a lo más difícil que se me presente en la vida.

Amén.

CROMOS Y NOVEDADES DE MEXICO, S.A. DE C.V.

A *cédula* or prayer with a printed frame, addressed to Pancho Villa. The translated prayer reads: "In the name of God our Lord I invoke the spirits that protect you, that they might help me. / Just as they helped you in this earthly world to what was necessary. / Just as you conquered the powerful. / Just as you made your enemies fall back. / Thus I request your spiritual protection, so that you free me from all evil and give me the courage necessary to confront the greatest difficulties that I am presented with in life. / Amen." Published and copyrighted by Cromos y Novedades de Mexico, S.A. de C.V., reprinted with permission. Purchased in Mexico City, July, 1997, by John Thompson. (David Burkhalter photo)

PRAYER TO NINO FIDENCIO

BEAUTIFUL HOLY CHILD FIDENCIO WITH THE BLESSINGS OF OUR LORD JESUS CHRIST YOU ARE MY HOPE AND MY FAITH. HOLY CHILD FIDENCIO S. CONSTANTINO, KEEP ME HEALTHY AND PURE, REMOVE ALL EVIL AND GIVE ME PEACE OF BODY AND SOUL. CHILD FIDENCIO, HELP ALL PEOPLE WHO, LIKE MYSELF, HAVE FAITH IN YOU AND NEVER FORSAKE THEM. PRAY ONE OUR FATHER AND ONE HAIL MARY. (CONCENTRATE ON YOUR DESIRES)

Prayer to el Niño Fidencio, photocopied on white paper and laminated in plastic. Purchased in Corpus Christi, Texas, in April, 1995, by Cynthia Vidaurri. (David Burkhalter photo)

ORACION AL TODOPODEROSO Y EVOCACION AL ESPIRITU PURO

D·PEDRITO JARAMILLO

Prayer leaflet to Don Pedrito Jaramillo. This folded, 4½" x 7½" piece of newsprint bears no printer's name. The title reads in translation, "Prayer to the Allpowerful and evocation of the pure spirit of D. Pedrito Jaramillo." Interior headings include "Prayer for the Medium" (English word used) and "To the Guardian Angels and Protective Spirits." Purchased in Chimayó, New Mexico, 1993. (David Burkhalter photo) others doubtless exist elsewhere in the borderlands, but Juan Soldado is the only victim intercessor I am aware of to have devotional aids printed in his name.

Jesús Malverde, an example of the social bandit, is said to have robbed from the rich and given to the poor in turn-of-the-century Sinaloa (Lopez Sanchez 1995, 32–40; Grant 1995). He was captured and hanged near Culiacán, the state capital, in 1909. His chapel is now one of the landmarks of Culiacán, and many people, including but not at all limited to drug traffickers, pray to him for miracles. He is represented as a youngish man with black hair and mustache, dressed in a light-colored "Western" shirt with dark pocket flaps and a dark-colored neckerchief. While Culiacán is a long way from the Arizona-Sonora border, Malverde has a growing number of devotees in the borderlands. I have seen a prayer to him pinned to a saint's statue at Mission San Xavier del Bac, just south of Tucson, and his statue appears on at least one home altar in Tucson. Cards to and statues of Malverde may be purchased in Tucson's *botánicas* and religious articles stores.

Another social bandit who appears in printed prayers is Francisco "Pancho" Villa, the famous revolutionary leader from the northern Mexican state of Chihuahua. Known as *"el centauro del norte"*—"the Centaur of the North"—Villa has entered national and regional Mexican legendry as a champion of the rights of the common people, as a fierce and skillful fighter, and as a man of great physical strength and courage. A prayer card to Villa, on file at the SWFC, dwells on how he helped the needy, conquered the powerful, and paid back his enemies in this world, and requests assistance of him and his protecting spirits. (Interestingly, social bandits—or at least bandits—have been elevated to sainthood by Christian folk since at least 400 A.D.; a life of St. Martin of Tours describes an incident in which the saint revealed the supposed shrine of an early Christian martyr to be in fact the gravesite of a notorious robber [Schmitt 1983, 22, 23].)

With Pancho Villa, another dimension enters into the picture. Not only is Villa asked for supernatural assistance, but spiritualists of various sorts are accustomed to call upon and be possessed by his spirit at seances (Cynthia Vidaurri, personal communication). Some of the mediums who do so are *fidencistas*—followers of a deceased faith healer (our third category) known familiarly as "el Niño Fidencio."

El Niño Fidencio—"Fidencio the child" ("of God" is understood)—was born José Fidencio Sintora Constantino in Guanajuato, Mexico, in 1898 and spent most of his adult life on a hacienda in Espinazo, Nuevo León. Interested in traditional curing from an early age, Fidencio gained the reputation of being an extremely powerful *curandero*—almost a miracle worker. He never married and is remembered as a gentle, generous man with a strong sense of play and drama. He concentrated on healing, even while his reputation as a spiritual person grew, and did not produce any sort of doctrinal statements.

He is said to have cured Plutarco Elías Calles, then president of Mexico, of a chronic ailment. He died (some of his followers say he was murdered by jealous doctors) in 1938, the most famous healer in Mexico (Gardner 1992; Macklin and Crumrine 1973, 89–105).

His influence did not stop with his death. Today, his spirit is called upon (and assumed) by mediums (*materias* and *cajones* are the terms commonly used) all over northern Mexico and the U.S. borderlands. There are communities of *fidencistas* from the Gulf of Mexico to Los Angeles. Annual pilgrimages to his homesite at Espinazo, a sacred place for *fidencistas*, number well into the tens of thousands. One group of *fidencistas* has registered itself as a separate church in Mexico, while others simply add the devotion to el Niño to their Catholic beliefs. While most *materias* only serve as vehicles for the spirit of el Niño, a few call upon other spirits as well, including several of those mentioned in this paper (Cynthia Vidaurri, personal communication).

Don Pedrito Jaramillo, another famous healer, is said to have been born in Guadalajara. He arrived in South Texas in 1881, announcing himself as a *curandero* and settling at the Los Olmos ranch near present-day Falfurrias, Texas. Claiming that he was appointed as a curer by God, he commenced a long career of curing anyone upon request for only voluntary recompense. He acquired a widespread reputation for his saintliness and curing abilities, and died in 1907 (Dodson 1951). He was buried in the cemetery near Paisano, Texas, and his grave is still well kept and visited (Cynthia Vidaurri, personal communication). In the SWFC are two separate prayer cards to him that include a request for blessing the medium who is calling his spirit. Both cards appear to have been produced by small printshops. A third card is printed in color on slick paper and was made in Italy! According to Cynthia Vidaurri (personal communication), Don Pedrito is among those spirits who are called upon for advice and assistance by some *materias* of el Niño Fidencio.

A third faith healer, Teresa Urrea, often known as "Teresita Urrea, la Santa de Cabora," was born in 1873, the illegitimate daughter of a Sonoran *haciendado*. At about the age of sixteen, she underwent a traumatic illness and, upon recovery from it, commenced curing people. She was said to be gifted with second sight and the power of bilocation, along with her spiritual curing powers. As a healer, her fame spread through Sonora and Chihuahua, attracting both Mestizo and Indian followers. In the 1890s she became the (probably unwilling) figurehead for a series of uprisings in Northwest Mexico, and in 1893 she and her father were expelled from Mexico. After marriage and a tour of the United States, she died in Clifton, Arizona in 1906 (Holden 1978; Macklin and Crumrine 1973). Her grave has been moved at least once, and in the early 1990s a site in the Clifton cemetery was declared to be her gravesite. At least one request has since been received by the Clifton church for dirt from Teresita's grave. A postcard of her curing an Anglo banker's child has been printed and has sold extremely well. Interestingly, she is among the spirits called upon by *fidencista mate-rias* (Cynthia Vidaurri, personal communication). Like Fidencio, she was regarded by some as a "living saint" during her lifetime.

Far from dying out, folk devotions to unofficial saints are growing rapidly. One indicator is the fact that, while older prayer cards and devotional images show all the signs of having been printed in small shops, major print-ing houses have now started printing and distributing pictures of many of the individuals mentioned above. I mentioned above a full-color, laminated card to Don Pedrito that was printed in Italy. On a recent trip to Mexico City, my colleague John Thompson visited the headquarters of Cromos y Novedades, S.A., "one of the largest, if not the largest," producers of devo-tional cards and pictures in the hemisphere (John Thompson, personal communication). They have recently started a line of what they call *cédulas* (certificates)—full-color chromos which include both a prayer and a picture within a printed frame made to look like wood. Thompson procured a full list of these *cédulas*, which includes, along with mainstream saints and sacred scenes and figures, Pancho Villa, el Niño Fidencio, Don Pedrito, and Jesús Malverde. Inclusion in the line is determined, Thompson was told, by popular demand.

There seems to be one major point of intersection between the folk beliefs that have produced this rich array of souls and saints and the doc-trine of the Roman Catholic Church. That point concerns the Holy Souls in Purgatory. These souls are said to be bound for heaven but to need a period of purification before they can enter into the presence of God. It is custom-ary to pray for the souls who are in Purgatory, in the belief that such prayers will shorten their time of suffering. It is also permissible to pray *to* them, in the hope that, once they enter into God's presence, they might intercede on behalf of the petitioner. If the individuals described in this essay are consid-ered to be in purgatory, prayers and petitions to them are within the range of behavior permitted by church doctrine (Charles W. Polzer, S.J., and Thomas Steele, S.J., personal communications).

Although I have lumped all these deceased helpers under the rubric folk saints, they seem, in truth, to be of more than one sort. The victim inter-cessors are closest to the Catholic concept of saints in their behavior, although they would certainly not qualify for consideration for that status within the church; the woman who first told me about Juan Soldado made a point of emphasizing that he was an *alma* rather than a *santo*. Nevertheless, both Juan Soldado and el Tiradito seem to intercede with God on behalf of the petitioner just as regularly canonized saints are believed to do. The social bandits Jesús Malverde and Pancho Villa appear to be thought of as behaving in much the same way, although the printed prayers I have

seen addressed to both these men ask for direct assistance rather than inter-
cession. In addition, Villa is called on by spiritualists for direct help and
advice. Finally, the three faith healers seem to function as helpful spirits in
communication with this world through mediums and only secondarily as
powerful helpers to be petitioned. Although both el Niño Fidencio and Santa
Teresita were referred to as saints during their lifetimes, it is not really clear
to what extent their followers consider them to be intercessors in the way
that Roman Catholic saints are.

Something should be said about the ways in which the individuals I
have been describing seem to differ from folk saints in other parts of North
America. Folklorists working in places as disparate as upstate New York and
southern Louisiana have written about local folk saints. However, these are
much more within the model of Catholic saints than are the figures I have
been discussing. For example, Father Baker, a priest in Lackawanna, New
York, changed his working-class community through acts of great love and
charity. Although he is considered a saint by many members of his former
community, there is no serious movement towards canonization, a step that
might well be impossible due to the current tendency to canonize only those
whose cause is supported by one of the religious orders (Fish 1984 and personal communication). A second example is Charlene Richard, a young
Cajun girl who died of leukemia in 1959, moving all who knew her by the
loving resignation with which she met her fate. She is the subject of a
groundswell movement for canonization among both clergy and lay people
in her part of Louisiana (Gaudet 1994). These two examples of folk saints
from other regions in North America present a considerable contrast to the
borderlands' victim intercessors, social bandits, and faith healers whose
devotions make up the body of this paper, for both Father Baker and
Charlene Richard functioned within the framework of the Catholic Church,
Butler as a priest and Charlene as a little Catholic girl who impressed priests
and sisters by her willingness to offer up her sufferings for the benefit of others. Each strongly represents values of the formal church.

A possible explanation for this difference might be found in the contrast
between the Catholic experience in the United States on the one hand and
that in Mexico on the other. European Catholic populations in the United
States are mostly descended from eighteenth- and nineteenth-century immigrant groups who remained as Catholic enclaves within a basically Protestant
country. They kept their ties with the church and, partly because they were
enclaves, emphasized their Catholicness. Mexico, however, was colonized and
evangelized in the sixteenth century by Spain, a significant political force in
the Counter-Reformation. Missionary priests worked for three hundred years
to turn Mexico's indigenous populations into Catholic subjects of the Spanish
crown. Mexico remains a predominately Catholic country with a huge indigenous population. Much of the distinct flavor of Mexican popular Catholicism

seems to be a result of two factors: the size and intense regionality of the country and the presence within the population of large indigenous groups who have managed to preserve portions of their traditional belief systems through almost five centuries of Catholic dominance.

Beyond this blending of indigenous and Christian belief systems are other dynamics. The fact that the Catholic Church was the largest property owner in Mexico well into the second half of the nineteenth century, coupled with the popular perception of the Catholic hierarchy as supporting the upper classes, has led to a kind of devout anticlericalism that is still a feature of much Mexican religiosity. Spiritualism gained a strong foothold in late nineteenth-century Mexico, and remains as an important influence. The history of Mexican popular Catholicism, especially in non-Indian communities, is complex in the extreme. All this and more must be taken into account in any thorough study of the materials introduced in this short paper.

It is obvious that one can find out quite a bit by starting off with such material objects as prayer cards and holy pictures. I have discovered that certain saints—St. Martin of Tours and Saint Alexis—are asked by some people for favors of a sort not in keeping with the ethics of mainstream Catholicism. I have also discovered that the various folk saints I have mentioned—Juan Soldado, Jesús Malverde, Pancho Villa, el Niño Fidencio, Don Pedrito, and Teresita, la Santa de Cabora—are petitioned either as heavenly pleaders or as helpful spirits. Equally interesting, however, is what I did *not* learn through examination of the printed material. The complex of folk belief surrounding the composite statue of San Francisco in Magdalena, Sonora, is not even hinted at in print. Neither is the existence of el Tiradito, Tucson's important victim intercessor, whose shrine has been in existence since at least 1893, suggested by any printed devotional material. For knowledge of these important regional folk devotions, one must go to either the folk themselves or to the popular and professional literature concerning the region.

Another problem with relying on purchased devotional material as a research tool is that the existence of the material in a store or market stall does not necessarily prove existence of the devotion in that place. It might be available for purchase in a store or a stand precisely because nobody has purchased it. One way to approach this problem is by attracting collections of devotional material which have actually been amassed and used by someone. The SWFC does in fact have two such collections and is actively soliciting more. The knowledge that a particular Tucson woman owned, and presumably used, a printed prayer to Don Pedrito Jaramillo adds greatly to the collection's usefulness for discussion.

In this paper I have mentioned only folk saints, canonized saints, and manifestations of Jesus and Mary. The SWFC also contains, however, a number of prayer cards addressed to such spirits (if that is the correct term) as the Male Garlic, the Miraculous Hummingbird, the Holy Cigar, and the Secret of Most Holy Death. These, too, are sold and used along the border. These, too, are a part of the folk religion, but not necessarily the folk Catholicism, of the region.

What are some directions for further work with SWFC materials? One is to continue collecting as broadly as possible, both through purchase and through gift acquisition, increasing the already-rich possibilities for studies of borderlands iconography, traditional popular religious verse and prose, and related subjects. Another would be to engage in fieldwork to follow up on questions suggested by the extant materials, including questions raised in this brief paper—a progress report on the early stages of a project rather than any sort of definitive treatise. As such, one of its major functions has been to raise questions. The next step is to look for answers.

Note

An earlier version of this paper was read at the annual meeting of the American Folklore Society at Lafayette, Louisiana, October 1995. This enlarged and revised version has benefited greatly from comments by Erika Brady, the late Pack Carnes, Lydia Fish, and Cynthia Vidaurri. I am also deeply indebted to John Thompson of Tucson for generously sharing his field notes and observations with me. As he often has before, David Burkalter took all the studio photographs and printed the field photographs.

Icons of Immortality: Forest Lawn and the American Way of Death

Elliott Oring

They function the way good imagery and poetic diction do in literature: to convey and dramatize more fully those abstract matters which cannot be well articulated and reexperienced in any other way.

—Barre Toelken

In 1916, Hubert Eaton became the manager of a fifty-five acre rural cemetery in Tropico, California, called Forest Lawn. It was on New Year's Day of the following year that Eaton received the vision that led him to transform this little, failing cemetery into one of America's most famous cemeteries, second perhaps only to Arlington National Cemetery.

Today over 250,000 "loved ones" are entombed, interred, and inurned within the sacred grounds of Forest Lawn Memorial Park, Glendale. Twenty-five thousand weddings have been performed in its three churches, and more than half a million tourists visit it annually. Prior to the development of Disneyland, Forest Lawn was Southern California's most popular tourist attraction. However, Eaton's success with Forest Lawn was not without struggle, and in many quarters Forest Lawn's fame and reputation might be more properly described as notoriety.

A good deal of this notoriety was inspired by Evelyn Waugh's 1948 satire, *The Loved One*, and the even more excessive 1963 Hollywood film based upon the novel. Waugh viewed Forest Lawn as a product of the Southern California environment, heavily tainted by the artificiality, superficiality, and sentimentality of Hollywood. He saw Forest Lawn as banishing death and selling eternal life to those who could afford its cosmetic treatments for the deceased, its quilted caskets, and its earthquake-proof ventilated crypts. Stated Waugh, "The body does not decay; it lives on more chic in death than ever before, in its undestructible Class A steel and concrete shelf; the soul goes straight from the Slumber Room to Paradise, where it enjoys endless infancy" (Waugh 1947, 84).

Waugh's view has certainly conditioned subsequent responses to Forest Lawn, particularly in the national media. A writer in *Saturday Review* referred to Forest Lawn as "Ever-Ever Land," and *Time* sardonically dubbed it the "Disneyland of Death." (Sutton 1958, 24–26; "Disneyland of Death" 1959, 107). Even singer John Denver was not to miss out on the fun and recorded Tom Paxton's satirical song "Forest Lawn" on one of his early albums.

But there is something wrong in uncritically accepting a satirical portrait as the basis for understanding. And Waugh's portrait, though excellent and amusing as literature, leaves something to be desired as interpretation. It is appropriate, therefore, that a reconsideration of Forest Lawn begin, not with Waugh's interpretation, but with the set of questions he posed: "What will the professors of the future make of Forest Lawn? What do we make of it ourselves? Here is the thing, under our very noses, a first class anthropological puzzle of our own period and neighborhood. What does it mean?" (Waugh 1947, 77). Waugh's questions are substantial enough to merit a serious response, even if they are somewhat facetiously propounded. Although it will not be possible to render a complete and detailed portrait of Forest Lawn here, it should be possible to delineate the character of Forest Lawn sufficiently to offer some response to Waugh's query.

Inscribed on the twenty-five-by-twenty-eight-foot tablet known as "The Builder's Creed," which stands in the forecourt to the Memorial Terrace of the Great Mausoleum, is the substance of Hubert Eaton's vision for Forest Lawn.

I believe in a happy Eternal Life.

I believe those of us who are left behind should be glad in the certain belief that those gone before who believed in Him have entered into that happier Life.

I believe, most of all, in a Christ that smiles and loves you and me.

I therefore know the cemeteries of today are wrong because they depict an end, not a beginning.

I therefore prayerfully resolve . . . that I shall endeavor to build Forest Lawn as different, as unlike other cemeteries as sunshine is unlike darkness, as Eternal Life is unlike Death.

In fulfillment of these propositions, Eaton set out to create not only a safe repository and garden of memory for the dead, but also a place for the "sacred enjoyment of the living" (*Art Guide of Forest Lawn with Interpretations* 1941, 1). To this end he established a great park with green rolling lawns, unbroken by tombstones or other raised markers; with tens of thousands of shrubs, flowers, and trees (non-deciduous and forever green); replicas of Old World country churches; singing birds and splashing fountains; a great Mausoleum-Columbarium; and one of the largest collections of marble statuary and stained glass ever assembled in America.

The presence of all this beauty was to "dissolve man's fear of oblivion and bolster his faith in immortality" (*Art Guide*, 1). The "immortal" works of art in marble and glass, as well as the scientifically constructed mausoleums and columbaria, reinforce this belief. "We Build Forever," reads the inscription in the Great Mausoleum. The proposition, though Ozymandian in its claim, nevertheless seems sincere.

The message of immortality is communicated at Forest Lawn at different levels. At the level of formal mythology, it is represented in the Sacred Trilogy—three works of art that depict the dramatic and theological foci in the life-story of Jesus: the Last Supper, the Crucifixion, and the Resurrection. *The Last Supper* is a recreation of Leonardo da Vinci's famous fresco in a brilliant stained glass window set in the Memorial Court of Honor in the Great Mausoleum. *The Crucifixion* is a massive oil painting by the Polish artist Jan Styka. Its size (if stood on its side it is approximately the height of a twenty-story building) required the construction of a special hall to house and display it. Housed in the same hall is *The Resurrection*, a somewhat less massive painting that was commissioned by Forest Lawn to complete the trilogy. *The Crucifixion* itself is unusual, not merely for its size, but for its subject, which is not a crucified Christ but a Christ the moment before his crucifixion in a posture of serene faith and confidence in the eternal life that awaits him.

It may seem surprising, given the basic Christian orientation of Forest Lawn, as represented in the trilogy, that a negligible number of the hundreds of marble statues that grace the gardens, courts, terraces, and sanctuaries are explicitly Christian in theme. And very, very few of them depict the figure of Jesus. In fact there are only three: a reproduction of Michelangelo's *La Pietà*, Bertel Thorvaldsen's *The Christus* (there are several reproductions throughout Forest Lawn), and an original sculpture by Vincenzo Jerace, *For of Such Is the Kingdom of Heaven*. It was Hubert Eaton's vision of the Christ that limited its appearance at Forest Lawn. The greatest number of extant statuary tends to depict Christ on the cross, a joyless suffering Christ. What Eaton wanted was a smiling Christ, a Christ that "loved you and me," what Eaton called an "American Christ." Despite contests and competitions that were held, Forest Lawn never found its American Christ; but it acquired Jerace's *For of Such Is the Kingdom of Heaven*. Eaton was reputed to have said to Jerace, "It is not my smiling Christ, but it is a kindly Christ, a Christ to whom the little children came" (*Art Guide*, 81).

The centrality of the Sacred Trilogy substantially establishes the Christian context of Forest Lawn, despite the quantitative meagerness in the representation of explicit Christian themes in the remainder of Forest Lawn's large inventory of sculpture. Explicit Christian themes are reiterated, however, in the mosaics, stained glass, and inscriptions that appear throughout Forest Lawn's courts, churches, and mausoleums.

If Forest Lawn could not present the American Christ who smiled and loved you and me, it could present the love. The inscriptions proclaim it, the weddings celebrate it, and the statuary depicts or evokes it.

In the garden adjacent to the Court of David in the Triumphant Faith section of Forest Lawn stands Ernesto Gazzeri's *The Mystery of Life*, a large group of statues containing eighteen life-sized human figures. Through the center of the work flows the "mystic stream of life" (of real water), and each figure represents a person of different character, station, and circumstance in their moment of response to this great mystery. The work was created specifically for Forest Lawn, and Forest Lawn (with the approval of the royal superintendent of fine arts of Italy and Victor Herbert) offers its solution to the mystery: "Love is the end and all of living." The theology of Forest Lawn is a theology of love. "Love lives forever and is reborn," says Forest Lawn (*Pictorial Forest Lawn* 1953, 7). It is not only the basis of life in this world, but it is the key to life in the next. At Forest Lawn one depiction of love is romance. The Wee Kirk o' the Heather is a replica of Annie Laurie's church in Dumfriesshire, Scotland. The eight stained glass windows tell the story of Annie and Douglas of Fingland and their tragic love affair. The Ring of Aldyth, through which bridal couples clasp each other's hands and pledge their devotion, is reputedly based on some romantic Saxon legend with a happier climax. Over the chancel in the Church of the Recessional is inscribed, "Now abideth faith, hope love, these three: and the greatest of these is love."

The representations of love that are focal in the iconography of Forest Lawn, however, are those of domestic love. Death is not an end—it is a "going home," and Forest Lawn is virtually littered with images of idealized domesticity. The child—asleep, at play, mischievous, curious, content—is a primary image for sentimental reflection, as is the family group, invincible in its love and devotion, and the mother and child—the essence of love pure and uncomplicated. In this theology man is not depraved, nor is he judged. He is an innocent, as loving and as loved as the child—and it would seem that it is primarily within this structure of family sentiment that man is redeemed and reborn.

In a cemetery context it is difficult to ignore the overwhelming abundance of statuary that glorifies the human body. Scores of statues of young men, women, and children all emphasize the beauties of the flesh. It would seem to impute a physical referent to the immortality that Forest Lawn proclaims, not merely a spiritual one. Indeed, all contemporary embalming and cosmetic practices strive to present a physically pleasing last portrait of the deceased to family and friends. Scientifically designed crypts that promote "desiccation but not decay"(*Art Guide* 40) all contribute to a message that

Love's Treasure by Leone Tomassi. Printed with permission of
Forest Lawn Memorial Parks.

the life beyond involves not merely the immortality of the spirit but, in some unexplicated manner, the endurance of the flesh as well.

There is a brief and perceptive moment in the film *The Loved One* when the protagonist finds himself wandering about a hall filled with marble figures of nude and semi-nude women. Suddenly, when he is sure no one is watching, he plants a hasty kiss on the breast of one of the statues. Although Forest Lawn acknowledges the physical beauty of its statuary, it does not entertain the notion of its sensuality. Beautiful, yes; erotic, no. Consider the description of Harriet Whitney Frishmuth's statue *Joy of the Waters* in one of the editions of the *Art Guide of Forest Lawn Memorial-Park*:

> With upflung hands and windblown hair, this gay young girl eagerly greets the onrushing waves. Well known for her lyrical figures, Miss Frishmuth has displayed here a sound knowledge of human anatomy and a sincere desire to attain the ideal of beauty in her work. The basic theme is spiritual. This girl, by her action and by the evident keen enjoyment on her face, expresses the happiness that comes to a receptive and believing heart which accepts and receives the blessings of God's all-embracing love. (*Art Guide* 54–55)

The description is typical; while recognizing the beauty of the female anatomy, the statue is unambiguously assigned a spiritual context. Physical beauty should not evoke a physical response but a spiritual one. Sensuality is subordinated. The possibility of the erotic is denied. The surreptitious kiss bestowed by the protagonist of the film was a denial of this denial.

Forest Lawn is dedicated to the stirring of national as well as domestic sentiments. Representations of relics, personages, and ideals that evoke the spirit of American freedom and democracy permeate the park. Statues of George Washington, Abraham Lincoln, Henry Clay, Daniel Webster, and Theodore Roosevelt, as well as personifications such as *Pro Patria* and *The Republic*, can be found. In the Court of Freedom stands a re-creation of John Trumbull's painting *The Signing of the Declaration of Independence* constructed of more than 700,000 mosaic tiles. At the base of the statue of Washington stretches a piece of the Liberty Chain that was used to bar the British access to the Hudson River during the Revolutionary War.

Besides love, beauty, and patriotism, there are other virtues to which Forest Lawn is clearly committed—those that constitute and contribute to what might be called "good character." In the forecourt of the Church of the Recessional—a replica of the Parish Church of St. Margaret's in Rottingdean, England, where Rudyard Kipling worshiped for several years—are inscribed three of Kipling's famous poems: "The Recessional" (after which the church is named), "If," and "When Earth's Last Picture Is Painted." Tolerance, faith, humility, reverence, trust, truth, courage, vision, and determination—these are the virtues that are evoked in the poems and throughout Forest Lawn.

Joy of the Waters by Harriet Whitney Frishmuth. Printed with permission of Forest Lawn Memorial Parks.

Forest Lawn also evokes a sense of efficient organization and commercial success. It was one of the first cemeteries to utilize media advertising, stressing the economic and organizational benefits of Forest Lawn's services. Furthermore, the economic significance of the distinctions that are evident between the different plots, crypts, niches, caskets, urns, and memorials that are available at Forest Lawn serve as markers of individual material success. Anyone is entitled to the memorial they can afford. You may be buried simply or grandly. You may not be able to take it with you, but at Forest Lawn it is certainly possible to indicate that you once had it.

What then are we to make of Forest Lawn? What is the solution to the "first-class anthropological puzzle" that Waugh propounded? Is it some Hollywood fantasy, locally bred and born? I think not. In the first place we must recognize that in certain basic respects the concept of Forest Lawn is not new. In the early nineteenth century in reaction to the grim, gloomy, and neglected cemeteries of Puritan tradition as well as the offensive, over-crowded, and health-hazardous cemeteries of the city, the rural cemetery movement developed. The members of this movement advocated the acquisition of large, attractive acreage outside the city limits that would serve as sacred and inviolable resting places for the dead. The graves and memorials were to be set in beautiful foliage and landscaped surroundings. Fences that were constructed around family plots had to be made of durable metal or stone (not wood and not slate, the standard materials of the Puritan grave-yard.) The memorials themselves were to be artistically controlled by the cemetery trustees to ensure their aesthetic effect. It was hoped that such cemeteries might become schools "of instruction in architecture, sculpture, landscape gardening, and arboriculture."[1] Furthermore, these cemeteries were regarded as schools of religion and philosophy where the memorials to the dead were to serve as inspirations to the living. The symbolism on the memorials was not grim, and Christian symbolism was only infrequently used. It was expected that the amalgam of the beauty of nature and art would teach that death is not an end and time not a destroyer. It was also hoped that the art would make the lessons of history tangible and thus give people a sense of historical continuity and instill feelings of patriotism and national pride.

Beginning with Mount Auburn Cemetery in Cambridge, Massachusetts, in 1831, the rural cemetery movement rapidly spread: Laurel Hill Cemetery, Philadelphia (1836), Greenwood Cemetery, Brooklyn (1838), Allegheny Cemetery, Pittsburgh (1844), Spring Grove Cemetery, Cincinnati (1845). By the middle of the nineteenth century there were few major cities or towns that did not boast a rural cemetery.

These cemeteries were exceedingly popular. No visitor from abroad could visit the Boston area without being taken on a tour of Mt. Auburn. Laurel Hill Cemetery boasted 30,000 tourists a year. In the latter part of the century the internal fencing that had delineated the boundaries between family plots began to be removed, an innovation that resulted in an aesthetically integrated park and which gave rise to the "lawn cemeteries" popular after the Civil War.

Thus—Hubert Eaton's creed to the contrary—the Forest Lawn concept is not essentially new, but well within the tradition of the nineteenth-century rural cemetery. Like Forest Lawn, the rural cemeteries of the nineteenth century were not merely areas for the disposal of the dead, but also cultural institutions that served to instruct, inspire, and ennoble the living.

But if Forest Lawn is within the rural cemetery tradition, it still does not appear to be a typical nineteenth-century American cemetery. Perhaps to answer Waugh's questions and to understand what Forest Lawn is, it might be best to view Forest Lawn not as a cemetery at all, but rather as a twentieth-century memorial to the tastes and values of the nineteenth century: a monument to the culture of Victorian America.

Victorian culture was essentially an Anglo-Saxon Protestant culture; [2] and Anglo-Saxon Protestantism is clearly reflected in Forest Lawn's rural English and Scottish churches, Saxon legends, Tudor architecture, and in the overwhelming majority of its client population (until 1959, only members of the "Caucasian" race were permitted to be interred at Forest Lawn).

The artistic tastes manifested in the art and architecture of Forest Lawn are those commensurate with the popular tastes of Victorian America. The idealized subject matter, sentimentality, use of literary and classical associations, didacticism, and use of extraneous symbolism are all characteristic of the artistic expectations of Victorian culture. It is no accident that there is virtually no modern or abstract sculpture in Forest Lawn. The patriotic strains, the encouragement of the "inner-directed personality"—i.e., the building of good character—and the subordination of sensuality are well-known Victorian attributes. The focus upon the family, the child, and the mother-child relationship can be associated with the Victorian emphasis on the sanctity of the family unit, the importance of childhood, and the exaltation of motherhood.

What might appear to be the naive theology of Forest Lawn, which seems to stress a rather simplistic immortality of flesh and spirit, reuniting innocent loved ones in some kind of domestic Heaven, is entirely in keeping with conceptualizations of the afterlife that were propagated in the huge consolation literature of nineteenth-century America.[3] If anything, Forest Lawn's vision is considerably less extreme.

Love, Death, and Success are the three great themes that Carl Bode sees running through much of the American culture of the mid-nineteenth century—a "Trio for Columbia," as he called it (Bode 1959, 269–276).[4] And these indeed are the great themes of Forest Lawn as well. In viewing Forest Lawn, it is necessary to see Death simply as another of Forest Lawn's themes, like Love. What emerges from our perspective, therefore, is not a cemetery, nor even a Victorian cemetery, but a twentieth-century exhibition of and memorial to the culture of Victorian America.[5]

Since the 1970s, the clientele of Forest Lawn has changed dramatically. Hispanics, Armenians, Koreans, Chinese, and Japanese have become major consumers of Forest Lawn services and properties. The change in the population in part reflects the change in the population of southern California generally and the Glendale area specifically. But considering that Forest Lawn was restricted to Caucasians until 1959, the change is dramatic. Yet it would be wrong to say that the park has changed in its style or spirit. Chinese characters may appear on bronze grave markers, and neo-classic statues may bear Korean or Hispanic names on their pedestals, yet the park, the structures, the art, the thematic emphases have not changed. They remain as before. It seems that the Victorian values and tastes represented by Forest Lawn are precisely those that these populations respect. Despite the fact that Victorianism had declined before many had come to this country, they appreciate the beautiful landscapes, the representational art, the spiritual tone, the respect for family, nation, and character. Perhaps they are misreading the park, but I suspect not. It is rather that Victorianism never succumbed to modernism. If Victorian values were consciously repudiated by the cultural elite, they never lost their hold in the largest segments of American society. These values continue to be significant for those who have never identified with the cultural vanguard, and for immigrant and ethnic communities whose traditional values are close to those that Forest Lawn would conserve.

It, of course, becomes no less easy to satirize Forest Lawn. For those who do not share the artistic tastes, moral righteousness, and philosophical dispositions of the previous century, Forest Lawn will continue to seem curious, comical, or pathetic. But Forest Lawn is not the invention of some Hollywood studio, some whole-cloth fabrication for mass consumption. It is rather a genuine reflection of a well-established and powerful movement in the culture of Anglo-America.

Notes

1. The quotation is from John C. London's book, *On the Laying Out, Planting and Managing of Cemeteries* (London, 1843), cited in Stanley French (1975, 69–91). See also Edmund V. Gillon, Jr., *Victorian Cemetery Art* (1972, v–xiii), and Neil Harris, *The Artist in American Society* (1966, 200–208).

2. For overviews of Victorian American culture, see *Victorian America*, ed. Daniel Walker Howe (1976b), particularly Daniel Walker Howe, "Victorian Culture in America," (1976a, 3–28), and Stanley Coben, "The Assault on Victorianism in the Twentieth Century," (1976, 160–81).

3. For an excellent description of nineteenth-century "consolation literature," see Ann Douglas, "Heaven our Home: Consolation Literature in the Northern United States, 1830–1880," (1975, 49–68).
4. Bode's "Aside to the Reader," ix–xv, develops some other points concerning Victorian culture.
5. For the influence of the exhibition complex on Hubert Eaton, see Barbara Rubin, Robert Carlton, and Arnold Rubin, *Forest Lawn* (1979, 1–12).

Ride 'Em, Barbie Girl: Commodifying Folklore, Place, and the Exotic

Jeannie B. Thomas

In 1959, Ruth Handler of Mattel—inspired by paper dolls and a German sex doll—created an adult doll for little girls and named her Barbie. According to Mattel, the doll's full name is Barbie Millicent Roberts, and she attended Willows High School in Willows, Wisconsin, and then went to "State College" (Robins 1989, 26). Barbie M. Roberts has come a long way since those early days. In 1996 Mattel's net sales reached $3.8 billion, and Barbie dolls represented nearly one-half of these sales (Sarasohn-Kahn 1998, 1). If all the Barbies sold as of 1997 were lined up head to toe, they would circle the earth more than eleven times (Tosa 1998, 107). Today, two Barbies sell every second somewhere in the world ("Twin Fates" 1999, 121). Clearly Barbie is a sales success.

In this paper, I look at one strategy used in selling Barbie: the marketing of folkloric themes. Of course, these are not the only themes used in marketing Barbie; popular culture and fine art are drawn on as well. For example, there's *Star Trek* Barbie and Ken; Barbie Loves Elvis; Barbie as Marilyn Monroe, complete with white halter dress flying up as she stands above the subway grill in *The Seven Year Itch*; Barbie as Marilyn Monroe as Lorelei Lee in *Gentlemen Prefer Blondes*; and *X Files* Barbie and Ken. There is even a Harley-Davidson Barbie.[1] Barbies are also born of famous artistic masterpieces; for example, there's a Barbie inspired by a Vincent Van Gogh's painting, "Sunflower Barbie." She wears a yellow chiffon petal skirt and has "delicate leaves of green and green satin tendrils" encircling her waist, according to Mattel's description of her (Mattel 1999).

Mattel mines all levels of culture in its attempts to sell Barbie, and the folk level has proved a particularly rich source. Examining the use of folkloric currents in the selling of Barbie allows us to see how those involved with an important aspect of American culture—marketing of goods for capitalist consumption—select aspects of folklore that they think will have dollar value.[2] What I talk about in this paper is what could therefore be

called *commodified folklore*; that is, folklore and folkloric themes translated
into marketable objects. My use of the appellation commodified folklore
here is deliberate; I could have resorted to the more common phrase "folklore in popular or mass culture," but that evokes folklore embedded in
something larger. Commodified folklore, by contrast, connotes the historical
primacy of folklore; the phenomenon I'm calling commodified folklore was
created *from* folklore, and the folklore existed before the commodified version of it.

To be considered commodified folklore, the object of study must have
folk antecedents and also be mass produced with the intent of sales or promotion. We may, in general, consider mass-marketed dolls to be commodified
folklore because most dolls were originally created through informally
learned, folk processes and only later mass produced and sold for money
(Fennick 1996, 9–10). Regardless of origins—whether dolls were created
through folk means or mass production—children's play with dolls was and
continues to be folk behavior.

I will focus my discussion of commodified folklore on the merchandising of the Barbie doll. First, I argue that folklore is a significant component
in Mattel's marketing of Barbie. Second, I identify some of the major folkloric currents in Barbie merchandising. Finally, I examine the manner in
which Mattel presents this commodified folklore, paying specific attention to
Barbie and the construction of the ethnic Other, the tourist gaze, exoticism
and sex, the West, and the folk conflation of horse and woman.

The folkloric currents utilized in Barbie merchandising include legendry, fairy tales, mythology, rites of passage, holidays, costuming, and
notions of place. Barbies drawn from the category of legend include Tooth
Fairy Barbie, various mermaid Barbies, and angel Barbies—like Angel
Lights Barbie, issued in 1992, who lights up and serves double duty as both
a toy and a Christmas tree topper (Sarasohn-Kahn 1998, 118). Greek
Goddess Barbie draws on mythology, while Barbie as Rapunzel and Barbie
as Sleeping Beauty emerge from the exotic and otherworldly realm of the
fairy tale.[3] Barbie also participates in folkloric events such as rites of pas-
sage. Weddings are her all-time most popular rite of passage, but one can
also purchase a graduation Barbie.[4] She celebrates holidays including
Christmas, Mardi Gras (Summers 1996, 39, 67), and Valentine's Day.
Indeed, in 1988 a doll named Holiday Barbie, which went on the market at
Christmastime, helped Mattel make a profit during difficult financial times
(Sarasohn-Kahn 1998, 118). This first Holiday Barbie was quite successful,
and it remains a collector's find. It has been known to fetch as much as
twenty times its original value (Fennick 1996, 92).

After their success with dolls associated with holidays, Mattel yearned
for a holiday that occurred all year round. It was this longing that led to the
conception of Birthday Barbie (Sarasohn-Kahn 1998, 14). The birthday

theme can also be seen in Barbie's friend *Quinceanera* Teresa, created to celebrate fifteen years of Hispanic Barbie and her family of dolls (Sarasohn-Kahn 1998,156). As early as 1963, Mattel created the Halloween-party-style Masquerade costumes for Barbie-and-family dolls (Westenhouser 1994, 34). In 1968, Talking Barbie said, "Let's have a costume party" (Fennick 1996, 41). Barbie's 1964–65 Little Theater costumes relied on folkloric texts and figures: the Arabian Nights, King Arthur, Guinevere, Little Red Riding Hood and the Wolf, and Cinderella and her prince (Tosa 1998, 122–24, 126; Theriault 1992, 9).

Folklore continues to be important in Barbie's association with place. For example, reliance on place and its folk and popular associations can be seen with Country Rose Barbie, whose cowgirl costume recalls romantic notions of the American West. In the Dolls of the World series, Barbie hails from places like Peru, Puerto Rico, Thailand, and Poland, and she is often sold in her "authentic" folk costume. To use a western metaphor, Barbie rides herd on a large number of images and meanings, but Mattel's use of place and folkloric themes to construct Barbie as an attractive, non-threatening exotic Other is my interest here. Lore related to place—specifically foreign countries and the West—helps sell Barbie.

Looking at the thousands of different identities through which Barbie has been marketed makes me wonder if today she wouldn't be more aptly named Sybil. But it's just this ability to generate new identities that has led to Barbie's survival and success. In its 1987 *Annual Report*, Mattel says, "Barbie remains the highest volume brand in the industry, due in no small part to our ability to reintroduce the product line year-after-year to fit the current lifestyles of girls" (Sarasohn-Kahn 1998, 35). In the 1988 *Report*, it says, "She's a new doll every year, and yet she's always glamorous and fun" (Sarasohn-Kahn 1998, 39). The 1992 *Annual Report* reads, "The key is to make Barbie fresh and new every year, to develop multiple doll segments based on established play patterns, and to drive sales through effective advertising, promotion and merchandising" (Sarasohn-Kahn 1998, 63). Barbie has been very successful with children, in part because she addresses major issues that children work through via folkloric venues, which Mattel calls "play patterns": in particular, kids play at being an adult and learn how to be an adult through their play (Mechling 1986, 97, 114).

Barbie is not only for kids, though; many Barbies today are specifically marketed to adults, which illustrates the company's attention to market segments. Their 1995 *Annual Report* says, "With a number one share in most every major global market, Barbie penetration continues to grow. . . . Most of the 100 dolls in each year's product line are designed for little girls, but the adult collector market also provides excellent opportunity for Mattel. There are 83 million women in the world today who grew up with the Barbie doll, and every one of them is a potential collector" (Sarasohn-Kahn 1998,

87). One group of Barbies is heavily marketed toward adult collectors, although many of these dolls are also available to children in the aisles of major chain stores like Wal-Mart, K-Mart, and Toys "R" Us.

International Barbie

In 1964, Mattel released "colorful costumes created to simulate pretend travel" for Barbie and Ken (Westenhouser 1994, 33). At that time Barbie and her boyfriend were off to see the world; in 1980 Barbie became the world. As Mattel tells it, "Barbie went international [with the Dolls of the World Collection in 1980]. . . . The dolls in this series combine *authentic* outfits with unique cultural profiles" (Mattel 1999; emphasis added).[5] Both the selling of Barbie as tourist—a practice that continued with dolls like 1986's Vacation Sensation Barbie (Summers 1996, 99)—and the selling of Barbies in the contemporary Dolls of the World Collection as natives of varied places (which are frequently tourist destinations) rely on tourist perceptions. Whether Barbie is presented as a tourist or a native may encourage the consumer to identify with her role, or persona. However, the intricacies of the native's position are frequently hard to grasp from an outsider's vantage point, especially if the outsider knows little about the culture. Therefore, it is likely that at least some consumers look upon these Barbies with the gaze of a tourist. By *gaze of a tourist*, I mean simply an outsider's gaze at an Other person, culture, object, or place that is seen as distinctive and different from the outsider in significant ways (for more discussion of the tourist gaze, see Urry 1990, who breaks the gaze down into specific categories). The context for this perception on the part of the outsider is often one of play (i.e., the tourist's vacation). John Urry says, "I have strongly argued for the significance of the gaze to tourist activities. This is not to say that all the other senses are insignificant in the tourist experience. But I have tried to establish that there has to be something distinctive to gaze upon" (1990, 128).

Interestingly, Barbie and Ken's tourist costumes from 1964 foreshadow the use of native costumes in the contemporary Dolls of the World series. For example, the 1964 Ken in Switzerland outfit includes lederhosen, a black felt Tyrolean cap, and a beer stein (Theriault 1992, 121). These native costumes effectively turn the dolls into "something distinctive to gaze upon" (Urry 1990, 128). Creating something distinctive to capture sales was clearly the intent behind the contemporary Dolls of the World, which are more expensive than regular Barbies. The target audience, collectors, usually display dolls more than they play with them. This is a lucrative market segment; in 1995, adult collectors spent $175 million on Barbie dolls (Sarasohn-Kahn 1998, 1). The idea of doll as native draws on constructions of natives as doll-like—cute and adorable, costumed indigenous peoples presented for the entertainment and consumption of tourists—and in the process commodifies them.

The Dolls of the World Collection relies on references to place and the traditional folk customs and costumes associated with that place. The dolls are generally named after a place, and the collection includes the following: Arctic Barbie (1997), Australian Barbie (1993), Brazilian Barbie (1990), Canadian Barbie (1988), Chilean Barbie (1998), Chinese Barbie (1994), Czechoslovakian Barbie (1991), Dutch Barbie (1994), East India Barbie (1982), English Barbie (1992), Eskimo Barbie (1982), French Barbie (1997), German Barbie (1987, 1995), Ghanaian Barbie (1996), Greek Barbie (1986), India Barbie (1982), Indian Barbie (1996), Icelandic Barbie (1987), Irish Barbie (1984, 1995), Italian Barbie (1980), Jamaican Barbie (1992), Japanese Barbie (1985, 1996), Kenyan Barbie (1994), Korean Barbie (1988), Malaysian Barbie (1991), Mexican Barbie (1989, 1996), Moroccan Barbie (1998), Native American Barbie (1998), Nigerian Barbie (1990), Norwegian Barbie (1996), Oriental Barbie (1981), Parisian Barbie (1980), Peruvian Barbie (1986, 1998), Polish Barbie (1998), Polynesian Barbie (1995), Puerto Rican Barbie (1997), Royal U.K. Barbie (1980), Russian Barbie (1989, 1997), Scottish Barbie (1981), Spanish Barbie (1983), Swedish Barbie (1983), Swiss Barbie (1984), and Thai Barbie (1998) (Tosa 1998, 146; Mattel 1999).

From the perspective of an American tourist, these dolls are all associated with exotic locations. Urry argues that there is a hierarchy of tourist sites:

> Travel had always been socially selective. It was available for a relatively limited elite and was a marker of social status. But in the second half of the nineteenth century there was an extensive development of mass travel by train. Status distinctions then came to be drawn between different classes of traveler, but less between those who could and those [who] could not travel. . . . The car and the aeroplane have even further democratised geographical movement. As travel became democratised so extensive distinctions of taste came to be established between different places: where one traveled to became of considerable social significance. The tourist gaze came to have a different importance in one place rather than another. . . . Certain places were viewed as embodiments of mass tourism, to be despised and ridiculed. (1990, 16)

In general, international Barbies are from places that are now seen as respectable tourist destinations—unlike the working-class, nineteenth-century British seaside resorts Urry studied. However, cultural commentators still criticize many of the dolls on the basis of their shallow approaches to the cultures they represent:

> Far from authenticity, these dolls have the theme-park bogusness of the "foreign lands" at Disney's Epcot Center. . . . To be sure some of the Dolls of the World are less reductive than others. Malaysian Barbie, which the workers in Mattel's Malaysian factory helped design,

gets high marks for authenticity and attractiveness. . . . But Jamaican Barbie is another story. "She looks like a mammy," [Yla] Easton told me. "She's got the head rag and the apron, and I'm like, 'Why did they pick that slice of life?' When they did the Nigerian Barbie at least they made her a regal person." [Ann] Ducille is blunter: "That's the one I call the anorexic Aunt Jemima." The phrase book of "foreign expressions" on Jamaican Barbie's box seems almost calculated to patronize. It includes: "Howyu-du (Hello)," "A hope yu wi come—a'Jamaica!" (I hope you will come to Jamaica!). (Lord 1994, 176, 177)

This Jamaican doll box depicts vernacular language in its description of the doll. Language associated with folklore also appears frequently on the doll boxes in the series. For example, the box of the recent Peruvian Barbie says,

¡Hola! (Hello) I'm Peruvian Barbie and I'm proud to welcome you to one of the most beautiful and mysterious countries in South America. . . . Of course you will want to enjoy our delicious Peruvian foods, especially the wonderful smells and yummy flavors of Creole cooking (highly spicy rice dishes). For fun, we love to watch soccer and volleyball. We also love to attend festivals and to dance the marinera and huaynos (two typical Peruvian dances), guaranteed to make you smile! Today I am wearing an authentic Peruvian dress shawl in vibrant multi colors, which reflect the excitement, passion and beauty of my country.

The box of Puerto Rican Barbie (1997) reads,

I live in Puerto Rico, a beautiful place often called the Island of Enchantment. . . . We love good food in Puerto Rico. Seafood like squid, shrimp, and codfish is a popular choice and often mixed with rice. . . . I hope you like the special white dress I'm wearing. It is very typical of a dress I might wear to a festival or party. . . . Tourism is a very significant part of our economy. Many cruise ships dock in the harbor of our capital city, San Juan. Long ago, pirate ships used to dock here too! Today, people from all over the world come to enjoy our beautiful country, delicious food and friendly people.

Thai Barbie also lives in a "beautiful country"—in fact, *beautiful* is a word used many times on these boxes, which is not surprising since beauty is a big part of Barbie, who was conceived as a fashion doll. Thai Barbie's box says,

I'm Thai Barbie. I live in a beautiful country. . . . Many exotic animals like rhinoceros, leopards, and elephants live in the jungles and forests of Thailand. . . . My beautiful costume is created from the ceremonial clothing we wear to perform a traditional dance,

Figure 1. Polish Barbie (J. Thomas photo)

called the Lacon. . . . I have golden bracelets on each arm and my feet are bare, just like a real Thai dancer!

Then there is the narrative on Polish Barbie's box (figure 1):

Let me tell you about my beautiful country. . . . The Polish countryside is scenic and full of fun! We love to celebrate and have many festivals, where everyone dances the polka, a dance we invented in Poland! There are also many beautiful animals in the Polish forests. . . . My traditional folk costume is a lovely example of festival attire. My blonde hair is worn in two thick braids. I have a beautiful crown of flowers in my hair, tied with a pretty ribbon. I hope one of the boys will ask me to dance with him!

Of interest here are the references to the exotic, the authentic, and the traditional: foodways, the festival, and the folk costume—all of this in a narrative that sounds as though it could appeal to tourists as well as to doll collectors. These terms appear in scholarly folkloristic discourse, but in relation to Barbie, they're used in a fashion that creates a stereotypical image of the Barbie doll as the singing, dancing, happy native. Such language also helps conjure an image of Barbie as the ethnic Other. In her article about the tourist folklore surrounding the Hawaiian goddess Pele, Joyce Hammond writes, "Pele's power as a symbol of the Other derives most clearly from the replication of Otherness which is constructed for native women. The overwhelming number of photographs of island women in promotional tourist material for Hawai'i, as well as the predominant use of 'ethnic' women to greet tourists, dance for tourists, and serve tourists, attests to the tourists' equation of the native woman herself with the exoticism sought in the tourist quest" (1995, 163–164). The international Barbie dolls are presented in a similar manner. However, for tourists to Hawai'i, Pele is frequently constructed as a threatening, exotic, native Other (Hammond 1995, 162–163). Barbie is not constructed this way for her consumers. The descriptions of her create a non-threatening, ingratiating Other: The Barbies say, "Enjoy our delicious Peruvian foods." "Guaranteed to make you smile!" "I hope you like the special white dress I'm wearing." "I hope one of the boys will ask me to dance!" As native Other, Barbie invites the consumer to enjoy her beautiful country's delicious food and friendly natives. In short, Barbie is saying, "Let me please you." "Look at me with the gaze of a tourist and enjoy." Ann Ducille notes, "We are living in a moment where 'the other' has a certain kind of commercial value" (Lord 1994, 171). Barbie embodies this; she particularly represents a kind of accessible, inviting Other.

Folklorists and anthropologists have provided thoughtful definitions, discussions, and critiques—in folkloric and historical contexts—of terms that get used in the marketing of international Barbies, such as *authentic, traditional,* and *festival* (Bauman et. al. 1992; Bendix 1997; Duggan 1997; Dundes and Falassi 1975; Evans-Pritchard 1987; Falassi 1987; Glassie 1995; Kirshenblatt-Gimblett 1998; Posen 1993; Turner 1982). Of course Barbie is neither a scholar nor a folklorist and neither are her marketers. Instead they draw on and present folk factors in a superficial and digestible form because this constellation of dolls, with its commodified versions of folklore and associated terms, sells. One doll in the series has sold so well that there have been several editions of her over the years. She is interesting because even though she's considered exotic enough to belong to the Dolls of the World Collection, her place, the American West, is a little closer to home.[6] Her name is Native American Barbie.

The Barbie West

Mattel's internet web site shows images of six different Native American Barbies introduced in the last few years, not including the Eskimo and Arctic Barbies that also are a part of the Dolls of the World series. Other Native-American-themed dolls not in that collection include Nia, Barbie's first Native American friend (Augustyniak 1996, 30), and Barbie Olé, who wears a Navajo-style dress with a dreamcatcher around her neck and was a special convention Barbie designed by the Barbie Friends of Albuquerque Doll Club (Fennick 1996, 129). Invariably the Dolls of the World version of Native American Barbie (figure 2) is dressed in what—under the influence of Hollywood's frequent emphasis on Plains-Indian-style dress with a little Southwest color thrown in—has come to be pervasive in popular culture and could be described as an Anglo's construction of a generic Indian: buckskin, feathers, fringe, and turquoise. Mattel describes one Native American Barbie as "dressed in a festive outfit for ceremonial events. Native American Barbie doll looks authentic from head to toe. She's wearing a 'buckskin' fringed top with a matching skirt. Silver-color braided trim highlights her outfit. Her long black hair is adorned with a headband and turquoise-colored feather. In keeping with Native American traditions, she has soft 'buckskin' moccasins on her feet" (Mattel 1999). Mattel described a previous Native American Barbie introduced in 1996 with similar stereotypical images but also mentioned accessories not associated with Indians wearing pre-contact early contact period clothing: "This Collector Edition Barbie wears a tan buckskin-like dress with matching boots. The tiny papoose she carries has a 'buckskin' headband and diaper and comes with a matching backpack." The Barbie introduced in 1997 is described as "beautiful in her turquoise-colored dress with matching moccasins. Her baby sister comes with her own carrier so Barbie can take her to a *'picnic'*" (Mattel 1999).

Mattel's Native American descriptions are further examples of the commodification and simplification of such terms associated with folklore studies as authentic, ceremonial, and tradition; they are also combined with idiosyncratic contemporary terms. For example, there is not a long historical record of pre-contact and early contact (the time periods to which Native American Barbie's clothes link her) Native American picnics. Picnics, diapers, and backpacks are commonplace for Americans of many ethnic backgrounds today, but here they are combined with an earlier, exotic era of buckskin and

Figure 2. Native American Barbie (J. Thomas photo)

turquoise. As M. G. Lord argues, Native American Barbie presents an out-sider's interpretation of Native Americans (Lord 1994, 186).[7]

    Native Americans joke that for every Indian and his or her dog, there are five anthropologists studying the Indian and two studying the dog.[8] Well, even in Barbie's world there are such scholars studying out West:

Figure 3. Paleontologist Barbie (J. Thomas photo)

Paleontologist Barbie, to be specific (figure 3). While not a part of the Dolls of the World series, she is linked to place by the landscape depicted in her box. That place looks like the western desert, a locale for dinosaur bones, which is where Paleontologist Barbie's vocation leads her. It is apparent that some Barbie aficionados have an *Indiana Jones* view—a romanticized view—of anthropology. For example, Sarasohn-Kahn describes an exotic leopard-print Barbie ensemble as "perfect for those glamorous anthropological outings!" (1998, 42). Even in its presentation of a career choice that is frequently tedious and dirty, Mattel plays up the romantic side, and the idealized association of place assists in this process. Frequently, the West has been construed as a romantic and exotic place. This is the West constructed for tourists to gaze upon. I use exotic here not just for its connotations of unusualness but also for its sexual evocativeness (as in exotic dancer) because part of Barbie's attraction is sex. Indeed, Barbie owners of different ages have used the dolls to explore issues related to sexuality (Stern 1998). Even on the job out in the field, Paleontologist Barbie has big hair and sexy short shorts. At this juncture, it's also pertinent to remember that Barbie was originally inspired by and closely modeled after a German sex doll, Lilli (Tosa 1998, 27–29; Deutsch 1996, 21).

Some of these notions of the West as alluring and even sexy could also be seen in Mattel's 1981 Western Barbie. Pushing a button on her back caused her to wink an eye. Judy Shackelford, the first female vice-president of Mattel, observes, "Girls didn't care if Barbie winked or not. Guys cared. They said, 'God, look at that doll wink'" (Lord 1994, 112). Western Barbie also had glamour and star quality: "Western Barbie. . . dressed in a silver-trimmed western jumpsuit, cowboy hat and boots, came with a unique 'autograph-signing' feature. This was accomplished through an autograph stamp, included with the doll, which attached to her hand. . . . Positioned as a Western star, she came with small pictures of herself to 'autograph' for her adoring fans" (Sarasohn-Kahn 1998, 13). Mattel also produced Western Ken and Western Skipper ("Make her twirl her lasso!") at the same time (Deutsch 1996, 93). Since the advent of the Western Barbie doll in 1981, western influences have been omnipresent in Barbiedom (Sarasohn-Kahn 1998, 13). The West is one of the most highly represented American regions in Barbie's world outside of the beach, which is usually a generic beach. When the beach is located in a specific region, it is often a western locale, California (as in Malibu Barbie and California Dream Barbie).

In the 1990s, a western emphasis continued in Mattel's marketing strategy; Mattel's web site includes a list of categories like Angels, Bridal, and Fashion Designer for collectors to check, indicating their areas of interest. The categories also include Native American and Western. Mattel's 1989 *Annual Report* says, "Western Fun is the theme for a new Barbie line which captures the popular fashion style of the American Southwest" (Sarasohn-Kahn 1998, 44). As of 1999, I was able to locate several western-style outfits for Barbie in a local Wal-Mart store. I purchased five representative western fashions for Barbie (figure 4). Four are dresses with accompanying cowboy boots in colors that include pink, purple, red, and brown. Three outfits have fringe and expose Barbie's midriff, two of these three are sleeveless, and all have very

Figure 4. A few of Barbie's western fashions (J. Thomas photo)

short skirts. Even the jeans outfit I bought for Barbie (which comes with white cowboy boots) includes a pink gingham top that reveals Barbie's belly.

As I looked at these outfits, I realized that Barbie would probably suffer hypothermia and/or frostbite if she actually had to wear this wardrobe in the West regularly. Obviously, these are not the clothes worn in the West on a daily basis; they're not the traditional, authentic western outfits worn for living and working in western climates. Jeans, a long-sleeved shirt, a hat, and work or cowboy boots would be more common garb. Barbie's western clothes are, to borrow from Thomas Adler, "more festal than ferial" (1981, 51). In the actual West outside of Barbie's dream house, clothes that appear most frequently and mundanely, that are routinely worn, would be traditional outfits. However, Barbie's clothes might be seen in the West during the summer in country-western dance clubs or on the backs of some tourists (figure 5). Indeed, Jane Fennick describes Barbie of the 1980s as a tourist in the American West: "For recreation, the 1980s Barbie doll could do aerobic exercise or roller-skate. Then she might go swimming, camping, or horseback riding on vacation in the West" (1996, 81).

A year after the creation of Western Barbie in 1981, Mattel brought forth a second western-themed Barbie, Horse Lovin' Barbie. Designed to appear as more of a native to the West, Horse Lovin' Barbie wore rather shocking red vinyl pants, a red and tan checked shirt, and an equally jarring vest trimmed

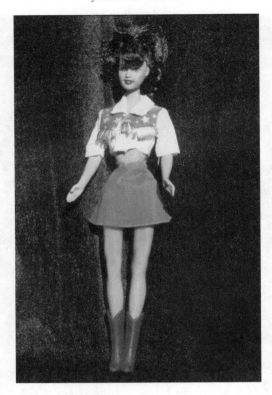

Figure 5. Barbie in western garb
(J. Thomas photo)

with wildly unruly fur. According to Barbie collector Kitturah Westenhouser, "With a western hat and saddlebag, she was ready for the rodeo" (1994, 111). However, she really looked as though she'd be more at home on the set of the 1980s TV show *Dallas*, with its oil-rich Texans, than on a the floor of a rodeo arena. This line of Barbies also included Horse Lovin' versions of Ken and Barbie's little sister, Skipper. Mattel sold horses for each doll separately: Dallas, Midnight, and Honey, respectively. Dallas had a colt named Dixie that was also sold separately. Finally, Mattel marketed a travel trailer for the horses and a jeep to pull it (Westenhouser 1994, 111). So not only did the West hold an outdoorsy, exotic-but-in-America's-backyard sort of appeal, but Mattel found that it could be accessorized quite effectively too. The western theme also appears in Barbie-related merchandise. There have been numerous Barbie coloring books over the years, and some of these from the 1980s and 1990s feature a Western Barbie on the cover; for example, one is titled *Barbie: A Trip to Santa Fe* and shows Barbie in western clothes and cowboy hat holding a Native American pot (Summers 1996, 206). There are Western Barbie paper dolls (Summers 1996, 150) and Native American Barbie Hallmark Christmas ornaments (Olds and Harrias 1997, 263).

In the 1990s, more Western dolls appeared. They included Western Fun Barbie, Western Fun Ken, Western Fun Nia—an African-American Western Fun Barbie—and a Western Fun gift set including Barbie's horse, Sun Runner (Augustyniak 1996, 30). Western Fun Barbie ("Blazing new trails in fashion and fun!") was dressed in "turquoise tights, pink fringed jacket, pink, magenta, yellow, and turquoise western print skirt, pink felt hat, and pink cowboy boots" (Summers 1996, 100; Jacobs 1998, 230). In 1991 there was Trailblazin' Barbie who was "advertised as 'steppin' lively in cowgirl-cute Western wear'"; she came with red cowboy boots (Summers 1996, 96). In 1993, retail chain Toys "R" Us exclusively sold Western Stampin' Barbie (both Anglo and African-American versions), Western Stampin' Ken, Western Stampin' Tara Lynn, and Barbie's horse Western Star—"Stamp trails of fun with Barbie boots and horse hooves!" Other western-theme dolls included retail chain Wal-Mart's 1994 Country Western Star Barbie, who came in Anglo, Hispanic, and African-American, and Denim 'n' Ruffles Barbie with High Stepper ("Horse really walks!") Gift Set, a B.J.'s Club exclusive in 1995 (Augustyniak 1996, 54, 103, 30, 107, 74). In 1997, the Grand Ole Opry Collection included Country Rose Barbie, a glamorous western star in the singing cowgirl mold. She is described by Mattel as dressed in a "stunning red satin ensemble highlighted by a black 'suede' yoke and cuffs edged in golden trim. Beautiful embroidered roses, a white chiffon scarf and dazzling rhinestone accents add an elegant touch to her western outfit. From her rooted eyelashes and clear blue eyes, to her 'suede' western [cowboy] hat, Barbie is simply show-stopping. She even has her own guitar" (Mattel 1999). This Nashville vision of Barbie as the singing cowgirl includes key accessories like a cowboy hat and guitar. The guitar, an important part of western cowboy lore (especially associated with the image of the singing cowboy), is an accessory not usually marketed with western-themed Barbies or Barbies in general.[9]

There is one component of western lore that Mattel frequently markets to accompany Barbie—the horse, also a part of the romance of the West. This notion can be seen in Jill McCorkle's comments about her childhood play with Barbie: "My Barbies went horseback riding. . . . I never owned a horse and rarely got to ride one. It was my fantasy. Ken didn't go. He belonged to my sister and stayed in his box most of the time while my Barbies rode through the wild West" (1994, 13–14). Mattel's web site reveals that Barbie and her family own sixteen horses and ponies (plus one sea horse): Dancer, Dallas, Midnight, Dixie, Prancer, Honey, Blinking Beauty, Sun Runner, All American, Rosebud, Stomper, Western Star, Butterfly, Chelsea, Prancing Horse, and Nibbles (Mattel 1999). Barbie and her family have owned more horses than either cats or dogs. Several Barbie coloring book covers also depict her with horses (Summers 1996,199). Barbie has not only owned horses, but a look at the manes that she has sported since the 1980s makes one start to wonder if Barbie is part horse.

Figure 6. Four-year-old girl engages in hair play: "curling" the
family dog's hair (J. Thomas photo)

Hi Ho Barbie!

Every time I walked down a Barbie aisle in a Wal-Mart, K-Mart, or Toys "R"
Us in the 1990s, I was overwhelmed by two things: the pervasiveness of big
hair and the color "Barbie pink." A wall of Barbie pink is a merchandising
tactic that began in 1991 (Sarasohn-Kahn 1998, 219); Barbie's big hair is also
a marketing strategy. Hair is a central part of Barbie's being, despite the
many difficulties it has presented Mattel over the years. For example, in the
early days, Ken's flocked hair came off in water, so many Kens were bald
before their time. Mattel responded to this problem by introducing Ken with
molded painted hair (Fennick 1996, 45). The 1969 Julia doll's short hair was
originally dark brown, but the fiber frequently oxidized, causing her hair to
turn a dramatic shade of red (Fennick 1996, 61). The hair of Color Magic
Barbie often became brittle, broke, and then fell out (Fennick 1996, 32).
Mattel continued to research and develop new kinds of hair for Barbie and
her friends (Westenhouser 1994, 52–53), and by the 1990s, all Barbies had
extra-long tresses (Sarasohn-Kahn 1998, 50).

When focus groups during the 1970s revealed hair play to be a key
component in the play value associated with Barbie, Barbie designers began
to incorporate hair play features in the dolls. According to Sarasohn-Kahn,
most mainline Barbie dolls targeted today to girls under ten years of age are
hair-play dolls (1998, 129). Imaginative play, play with dolls, and play that
uses patterns seen in the adult world are all folk behaviors of children that
Mattel has capitalized upon in the creation of the Barbie doll. Hair play is

such a folk behavior; little girls learn from their parents, siblings, and friends how to comb and style their own hair and the hair of others. They often spend time styling and playing with the hair of family members, household pets, and friends (figure 6). For example, it is not uncommon to find girls braiding and styling each other's hair at slumber parties. After all, to groom is often to bond. Hair play is another folk activity that Mattel has commodified in the form of a Barbie doll.[10]

The list of official hair play dolls includes Beauty Secrets Barbie (1980), Pretty Changes Barbie (1980), Golden Dream Barbie (1981), Magic Curl Barbie (1982), Twirly Curls Barbie (1983), Super Hair Barbie (1987), Perfume Pretty Barbie (1988), Style Magic Barbie (1989), Totally Hair Barbie (1992), Hollywood Hair Barbie (1993), Troll Hair Barbie (1993), Glitter Hair Barbie (1994), Cut 'n Style Barbie (1995), Sparkle Beach Barbie (1996), Splash 'n Color Barbie (1996), and Hula Hair Barbie (1997) (Sarasohn-Kahn 1998, 129). According to Sarasohn-Kahn, a doll called My First Barbie was designed in part to help prepare the young Barbie consumer for future hair-play dolls (1998, 13–14).

This emphasis on hair play explains why so many African-American Barbies have the long flowing hair so emphasized in white culture instead of hairstyles that are more Afrocentric (figure 7). Kitty Black-Perkins of Mattel says, "The first Black Barbie that we did had short hair. . . . I thought the short haircut was adorable. What I didn't know at the time, because at that time we didn't rely on a lot of market research, was that half of the play with the doll was (and still is) in the hair. What we know now through our market research is that it doesn't matter what color the child is, they like that long hair! That's one reason why a lot of black kids will buy Barbie—for the length of the hair" (Sarasohn-Kahn 1998, 189).

One notable doll defined completely by her hair is Totally Hair Barbie. At the time of her production, her hair was the longest ever on a Barbie: at ten inches it reached her ankles. Totally Hair Barbie generated some parental disdain; Lord describes her as a "woolly object reminiscent of Cousin It from the *Addams Family*" (1994, 77) and cites an article in *Allure*, which describes the parental dismay generated by this doll: "These mothers have, in fact, singled out . . . Totally Hair Barbie, with her ankle-length tresses and tight, thigh-high minidress, as particularly horrifying; she looks, one observed, like 'a professional fourth wife'" (1994, 185). Despite parental misgivings, Totally Hair Barbie generated $100 million in worldwide sales during 1992; she was the most successful Barbie ever sold to that date (Sarasohn-Kahn 1998, 73–74). These dramatic tresses contribute to the vision of Barbie as exotic and sexy. Lord argues that, along with its play value, all this Barbie hair is sexy, which is part of its attraction, and she notes that historically hair has been seen as a sexual characteristic: "Ever since Milton's portrait of Eve in *Paradise Lost*, with her 'golden tresses'

Figure 7. African-American Jewel Hair Mermaid
Barbie (J. Thomas photo)

falling 'in wanton ringlets' to her waist, long hair has been part of the arse-
nal of seduction" (1994, 210).[11]

At the end of the previous section, I compared Barbie to a horse because
of her massive manes. This association of horse and female is not so far
fetched; it certainly exists in the folk tradition.[12] Jan Brunvand talks about this
motif in his study of *The Taming of the Shrew* tale in the United States (1968,
304; see also 1991). It can also be found in the cowboy poetry of Howard L.
Norskog (1990, 83) and Lucky Whipple (1985, 134, 135). Elsewhere I discuss
this motif's appearance in western folklore and some of its sexual overtones
(Thomas 1995). The German ads for Lilli, the sex doll that was the prototype

for Barbie, support this association. Some of these ads include risqué slogans like *"Ob mehr oder minder nackt Lilli bewahrt immer Takt,"* ("Whether more or less naked, Lilli is always discreet"). There is also an ad that conflates woman with animal, and it is a clear double entendre. It shows Lilli riding on a donkey and says, *"Sicher gefällt Lilli dir mit einem schönen Tier"* ("Lilli will please you with a beautiful animal") (Lord 1994, 30, 28). Also, Barbie on her horse is somewhat reminiscent of Lady Godiva.

If Barbie is part horse, then toy horses these days are part Barbie. When I was a child, all my horses had molded and painted manes and tails. This kind of horse made up the bulk of the toy horses I saw in stores. The horses owned by my children today have voluptuous, flowing, multicolored, big-hair manes and tails that can be combed and styled endlessly. Toy horse manufacturers, it seems, have discovered the profitability of commodifying hair play as well. Of course, many of Barbie's horses have big hair to the hilt. When Western Fun Barbie stands next to her horse Sun Runner or when Blazing Trails Barbie and "her horse blaze a trail through the colorful canyons of the West,"(figure 8), their combined sea of hair is almost enough to drown out the Barbie pink so pervasive in the toy aisle (Summers 1996, 155; Mattel 1999).

Selling Barbie

I have argued that in its marketing of Barbie, Mattel employs many folkloric themes, images, terms, and customs ranging from hair play to holidays to the Tooth Fairy to the use of words like *traditional*. In other words, Mattel is commodifying folklore. The company uses both folklore and place—foreign countries and the West—to help construct a sense of the exotic. That is, they use these things—borrowing an axiom from the tourist industry—to help create something distinctive for the consumer to gaze upon and then hopefully purchase (Urry 1990, 128). This has been an effective marketing strategy. In terms of sales, Barbie continues to ride tall in the saddle across the terrain of toyland.

However, some of the uses to which folklore is put in the designing and promotion of Barbie are troubling; many times they are superficial, manipulative, and stereotypical. When studied closely, though, Barbie frequently resists easy judgment. Part of the interest she generates as a cultural symbol emerges from her multivocality and her ability to be remade—the play and associations made with Barbie by her owners are conventional, unconventional, surprising, stereotypical, complex, shocking, delightful, puzzling, predictable, and unpredictable, depending upon the situation (see Lord 1994; Stern 1998). Initially in the mass media, males were most critical of Barbie; of concern was her "predatory behavior." An early piece in *The Nation* argued that Barbie threatened to create a generation of "viperous" women; she was

Figure 8. Blazing Trails Barbie and her horse (J. Thomas photo)

just too independent (Mitchell and Reid-Walsh 1995, 152, 154). Stern and Schoenhaus argue that Barbie was seen as "a perfect bitch" in the 1960s and as a "complete bimbo" by the 1990s (1990, 63). Much of today's criticism revolves around Barbie's unrealistic figure and the troubling messages about body-size expectations that the doll could be sending to little girls. Researchers have found that both Barbie and Ken are "relatively thin" compared to the non-plastic, human population. The possibility of having a body shaped like Ken's is one in fifty; the possibility of having a body shaped like Barbie's is less than one in 100,000 (Norton, Olds, Olive, and Dank 1996, 287). On the other hand, Kitty G. Abraham and Evelyn Lieberman studied children's play with baby dolls and Barbie dolls and actually found that "nonfacilitative play" with other children (grabbing, hitting, kicking, pushing, glaring, shouting, screaming, teasing, commanding, and name calling) was observed much more frequently during baby-doll play than during Barbie-doll play. They discovered that the children's "imaginations were consistently at work" during play with Barbie dolls. The children shared more, positively reinforced each other more, and made more mutual exchanges during Barbie play (1985, 13, 14). In 1995, Mitchell and Reid-Walsh also observed that Barbie collector cards focused on feminist history (1995, 148).

My discussion of the presentation of Barbie in this article and the research that documents the uses and types of play to which she is put demonstrate that Barbie truly does ride herd on a complex and multivalent variety of images, issues, and associations.[13] Ironically, the Barbie phenomenon also speaks to the power of folklore. American culture assigns cultural importance to things that generate money. In Barbie's case, we can see that folkloric themes and presentations, whether positive or negative, are compelling enough that millions are willing to pay for Barbie-ized versions of them. This commodification of folkloric themes has helped make her the reigning princess of plastic. In a country where money talks, these purchases speak to us of the import of folklore through what seems the most unlikely of sources: a mass-marketed, plastic doll named Barbie.

Notes

Grateful thanks are due to Utah State University's FHE group for their insightful readings and suggestions.

1. Mattel marketed celebrity dolls, including dolls like 1977's Donny and Marie Osmond, from the 1960s onward (Deutsch 1996, 76). However, later they started foregrounding TV shows with Barbie taking over the personae of some of the show's characters. The first TV show Barbie was matched with was *Baywatch*, and many believed *Baywatch* Barbie resembled Pamela Anderson Lee (Sarasohn-Kahn 1998, 90).

2. Peter Stromberg (1996, 290–91) argues that consumerism is such an important part of American culture that it actually constitutes the "real religion" of many Americans. Grider (1996) discusses the commercialization of Halloween.

3. Mattel has started lines of dolls intended to engage little girls in the collector mode. The fairytale-themed Barbies fall into this category as does the American Stories series (Fennick 1996, 107).

4. According to Jill Elikann Barad, former Mattel chief operating officer, the wedding gown is one of the most popular pieces of Barbie clothing, but Barbie has never been truly married. "Little girls are marrying and unmarrying her all the time. If we were to officially set it, it would cut off some of the fantasy" (Sarasohn-Kahn 1998, 115).

5. To determine which countries appear in the series, Mattel identifies at least one nation or region in which they have a production plant, subsidiary, or large or emerging collector population (Sarasohn-Kahn 1998, 123). Mattel also produces dolls especially for an international market; these are marketed abroad and not generally in the United States. For example, special less sexy Barbies resembling figures in Japanese cartoons and comics have been marketed in Japan (Shibano 1994, *passim;* Fennick 1996, 109). Also, Freundschafts Barbie commemorated the fall of the Berlin Wall (Sarasohn-Kahn 1998, 49). Of course, prior to the fall of the wall, Eastern Bloc countries had prohibited the importation of Barbies, which "exemplified every aspect of Western decadence and bourgeois culture" (Fennick 1996, 113). The fall of

the wall prompted Mattel to host an international summit for children: "In 1990, Mattel invited 40 children from 28 countries to the first Barbie Summit. . . . The conference featured tots as young as 6 years old discussing world hunger, degradation of the environment, and war and peace issues. . . . Mattel's idea for creating the Barbie Summit and the accompanying television ad campaign was an indirect result of the fall of the Berlin Wall. Mattel's management team was impressed with photos of Anika Polzin, a six-year-old whose first goal after crossing into West Germany was to buy a Barbie doll" (Sarasohn-Kahn 1998, 51). Mattel issued a special Summit Barbie to commemorate the occasion, which was sold in the United States.

6. Initially I thought that the South and the Southern Belle, due to their legendary and iconic qualities, would appear as much as the West and Western Barbie; this was not the case at all. The West is far more a part of Barbie's world than is the South.

7. Jaune Quick-to-See Smith gives an insider's perspective in her work of art called "Paper Dolls for a Post-Columbian World with Ensembles Contributed by the U.S. Government." The "dolls" she depicts are Ken and Barbie Plenty Horses of the Flathead Tribe; ensembles include "matching smallpox suits" (Lord 1994, 238–39).

8. This theme can be seen in the humorous list, "Being Indian Is," that Kenneth Lincoln includes in his 1993 book, *Indi'n Humor: Bicultural Play in Native America*; one of the entries is "Being Indian is meeting at least two dozen anthropologists before you're 21" (317).

9. Olds and Harris (1997) provide a comprehensive listing of Barbies and their accessories and clothing up to 1996.

10. McCracken (1996) offers an extended discussion of the social significance of hair.

11. Steele (1995, 21–22) discusses sex appeal and its relation to Barbie.

12. The subtitles "International Barbie" and "Hi Ho Barbie!" are puns that associate Barbie with horses. Part of the title of this article is a Barbie-ized version of a line on a Barbie Collector card that says: "Ride 'em Ken" (Mitchell and Reid-Walsh 1995:147), which comes from the Western expression, "Ride 'em cowboy."

13. For other work revealing the range and complexity of the discussion about Barbie dolls and Barbie play, see Cunningham 1993; Cordes 1992; Hohmann-Delf 1985; Lord 1994; MacNaughton 1996; Margo 1997; Motz 1983; Ebersole and Peabody 1993; Rand 1994; Rossie 1994; Stout and Mouritsen 1988; Sutton-Smith 1986; Turkel 1998; Wason-Ellam 1997; and Yocom 1993, 129.

Tall Tales and Sales

Steve Siporin

I s there anything significant left to say about tall tales? The apparent sim-
plicity of the genre and the vast literature already written about it, some
of which will be addressed below, might lead one to think that the answer
must be no. Yet, as is the case with folklore generally, just when we think our
"simple" subject has been exhausted, we discover new layers of meaning
tucked away in a tale, in silence, or in newly emerging uses.

In this essay I will argue that in spite of the attention scholars have
paid to tall tales, a fascinating function remains unexplored—the mercantile
function of marketing a region. My hypothesis is that in North America, tall
tales have traditionally served economic ends and continue to do so today.
Before I demonstrate this hypothesis, I want to bring the literature on tall
tales into focus in order to contextualize my ideas within the discussion
about the special role of tall tales in North America.

Tall tales—also known by such local terms as windies, stretchers,
yarns, whoppers, and lies—comprise one of the best known and best loved
folklore genres in North America. Richard Dorson, in his *Handbook of
American Folklore*, went so far as to say that "as the *Märchen* characterizes
European storytelling, so the tall tale exemplifies American storytelling"
(1983, 290).

The Norwegian folklorist Gustav Henningsen, while acknowledging
that "America became for one reason or another a liar's paradise," considered American folklorists' perspective on tall tales to be a distortion,
reflecting publication history and national political publicity more than storytelling reality:

> While the European hunter, fisherman, and skipper stories . . .
> have led a decidedly unnoticed existence . . . . the genre in the U.S.A.
> has been an object of attention and of study without parallel right
> from 1829 when the tall-tale teller and hero Davy Crockett was elect-
> ed to Congress; and while all of Munchhausen's [sic] undiscovered
> cousins at home in Europe sat entertaining a small local audience,

Abraham Lincoln as president in the 1860's could illustrate the political situation with tall tales which he had learned in his youth in the
Midwest. (1965, 181)

Jan Brunvand qualified Dorson's statement, noting that *tales of lying*
(types 1875–1999 in the Aarne-Thompson index) are thought of by
Americans as "a peculiarly American product, just as Turks, Germans, and
Scandinavians each think of [tall tales] as peculiarly *their* national invention, all of them forgetting that there were tall tales before any of their
nations was thought of" (1998, 246). Brunvand was certainly correct. Dan
Ben-Amos, for instance, has identified tall tales in the Talmudic-Midrashic
literature (1976), and others have found tall tales in Herodotus (Parton 1864,
468) and Plutarch (Henningsen 1965, 185–86). The most famous collection
of tall tales (recently given new life in a popular movie) is from Germany—
Singular Travels, Campaigns, and Adventures of Baron Münchausen, first
published in English by Rudolph Eric Raspe in 1785 (Dégh 1972, 71).

It is hard to know if North Americans really do favor tall tales more
than other peoples do or if the numerous and extensive American tall-tale
collections simply reflect American folklorists' collecting habits, ideas, and
expectations. Cecil Sharp, after all, during his famous field trip in
Appalachia, asked for ballads and got ballads; he didn't ask for Jack tales,
and he didn't collect any. Other field workers collected Jack tales from the
same informants nearly a decade later (Dorson 1964, 164–65). Thus, as many
scholars have pointed out, folklore archives do not necessarily reflect local
or national repertoires—how can they when personal preference, enthusiasm, the seeking of excellent rather than average performers, and chance
rather than random sampling shape folklore collecting?

This much, however, *is* clear: tall tales were told and recorded in North
America from colonial times onward, and today they remain vital and lively, particularly in the form of postcards and other objects.

What is a tall tale? Suzi Jones, in her landmark article "Regionalization:
A Rhetorical Strategy," defines the tall tale as "a humorous exaggeration of
some aspect of the local environment, told by an insider to an outsider for the
amusement of the insider, . . . a ludicrous image which rests on truth" (1976,
115). To further clarify the nature of the tall tale, let's compare it to the legend. Structurally, these two forms operate in amazingly similar ways for such
different genres. A legend is a story about something out of the ordinary,
something that challenges belief. Its teller usually believes that the story is
true and tries to convince his/her audience of its truth. A tall tale is also about
something unusual, but in the case of the tall tale, the narrator definitely does
not believe his/her own narrative, yet he/she wants the audience to believe it,
at least for a while:

Once a stranger stopped to ask about the country. His interest was stirred by the utter absence of anything in sight to show it had rained around Fort Rock. He said, "Has it *ever* rained here?"

I [Reub Long] told him, "Yes, once. Do you remember how Noah, the first long-range weather forecaster, built the ark and floated it during forty days and nights of rain?" He said he had knowledge of that. I told him, "That time we got a quarter of an inch." (Jackman and Long 1964, 348)

Jones's approach focuses on the rhetoric of the tall tale. Exaggeration, for instance, cannot be random; usually some true aspect of the local environment is "stretched" in order to fool the outsider. As she says, referring to Mody Boatright, "the liar's art is essentially realistic" (Jones 1976, 115). (And note that if Reub Long, the narrator, believed that it had really rained only a quarter of an inch in Eastern Oregon during Noah's Flood, we would call his narrative a legend.)

Jones also defined the tall tale partly through the social interaction surrounding its narration, demonstrating how the telling of a "windy" can be a way of drawing a boundary between insiders and outsiders in a given social context—ultimately to invoke and strengthen the bonds among insiders, who may feel threatened by outsiders and may desire to exclude them.

Patrick Mullen, in *I Heard the Old Fishermen Say: Folklore of the Texas Gulf Coast*, also sees more to the tall tale than just exaggeration. He identifies characteristic artistic devices and areas of specialized style such as (1) the use of concrete detail (in description and dialogue) to create a sense of reality; (2) the use of ludicrous imagery (the main device) which is vivid, appropriately incongruous, and absurd; and (3) the manipulation of point of view—a tendency to narrate in (or even shift to) the first person, creating a sense of immediacy and involvement. Mullen's fourth fictive device is the teller's adoption of a narrative persona that is not the personality of the actual teller himself but a standard character-narrator role he takes on.[1] This persona is a wide-eyed naïf—what Mullen calls "The American Everyman." The American Everyman bears witness to the unending bounty of nature in America through tales like "The Wonderful Hunt," in which a hunter kills an elk, a bear, a snake, several quail, and dozens of geese and ducks with one shot. His boots fill up with fish when he retrieves the geese and ducks from the river (Mullen 1988, 140–44).[2] Such tall tales express the idea of "unlimited good" and are an attractive symbol of the "limitless" natural resources of North America.

In terms of function, Mullen agrees with Jones about the creation of insider group solidarity through the telling of tall tales, although he sees this function as something that moved west as the frontier moved west. Tall tales provided a kind of initiation rite, bringing greenhorns into the group, and this function was contemporaneous with the frontier period as it transpired in each American region. In the 1960s, on the Texas Gulf Coast, Mullen observed a bait-shop owner, Ed Bell, telling tall tales to his customers—not so much as initiation but for the customers' entertainment and as a way to attract them and thus promote his business.

Both Jones and Mullen discuss the tall tale in its immediate, oral, inter-actional context. Mullen turns to a less context-bound, purely textual meaning of the tall tale when he interprets it as symbolizing the "limitless" bounty of North America and projecting the idea of "unlimited good." How that dimen-sion relates to the marketing of region through tradition brings us back to the hypothesis of this essay.

Today, recycled folklore is used to attract individuals to an area in the hope that, as tourists, potential home-buyers, investors, and consumers of all stripes, these individuals will spend money and thereby benefit the local economy. Mullen describes Ed Bell's tall tales functioning in this way on a small scale for his bait-shop business; but any folklorist who has worked for an arts agency since the late 1970s probably has heard a lot about the "mul-tiplier effect" of arts audiences on local economies and has felt the pressure to justify folk arts budgets in the same economic terms that are used to jus-tify arts expenditures in general. The multiplier effect is the notion that if people come into a region to see a play or visit a festival, for example, they will also spend money on lodging, food, and other services and commodities. Thus, tax money invested in the arts or in heritage as a means of attracting tourists is multiplied in the local economy. The burgeoning industry today called cultural tourism shows that the new economic argument of the 1970s has by now become a standard arts-and-heritage argument. It is not news that a region can be made attractive to outsiders through evocation of its dis-tinctive traditions—or that the resulting revenue can be enormous.

Not only is it not news, the multiplier effect (though never called that until recently) may be an old idea among ordinary people. As is often the case, folklore is ahead of mass culture, which perhaps only plays out folk ideas on a large scale (Dundes 1971). In North America, recounting tall tales may have sometimes acted as a *traditional* way of marketing a region. And it may still do so. This hypothesis of the tall tale as an elementary market-ing device may explain its widespread popularity in the commerce-driven United States and incidentally reveal the real divergence between the American and European tall-tale traditions. I can demonstrate this most readily with tall tale postcards and related paraphernalia.

Tall-tale postcards, or "boastcards," as well as other mass-produced tall tale objects, may not be folk artifacts themselves, but they are based on the folk tradition of the tall tale and often meet most of the criteria discussed by Jones and Mullen above. Such postcards, as mass-produced commercial

Figure 1. Postcard

items, provide a clear example of marketed traditions themselves: they are for sale. But their true economic impact may derive from their hyperbolic promotion of states and regions through the use of traditional tall-tale imagery.

The mermaid (figure 1), for instance, may promote travel to the destination that has been coupled with her image. No one today believes that mermaids actually exist, but the image deploys an old tall tale to convey a warm sense of welcome for (male) travelers to the region. A positive feeling lingers in the male mind: "Southern New England would be a good place for a vacation. . . ."

But catching the mermaid is also related to catching other dream fish (figures 2 and 3), parallel expressions of desire and fantasy. The big fish is probably the most common and one of the oldest of boastcard images around. It may sound far-fetched to hypothesize that such advertisements attract fishermen to a region, but the big fish possibility may operate like the mermaid, linking a positive association with a particular region. And note that—just as Jones and Mullen suggest for oral tales—sometimes it may be difficult for the outsider to know if the image of the fish is an exaggeration or not.

When I saw the postcards photographed in figures 4 and 5 during my first trip to Alaska, I was unsure if there really were fish of this size or if I was being taken in by a tall-tale postcard like those in figures 2 and 3. The ambiguity I experienced recalls the greenhorn's confusion and disorientation on the frontier and/or the West, where fertility was believed to be great and animals sizable and strange and the outsider was not quite sure if—or

Figure 2. Postcard. Caption reads, "Catch and Release Fishing in Montana."

Figure 4. Postcard.

Figure 3. Postcard. Caption reads, "Low-Water Fishing Gear, Montana."

Figure 5. Postcard.

Figure 6. Postcard.

Figure 7. Postcard.

Figure 8. Postcard.

Figure 9. Mosquito trap.

Figure 10. Postcard.

Figure 11. Postcard. Caption reads, "Oregon Toothpick."

Figure 12. Label from apple crate.

Figure 13. Postcard.

HICKEN'S FUR-BEARING TROUT
Clifford Lake

Figure 14. Postcard.

Figure 15. Postcard.

Figure 16. Postcard of jackalope.

Figure 17. A can of jackalope milk.

Figure 18. Stuffed and mounted jackalopes.

Figure 19. Postcard of *Wolpertinger.*

when—his leg was being pulled. Alaska remains one of the few frontiers where the greenhorn can still be confused because reality actually *is* so much bigger than elsewhere. What I thought was fake turned out to be genuine—salmon and halibut *can* weigh over a hundred pounds. Learning that fish could be unbelievably large in Alaskan waters made me vulnerable: what I might now be ready to accept as real, though unusual, could turn out to be a tall tale. In Alaska, and earlier western frontiers, reality sets you up to be fooled by a tall tale. The huge cabbages in some postcards (figure 6) are not tall tales, although the moose in the cabbage patch (figure 7) is.

Some exaggerations—like the mosquito as state bird (figure 8) or the mechanical mosquito trap (figure 9), based on a huge body of oral tall tales about mosquitoes—probably don't fool many people (Halpert 1990; Taft 1983, 42–45). And although giant mosquitoes are certainly a negative exaggeration, they have acquired a positive function through the tall tale because they allow the outsider a feeling of insiderness by being in on the joke. That sense of insiderness, no matter how ill-founded and unconscious, forms a subtle bond between the tourist and the Alaska of his/her imagination—and thus markets the region. An actual drawback has been turned into a draw by being converted to a joke, a cause for camaraderie.[3]

Fertility, in the form of giant agricultural products, is still among the most positive images western regions project in their postcards.[4] Typically, there is a one-to-one correlation between a hyperbolic product and a state or region, much as a logo identifies an institution. For Idaho there are dozens of different giant-potato postcards (figure 10); for Oregon it is logs[5] (figure 11). Washington State produces massive apples[6] (figure 12), while in Nebraska and

Iowa corn grows not only tall but wide (figure 13). Montana claims the fur-bearing trout (figure 14), and although pictures of gigantic fruit have appeared on California tall-tale postcards for perhaps a century, at least one recent card depicts giant marijuana plants (figure 15) as the regional crop of choice today.

The jackalope, however, must be considered the dominant pan-regional tall-tale image in the West. The jackalope has become ubiquitous throughout the western states (figure 16). According to the text reproduced on a variety of widely available postcards,

> the Jackalope is perhaps the rarest animal in North America. This strange little fellow defies classification. Were it not for the horns it might be a large rabbit. Were it not for its shape and coloring it might be a species of deer. It is not vicious usually, although coyotes have a fine respect for the sharp menace of its horns. . . . An odd trait of the Jackalope is its ability to imitate the human voice. Cowboys singing to their herds at night have been startled to hear their lonesome melodies repeated faithfully from some nearby hillside. The phantom echo comes from the throat of some Jackalope. They sing only on dark nights before a thunderstorm. Stories that they sometimes get togeth-er and sing in chorus is discounted by those who know them best.[7]

The jackalope also demonstrates the economic significance of today's regional tall tales. A resident of Douglas, Wyoming, claims that he and his brother created the original jackalope in 1934 to increase business for the La Bonte Hotel in Douglas. The jackalope seems to have succeeded in luring more tourists to the area, at least according to a 1977 newspaper article with the headline, "Tourists Love Jackalope: Hoax Jacks Up Town's Economy" (Dorson 1982, 51). A jackalope festival continues today as Douglas, Wyoming's major annual event.

The economy of the jackalope is fairly impressive at the micro-level, too. Today one can purchase not only jackalope postcards, but also jacka-lope hunting licenses (from the Douglas, Wyoming, Chamber of Commerce, allowing the hunting of one jackalope on June 31 between midnight and 2 A.M. only), cans of jackalope milk (figure 17), jackalope t-shirts, jackalope banks, jackalope eggs, and even stuffed and mounted jackalopes (figure 18).

The *Wolpertinger* (figure 19), a figure similar to the jackalope, exists in Bavarian folklore (Petzoldt 1995, 192–93). Although it looks like a jackalope, it has the additional features of wings, a coxcomb, and fangs. Maybe the Wolpertinger is an antecedent (or ancestor!) of the jackalope. Whatever its origin, the jackalope draws on earlier traditions of gigantic rabbits and their implicit, unstoppable fertility. In the North American West these soft creatures gained antlers and became oxymoronic symbols for the attractions of a region that can be both menacing and gentle, tough and sentimental—like the image of *the* regional icon, the cowboy himself.

These contemporary examples, from giant potatoes to antlered rabbits, are the latest versions of tall tales that have thrived in North America, not just in isolated pockets, but as part of the mainstream economic ethos that is central to American national character. Marketing America began early. Dorson wrote that "colonists readily credited accounts of New World fertility and fecundity, lushness and abundance, and transmitted them to their transatlantic kinfolk who waited cautiously before investing in or emigrating to these newborn settlements. . . . The historian of the Carolinas, John Lawson, told of a tulip tree so large that a lusty man moved his bed and household furniture inside" (1959, 9–11).

Fertility and fecundity, lushness and abundance—these are the themes of many tall tales, even if they are exaggerations, even if they are told, or visualized, in jest. These themes are communicated subliminally whether the tale is believed or not; for in the playfulness of the communication, an invitation has been extended. For those already in America or on the frontier, the motivation to attract new immigrants is easy to appreciate: as newcomers arrived, old-timers' property increased in value, transportation improved, the tax base grew, and markets developed. Americans still believe that the only good economy is an expanding economy. The tall tale, consciously or unconsciously manipulated, was an advertisement, an open invitation to draw in newcomers and to benefit the old-timers, the pioneers.

The ideas of bounty and unlimited good that we see in the tall-tale postcards of today were already present in nineteenth-century American oral tall-tale-telling contexts. Abraham "Oregon" Smith pioneered in Oregon from 1852 through 1859, but he regaled audiences in Indiana and Illinois with his Oregon tall tales until nearly the end of the century:

> One time when I was out in Oregon walkin along the foot of a hill, I came to a little cold stream. About halfway across I started noticing little bits of yaller stuff floating on the top of the water, and a bit further on down I saw a small pool of pale yaller churning around slowly. Well now, that interested me considerable.
>
> I looked at it and then, thinks I, it won't hurt none to taste the stuff. Well, I did and, do you know, it tasted just like butter—unsalted butter. (Halpert and Robinson 1942, 164–65)

Oregon Smith goes upstream until he finds a herd of buffalo cows stomping around in the water to keep flies away and, in the process, churning the milk that overflowed from their udders and creating a land perhaps even more fertile than the one that flowed with mere *milk* and honey.

Jacqueline Simpson remarks that a related motif was used nine centuries earlier. A mid-ninth-century Viking claimed that butter dripped from every blade of Iceland's grass (Jones 1968, 274). And according to *Eirikssaga*, Erik the Red called Greenland "Greenland, [because] he maintained that men would be much more eager to go there if the land had an attractive name" (Jones 1988, 129). That sounds like smart marketing. Simpson calls it a "bit of boastful advertising" (personal correspondence, July 4, 1994). In the twentieth century the same genre, tall tales, markets regions to tourists more often than settlers, largely by reasserting, through humor, that "pervasive feeling of optimism and enthusiasm" that cultural geographer Wilbur Zelinsky found to be so characteristic of North American worldview (1992, 63).

Wyoming's jackalopes, Montana's fur-bearing trout, Oregon's watermelons and pumpkins that grow so fast they have to be placed on skids to keep from getting bruised, and other instances of regional tall tales may suggest that using folklore to sell a region has a longer tradition than we had previously thought. Telling tall tales and selling tall-tale postcards and other tall-tale paraphernalia may be considered *applied* folklore in a fundamental way—as a traditional act of insiders, to benefit themselves, not an imposition of outsiders.

Today, we are deeply concerned about "the marketing of tradition," the "commodification of culture," and other materialist reductions of heritage. And we should be. But this tendency runs much deeper in our own culture than we might have suspected and is indeed traditional itself.

Notes

1. Using the first person over a long career of tall-tale telling can make one into a "Münchausen," a person with a reputation for telling tall tales about himself, like the original baron. American folklorists have studied several Münchausens in depth—Len Henry of northern Idaho, Abraham "Oregon" Smith of Indiana, John Darling of New York, Jim Bridger of the West, Gib Morgan of Pennsylvania and Oklahoma oilfields, and Hathaway Jones of Oregon, to name a few.

2. "The Wonderful Hunt" is "one of the most widely collected folktales in America" (Mullen 1988, 141). It combines one or more versions of tale types 1890 A–F, 1894, and 1896 in Aarne-Thompson (1987).

3. Oregon's "ungreeting cards" of the 1970s—which exaggerated rainfall through phrases like "Last year eighteen people drowned in Oregon." [open card] "They fell off their bicycles"—are other instances in which an unattractive regional characteristic was turned into an attraction through hyperbole.

4. For collections of early twentieth-century American tall-tale postcards with images of agricultural fertility, see Welsch 1976, Rubin and Williams 1990, and Henry 1995.

5. The Oregon tall-tale image is a bit different from the others because the exaggeration comes only in the language describing the logs as toothpicks. The logs themselves are not exaggerated in size as are most other tall-tale images.

6. This image is a label from a crate of apples rather than a postcard.

7. This identical phrasing appears on many jackalope postcards with a variety of images. I have not been able to identify the origin of the description.

Narrative

Jesse James: An American Outlaw

C. W. Sullivan III

Jesse James, born to Robert James and Zerelda Cole James in September of 1847 and killed by Robert Ford in April of 1882, is perhaps the most famous western outlaw in the United States. After the Civil War—during which he served for a time with Quantrill's men, as did his brother Frank—he and his brother became infamous as bank and train robbers, leading a gang which included, at times, such other well-known outlaws as the Younger brothers and the Miller brothers. There is substantial historical documentation for the major events of Jesse's life,[1] but this factual career is the stuff of history; the story of Jesse James that the people tell—which exists in ballads, folktales, dime novels, and films—is the stuff of legend, and the legend of Jesse James has its roots in British legend tradition. Although the deepest roots of the Jesse James legend may reach through Arthurian literature to the ancient Irish stories of Finn MacCumhaill, the most obvious links between the American and British outlaw traditions lie in the similarities between the stories of Jesse James and the stories of Robin Hood.

In *The American Songbag*, Carl Sandburg remarks that "Jesse James is the only American bandit who is classical, who is to this country what Robin Hood or Dick Turpin is to England, whose exploits are so close to the mythical and apocryphal" (1927, 420).[2] Sandburg was by no means the first to link Jesse James and Robin Hood; in fact, as William A. Settle notes in *Jesse James Was His Name*, such comparisons were already being made during Jesse's lifetime. The Lexington *Caucasian* published an extra edition on 1 September 1874 asserting that "in all the history of medieval knight errantry and modern brigandage, there is nothing that equals the wild romance of the past few years' career of Arthur McCoy, Frank and Jesse James, and the Younger boys" and then went on to describe the "Robin-Hood-like, rattling visit" which they had paid to Lexington (Settle 1966, 71–72).

The very first stanza of the ballad, which began to circulate almost immediately after Jesse's death and is popular to this day, may well have been created to invoke the Robin Hood image:

Jesse James was a lad who killed many a man.
He robbed the Glendale train.
He stole from the rich and he gave to the poor,
He had a hand and a heart and a brain.[3]

The general motif of robbing from the rich and giving to the poor, which appears in numerous tales about Jesse James, is the most direct link between Jesse and Robin Hood. In one tale with several variants, Jesse encounters a widow who cannot pay her mortgage and is about to lose her farm to the bank, which, it seems, Jesse and his gang have just robbed. Jesse gives the widow enough money to pay the banker when he arrives the next day, and as the banker heads back to town after giving the widow the title to her property, Jesse robs him again. An almost identical story is told of Robin Hood, his friend Sir Richard of Lee, and the Abbot of St. Mary's; and as Kent L. Steckmesser notes, "This floating anecdote is also assigned to Sam Bass" (1966, 351).

The legend of each man was constructed, therefore, on a perception of him as a hero of the people who "risked an outlaw's fate in order to rob the exploitive rich and give to the deserving poor" (Settle 1966, 171); but as each man's legend grew, he and his men came to stand for larger ideological concerns. According to the most popular form of the Robin Hood legend, Robin and his men battle the usurping King John and his allies, which include the Sheriff of Nottingham as well as the high officials of the church. In this fight, Robin and the Men of Sherwood not only defend the poor against John and his allies but also work for the return of the rightful king, Richard the Lionheart, who has been away at the Crusades. According to the Jesse James legend, the James Gang is battling the northern or Yankee carpetbaggers who have come south after the Civil War and are using the banks and other institutions to drive those who sided with the Confederacy off their lands. Jesse and his men, thus, rob the banks of the invaders and give the money to the residents so that the poor can keep their lands.

Whether English or American, then, the legendary outlaw hero is responding to or the result of "a recurrent social situation, namely, one in which the law is corrupt" (Steckmesser 1966, 348). In *Robin Hood*, James Clarke Holt traces the Robin Hood legend back to a "Robert Hode, tenant of the archbishopric of York, [who] fled the jurisdiction of the king's justices at York in 1225" (1982, 187), but Holt argues that most of the rest of the legend "is motley, derived from widely scattered sources" (62). As the story evolves over the centuries and takes on cultural overtones, Robin and his men become Anglo-Saxon partisans fighting against the Norman oppressors. Settle, with a great deal more historical record on which to draw, suggests that the legend of the James Gang is "deeply rooted and inextricably bound to the events of the Civil War and its aftermath" and includes such cultural situations as the "Granger's resentment of the practices of the railroads and the banks, the East's contempt for the West, [and] the economic rivalry between Chicago and the cities in Missouri" in the mix of events and emotions which aided in the legend's rapid growth (1966, 3). Jesse James and Robin Hood became legendary outlaw heroes battling the oppressive establishment on behalf of the victimized individual or minority.

The paradigm of the outlaw hero as well as specific incidents, such as the double robbery story mentioned above, then, link the legend of Jesse James to the legend of Robin Hood. But the connection between the two may be even deeper than that. From newspaper articles published during Jesse's lifetime which defended the James Gang's actions to the ballads, tales, and dime novels which circulated after his death, a cohesive legend was created. "A sampling of representative stories reveals that unusual shooting ability, courage in the face of danger, willingness to aid the unfortunate, deference to women, and ability to surmount all obstacles are common characteristics of the dime-novel James brothers" (Settle 1966, 190). Marksmanship, bravery, and the "ability to surmount all obstacles," would be a requisite for successful outlawry; but "aid [to] the unfortunate" and "deference to women" point to a code of behavior in addition to a level of skill, and this, too, links the James Gang with the Men of Sherwood.

These concepts, outstanding skill with weapons and what we might call a chivalric code of conduct, are important features of the legends of Robin Hood; in fact, the two most persistent images from the tales of Robin Hood involve skill with the long bow and robbing the rich to give to the poor. These concepts are present in the oldest recorded ballads of the famous outlaw, one of which, "A Lytell Geste of Robyn Hode," may have been written down as early as 1400 and is assumed to have been in oral tradition for years prior to that (Holt 1982, 15; Campbell 1853, 21). That the men of Sherwood were excellent archers is quickly established in the ballad:

> Lytell Johan and good Scatheloke
> Were archers good and fre;
> Lytell Much and good Reynolde,
> The worste wolde they not be
>
> Whan they had shot aboute,
> These archours fayre and good,
> Evermore was the best,
> Forsoth, Robyn Hode.
> Hym was delivered the goode aròw
> For best worthy was he. (Ritson 1823, 52–53)

The ballad also points out that Robin was a religious man:

> A good maner than had Robyn,
> In londe where that he were,
> Every daye or he wolde dyne
> Thre messes wolde he here;
>
> The one in the worshyp of the fader,
> The other of the holy goost,
> The thyrde was of our dere lady,
> That he loved of all other moste. (4)

And it is partly due to this religious nature that Robin set up a code of behavior by which all of the outlaws were sworn.

> Robyn loved our dere lady,
> For doute of dedely synne;
> Wolde he never do company harme
> That ony women was ynne.
>
> Mayster, than sayd Lytell Johan,
> And we our borde shall sprede,
> Tell us whether we shall gone,
> And what lyfe we shall lede;
>
> Where we shall take, where we shall leve,
> Where we shall abide behynde,
> Where we shall robbe, where we shall reve,
> Where we shall bete and bynd.
>
> Ther of no fors, sayd Robyn,
> We shall do well ynough;
> But loke ye do no housbande harme
> That tylleth with his plough;
>
> No more ye shall no good yemán,
> That walketh by grene wode shawe,
> Ne no knyght, ne no squyér,
> That wolde be a good felawe.
>
> These bysshoppes, and thyse archebysshoppes,
> Ye shall them bete and bynde;
> The hye sheryfe of Notynghame,
> Hym holde in your mynd.
>
> This worde shall be holde, sayd Lytyll Johan,
> And this lesson shall we lere;
> It is ferre dayes, god sende us a gest,
> That we were at our dynere. (4–5)

And as for Robin Hood himself, the ballad says that so "curteyse an outlawe as he was one / Was never none yfounde" (3). Like the James Gang, then, the Men of Sherwood were skilled warriors who lived by a code of behavior.

In the Robin Hood legends, however, that code has been formalized, referring specifically to expected conduct toward women and to which folk should be robbed and which let alone; in the Jesse James legends, the code is implied in the actions of the men as reported in a variety of media, from contemporary newspaper accounts to ballads, folktales, and dime novels. According to one story Settle reports, Frank James paid for lodgings with "a well-to-do farmer" during the days before the James Gang robbed the Deposit Bank at Columbia, Kentucky. The farmer's grandmother recounted James's interest in her Bible and a copy of *Pilgrim's Progress*, the latter of which he borrowed while there and returned before leaving. "A man of such courtesy and such reading habits, the grandmother believed, could not have been one of the desperadoes" (1966, 44). At the Gads Hill train robbery, the James Gang examined the male passengers' hands "stating, according to reports, that they 'did not want to rob workingmen or ladies, but the money and valuables of the plug-hat gentlemen were what they sought'" (1966, 49). During their subsequent escape from the scene, they traveled west, "and accounts were soon brought to the towns of their obtaining meals and lodging at farm homes along the way. Reportedly, they 'conducted themselves as gentlemen, paying for everything they got'" (Settle 1966, 49). Other stories, in which Jesse returns a preacher's valuables and says that they "never take from preachers, widows, or orphans" or in which Jesse is reported to be "a devout Baptist who taught in a church singing school" (Steckmesser 1966, 351; Croy 1949, 67–68), serve to reinforce the Robin Hood image.

The code by which Jesse James's men behave and Robin Hood's men swear is by no means original to those legends; in fact, perhaps the most completely articulated code of conduct in literature, and the one which is in the background of both the Jesse James and Robin Hood legends, was the one to which King Arthur's Knights of the Round Table swore.[4] Both skill at arms and a code of behavior are a part of the Arthurian materials from their literary beginnings. Geoffrey of Monmouth, Wace, and Layamon devote most of their "histories" to accounts of Arthur's battles, especially those on the European continent in which Arthur was victorious. But each author also comments that the knights who surrounded Arthur were the best to be found (Geoffrey 1969, 199; Paton 1912, 55, 209). In addition, the Round Table, which Wace and Layamon develop primarily as a means of settling the problem of seating for a group in which each man could claim to be deserving of a seat at or near the head of the table, quickly grew to become a symbol of peace, and the men who sat around it became examples of courtly breeding and behavior.

Wace relates that Arthur "ordained the courtesies of the court" (Paton 1912, 55) and Layamon writes that "Arthur was in the world wise king and powerful; good man and peaceful" and that his knights were "great in their mood" (Paton 1912, 211–12). And both authors were echoing Geoffrey's account:

> Arthur then began to increase his personal entourage by inviting very distinguished men from far-distant kingdoms to join it. In this way he developed such a code of courtliness in his household that he inspired peoples living far away to imitate him. The result was that even the man of noblest birth, once he was roused to rivalry, thought nothing at all of himself unless he wore his arms and dressed the same way as Arthur's knights. At last the fame of Arthur's generosity and bravery spread to the very ends of the earth. (Geoffrey 1969, 199)[5]

The two major elements of the pattern, "distinguished men" and a "code of courtliness," or "fame of generosity," are in Geoffrey's account.

By the time of Malory's writing, the "code" had been polished by French authors:

> [Then] the kyng stablysshed all the knyghtes and gaff them rychesse and londys; and charged them never to do outerage nothir mourthir, and allwayes to fle treson, and to gyff mercy unto hym that askith mercy, uppon payne of forfiture [of their] worship and lordship of kynge Arthure for evirmore; and allways to do ladyes, damesels, and jantilwomen and wydowes [socour:] strengths hem in hir ryghtes, and never to enforce them, uppon payne of dethe. Also, that no man take no batayles in a wrongefull quarell for no love ne for no worldis goodis. So unto thys were all knyghtis sworne of the Table Rounde, both olde and younge, and every yere so were the[y] sworne at the hyghe feste of Pentecoste. (Malory 1971, 75–76)

The disparity between the Arthurian legends and the legends of Jesse James and Robin Hood, of course, is that Arthur and his Knights were the emerging government and were establishing and enforcing the laws rather than breaking them. However, in Arthur's time most of the surrounding countryside was wild, not peaceful, and the land and people were being raided every summer by the Vikings, who, along with the Angles, Saxons, and other Germanic tribes, were trying to move in and take over—just as were the Normans, whom Robin Hood was fighting in some versions of the legend, at a later date. More important, Arthur and his knights, like Jesse James and Robin Hood, were defending all of the indigenous people against invaders who would, at best, take their lands and, at worst, take their lives.

If it is true that we remember Arthur and the Knights of the Round Table as defenders of Britain against the Anglo-Saxon invasion, it is also true that part of the Jesse James legend rests on the belief that the James Gang was protecting poor Southerners against the encroaching Northern interests. Settle admits that "the bandits did not differentiate between Northerners and Southerners" as a rule, but does note one situation in which the James Gang asked the victims if any "had served in the Confederate army. . . . One, G. R. Crump of Memphis, replied that he had. After further questioning, the bandit chief returned Crump's watch and money with the comment that the gang did not want to rob Confederate soldiers; Northerners had driven the members of the gang into banditry, and they intended to make Northerners pay" (1966, 49–50).

The existence of one actual instance in which the James Gang favored a former Confederate soldier is certainly more than enough basis for their legendary status as the defenders of postbellum Southerners.[6] This image, and its Arthurian overtones, was promulgated by the print media and especially by John N. Edwards, who saw these outlaws as being "as chivalrous as any character created by Sir Walter Scott" and as "men who might have sat with Arthur at the Round Table" (Settle 1966, 45–46).

Finn and the Fianna, the Irish group which may well be at the root of these legends of skillful and chivalric warriors, were an elite fighting force, the hand-picked troop of the king, who gained their initial fame defending Ireland from invasion. Finn and the Fianna are one of the earliest recorded non-familial or non-tribal groups to be formed in order to defend a specific geopolitical area, so whereas a warrior's previous primary loyalty was to the family or tribe, his primary loyalty was now contracted to a group and leader unrelated to him in any other way.[7] Being made a member of that group, like being made a member of the Round Table, was considered a high honor. To qualify, a man had to undergo a rigorous test to prove his skill as a warrior and also swear an oath which would, henceforth, govern his behavior at all times. Douglas Hyde comments that any man who "entered the Fenian ranks had four *geasa* [i.e., tabus] laid on him. . . . The first, never to receive a portion with a wife, but to choose her for good manners and virtues; the second, never to offer violence to any woman; the third, never to refuse any one for anything he might possess; the fourth, that no single warrior should flee before nine [i.e., fewer than ten] champions." Hyde also notes that there "was a curious condition attached to entrance into the brotherhood" which required that "[both] his father and mother, his tribe, and his relatives should first give guarantees that they should never make any charge against any person for his death. This was in order that the duty of avenging his own blood [wounds] should rest with no man other than himself, and in order that his friends should have nothing to claim with respect to him however great the evils inflicted upon him" (1967, 373).

Although Hyde does not mention it, this guarantee is an important step in the development of a society or culture, as tribal and familial rights—such as the right to individual revenge—were giving way to what might be considered the first stages of what would become a social contract, wherein primary loyalty was given to the state and not the family or tribe.[8]

In addition to these specific oaths, the candidate also had to prove himself as a man of learning and as a warrior. Hyde continues:

> not a man was taken until he was a prime poet versed in the twelve books of poetry.[9] No man was taken till in the ground a large hole had been made such as to reach the fold of his belt, and he put into it with his shield and a forearm's length of a hazel stick. Then must nine warriors having nine spears, with a ten furrows' width between them and him, assail him, and in concert let fly at him. If he were then hurt past that guard of his, he was not received into the Fian-ship. Not a man of them was taken until his hair had been inter-woven into braids on him, and he started at a run through Ireland's woods, while they seeking to wound him followed in his wake, and there having been between him and them but one forest bough by way of interval at first. Should he be overtaken he was wounded and not received into the Fian-ship after. If his weapons had quivered in his hand he was not taken. Should a branch in the wood have disturbed anything of his hair out of its braiding he was not taken. If he had cracked a dry stick under his foot [as he ran] he was not accepted. Unless that [at full speed] he had both jumped a stick level with his brow, and stooped to pass under one on a level with his knee, he was not taken. Unless also without slackening his pace he could with his nail extract a thorn from his foot he was not taken into the Fian-ship. But if he performed all this he was of Finn's people. (Hyde 1967, 373–74)

It may well be that the legends of Finn and the Fianna provide the ultimate source for the articulation of the ethical formula and the portrait of the skilled warrior which comes down through the Arthurian materials and the tales of Robin Hood to help structure the legend of Jesse James and the James Gang; and it is certainly clear from all of these tales of Finn, Arthur, Robin Hood, and Jesse James that the idea of an honorable band of men (regardless of their establishment or outlaw status) protecting the poor or common folk against an outside or invading oppressor has a long tradition in Europe and America. Although it may be specific historical and cultural situations which link the Jesse James and the Robin Hood legends so closely, it is an even longer tradition of European legendry from which the legends of the James Gang derive some support.

The legends surrounding Jesse James, though, whatever their corre-
spondences with European tradition, do break from their European precur-
sors in some important ways. The most important difference may center on
Jesse's death. Finn and Arthur, both heroes in an established and official
power structure, meet suitably heroic ends; Robin and Jesse are both treacherously murdered. But Robin's death at the hands of a cousin who was a nun
comes sometime after he and his men have entered into the service of the king
(Holt 1982, 74, 35). Although the reasons for the treachery are not clear, what
does seem to be clear is that Robin is no longer an outlaw at the time of his
death. In fact, modern versions of the Robin Hood story, and most especially
the film version starring Errol Flynn, end with Robin being pardoned by King
Richard, whom he has helped restore to the throne, and marrying Maid
Marian—neither of whom appear in any of the early versions of the legend.

Jesse James's murder, which, unlike the murder of Robin Hood, is a
matter of historical record,[10] is not preceded by any such rehabilitation. Jesse
dies an outlaw. The inability of the legend to counter this situation is certainly due in part to the better historical records surrounding Jesse James,
but it is also partly due to the American situation of the legend.

First, during Robin Hood's time, the government changed hands fairly
frequently among members of the royal family and among royal families
themselves; thus, an outlaw under one king might become a patriot with the
next, as the situation of Robin changes when Richard returns to take his
kingdom back from John. Like Richard, Robin, too, had been a Crusader
knight, and the status of both men, Richard and Robin, as Crusaders, creates a background which helps legitimize Robin's repatriation. Jesse, however, was not only outlawed by the established government (local, state, and
federal), which was not subject to change as England's government had been
in Robin's time, but Jesse was also a representative of a coalition, the
Confederacy, which had been defeated in its attempt to secede from the
United States. In March of 1874, a resolution was introduced in the Missouri
House to grant the James brothers and the Younger brothers amnesty "for
all acts charged or committed by them during the Civil War and to offer
them full protection and fair trials on charges of crime since the war" (Settle
1966, 81); the measure failed. There was no way that Jesse could, as Robin
did, become an official patriot—even in legend.

Second, the essentially Puritan attitudes which have structured so
much of the United States's legal and social policies mitigate against any
famous outlaw receiving amnesty and being pardoned, as Robin Hood was,
for his transgressions. Other American outlaws considered Robin Hoods in
their day—Billy the Kid and Pretty Boy Floyd, "The Robin Hood of the
Cookson Hills"—met violent ends, often gunned down at the hands of law-
men, without the opportunity for a trial, much less a pardon, even though

their legendary reputations, like Jesse's, as defenders of the poor are every bit as well established as the reputation of the original Robin Hood.[11] It is possible that Robin Hood—historically more remote, a product of English culture, and more immediately in the tradition of King Arthur, among others—was seen as deserving of pardon whereas the American outlaws, with more historical records available and viewed by an essentially Puritan society, could not be pardoned. Jesse, like the other American Robin Hoods, died an outlaw (Steckmesser 1966, 351).

Third, the America—society, government, economy, culture—of the late nineteenth century in which Jesse James carried out his outlawry was much more established and more highly organized, and its elements more interdependent than the English counterpart of the thirteenth and subsequent several centuries during which the Robin Hood legends took shape. In post-Civil War America, an individual acting outside the law to right establishment-imposed wrongs—as the legends have Jesse James doing in the manner of Robin Hood—was more obviously a threat to the system than was the outlaw of thirteenth-century England. Even the original Robin Hood, had he been practicing his outlawry in nineteenth-century America, would have won no pardons.

Finally, Jesse's unredeemed outlaw status is not only appropriate to the particular American culture in which it occurred, the nature of his "traitorous murder" may well be a part of the continued popularity of the legend. Settle notes that, in addition to traditional James apologists, such as John Edwards, many other newsmen as well as politicians expressed their disapproval of "the manner of the killing and the suspected bargain between the assassin and Governor Crittenden" (1966, 121). The assassination strengthened the James legend by creating, on the one hand, sympathy for Jesse and his family and by intimating, on the other, that the authorities had to hire an assassin because they could not accomplish the job through the properly designated agencies (121–22). "The manner of his death gave every admirer of the James band and every critic of the Governor an opportunity to praise their hero and condemn Crittenden. Soon, the cruel and unreasoning slaughter of innocent citizens and the pillaging of property were forgotten in a general admiration for the dashing highwayman" (Settle 1966, 123). It is also interesting to note in this context that Frank James—who eventually gave himself up to the authorities, stood trial, served a prison sentence, and lived peacefully until his death in 1915—does not have Jesse's reputation. It may be that Jesse's death as an outlaw was not only in keeping with America's basically Puritan attitudes but was also a key ingredient in his continuing popularity.

English legendry resolved the tension between hero and outlaw; American legendry could not. Jesse James and the other American outlaws like him will continue to be criminals in the eyes of the law, redeemed only in the larger arena of public imagination and popular culture.

Notes

1. William A. Settle Jr.'s *Jesse James Was His Name* (1966) carefully examines both the historical records concerning Jesse James and the development of the Jesse James legend in ballads, the popular press, and film and television.

2. Both William A. Settle Jr. in *Jesse James Was His Name* (1966), and James Clarke Holt in *Robin Hood*, comment that in these legends, as Holt says, "the criminal is made heroic" (1982, 11).

3. I heard "The Ballad of Jesse James" sung by Betty Waldren at the Roanoke Mountain Campground, Roanoke, VA, on 13 July 1997. The concert was one in the Mountain Music series sponsored by the Blue Ridge Parkway as a part of its mandate to preserve local Appalachian traditions. I am indebted to Professors Robert E. May and Jill P. May of Purdue University for making me aware of this series.

4. Settle discusses comparisons of Jesse James to such heroes of medieval romance as King Arthur and his Knights (1966, 45–47), and Holt compares the form and, in some cases, specific incidents of the Robin Hood stories to the tales of King Arthur (1982, 56, 115, and 125).

5. An explicit reference to the social skills of Arthur's knights occurs in the fourteenth-century poem, *Sir Gawain and the Green Knight*. Gawain, arriving at Bercilak's castle, is greeted enthusiastically by the local knights who are excited that they will be receiving lessons in manners (as opposed to warcraft) from the master of courtesy, Gawain himself: "Now pleasantly shall we see practised skill in knightly conduct and the perfect expressions of noble conversation, what profit is in speech unasked may we learn since we have welcomed here the fine father of breeding" (ll.916–919, my translation).

6. According to legend, Jesse could be chivalrous to his enemies as well. Once during the war, he and his men captured a young Union soldier who had sneaked into Missouri to see his mother. The Confederates were going to shoot him, when Jesse said: "He's come back to see his old mother. Any man ought to be willing to go through hell to see his mother, and that's what this boy has done. Let him live. He deserves it" (Croy 1949, 50).

7. Another war band formed to defend a geopolitical territory, the Jolmsburg Vikings, swore similar oaths and gave up the right to revenge as part of membership in this new kind of group. See *The Saga of the Jómsvikings*, translated by Lee M. Hollander (1990).

8. What emerged eventually as the social contract theory requires the individual to relinquish rights to officially empowered agencies of government, so that individuals were now supposed to seek justice in court rather than attempting personal vengeance and might be punished as criminals should they carry out such individual actions.

9. Although knowledge of poetry was certainly not a prerequisite for membership in the James Gang, it is interesting to note in this regard that Frank James was known to quote from Shakespeare's plays.

10. Settle discusses the substantial number of stories about sightings of Jesse James offered to suggest that he was not killed by Robert Ford but that the whole episode was a plot to allow Jesse to get away and live peaceably for the remainder of his life (1966, 117–19). Settle also discusses the claims of various men that they were Jesse James (169–71; Croy 1949, 247–53).

11. For additional discussions of the Robin Hooding of American outlaws, see especially: J. Frank Dobie, 1955, Helena H. Smith, 1970, and Kent L. Steckmesser, 1966 and 1965.

John Campbell's Adventure, and the Ecology of Story

Jarold Ramsey

For most of my adult life, I have been haunted by a story. Not so much a story, really, as the possibilities of one, lurking (or so I think) in a tangle of episodes, anecdotes, allusions, and conjectures that I've been carrying around in my head for years, until the urge to find a narrative order in the stuff, or impose one on it, has overcome my skepticism.

Lest I come off here at the outset sounding like a latter-day Ancient Mariner, or Conradian Marlow figure, forever doomed to seek the meaning of an experience by compulsively inflicting narrations of it on wedding guests, shipmates, and other unwilling listeners, let me explain that the story I am searching for is strictly secondhand to me. Its events happened only to some people I knew, or knew about, and long before I was born. So my interests are not immediately personal ones, nor are they (so far as I can tell) aimed at expiation or vindication of anything or anyone. In trying to work out these interests, I will in effect be endeavoring to create a kind of meta-narrative, a story around a story, in which the outer narrative will, maybe, stabilize and consolidate and clarify the inner one.

Before proceeding further, I should offer what will be the first of several provisional formulations of the original tale. It belonged, during his life, to a man named John Campbell, of Madras, Oregon. He told episodes from it and frequently made allusions to it to me and others over many years, so that it came to occupy a certain collective imaginative space amongst his familiars; but he never wrote it down, nor is there any record of his ever having told the whole story as a complete unit, so that it is not only totally oral (and on a very limited basis of oral tradition at that), but unformulated, unrealized, embryonic. If there is a compost heap of oral traditions, this one would surely be a candidate for composting! But instead, let's try to reclaim and reconstitute it. Stripped to its barest bones, the story would go like this:

Once, around 1906, three men spent several weeks in late summer wandering on horseback along the Cascade Mountains in Oregon between Mt. Jefferson and the South Sister. They were: a young unmarried rancher's son named John Campbell; a widower in his late thirties named Frank Stangland; and an older Wasco Indian named Jim Polk. Their intended destination was an alpine creek southwest of the South Sister where, according to Jim Polk, some of his people had once found gold nuggets; but just before the three reached the place, Jim Polk "spooked," having remembered another, sinister story about the location, and consequently refused to lead his friends to it. So they turned around and returned to the Warm Springs Indian Agency.

So much, then, for a provisional narrative peg from which to hang our enterprise. No sex, no violence, no heroic achievements or tragedies—in its apparently anticlimactic form, in fact, a kind of Shaggy Dog story. How to categorize what we are proposing to do with such material, according to academic domains and intellectual motives? In order to "identify" and conserve a story that never seems to have realized its full expressive form, in performance or otherwise, which specialists should we consult? The folklorists? The narratologists? Ethnohistorians? Literary theorists of many stripes? I confess I don't know—maybe all of the above, wherever help seems to be forthcoming—and perhaps such uncertainty as between intellectual domains is one good subversive reason to pursue the project in the first place!

Maybe the most sensible thing to do with such perplexing material would be to try to reinvent it as a short story, but instead I want to proceed on the assumption that the story can be reconstituted without recourse to tabulation or fictional inventions. What I want, no doubt impossibly, is the whole adventure as John Campbell might have told it, nothing left out, its scanty array of details identified and related as narrative facts, and contextualized as fully as possible through the exercise of whatever kind of research seems promising.

The term that the anthropologist Claude Lévi-Strauss uses to describe a characteristic mythic activity of Tricksters, *bricolage*, might aptly be applied to this project. *Bricolage* means a sort of "cobbling together" of a significant order out of "available materials," as performed by a *bricoleur* or handyman. So in Native American myth, Coyote or Raven sort of improvises the forms of reality, for better and for worse, as he wanders through a raw and unfinished, "unstoried" mythic world (Lévi-Strauss 1967, 250). I have I hope no tricksterish motives, but the image of a sort of handyman cobbling something together out of what's at hand is as good as any to describe what I want to do with the story of John Campbell, Frank Stangland, and Jim Polk.

How different, how much simpler the task would be, of course, if only they were alive to narrate the adventure, patiently answer our questions about it, and no doubt argue between themselves about what really happened in the mountains. But the fact that they can't do this, and that their story has virtually disappeared from all speech and memory, poses, I think, a special kind of obligation. Coming along behind them, inheriting pieces and shadows of what might be their story, we must do the best we can with what we've got; *and we must try*. I use the first person plural here, not as a rhetorical flourish, but to suggest that we are all potentially custodians and conservators of unwritten materials—stories, anecdotes, sayings, songs, from family and local tradition and elsewhere—material of such a nature that if we don't try to conserve it, knowing what we know, who will?

To undertake such work is crucial if we are going to maintain for ourselves and our inheritors an idea of a popular culture in the Far West or anywhere that is more localized and more nourishing to the imagination than, say, *Twin Peaks* or *The Guinness Book of World Records*. To the stern Biblical question, "Who shall inherit the earth?" lovers of folklore and local history must add, and act upon, a related question, "And what stories will they inherit about *this* corner of the earth?"

There is, I believe, an ecology of memory, imagination, and story, just as there is an ecology of land, water, and air. Indeed, as Gary Snyder has been saying for years, the two kinds of knowing and remembering are very closely related, and the moral imperatives of one are implied in those of the other. In Snyder's view, true conservation must involve the inner realms of the spirit and the imagination, as well as the outer realms of the biosphere. Cultivating and conserving the apparently inexhaustible but often wasted resources of the human spirit may well help us to conserve the all-too-clearly limited and exhaustible resources of the world around, under, and above us (Snyder 1974, 87–88; 1990).

In particular, as we work to conserve and understand the oral-traditional stories of Native Americans, we perceive that a crucial function of such stories has always been to help the people who knew and cherished them to maintain a proper imaginative relationship with the rest of the natural order. Native attitudes towards what we call "the environment" were clearly shaped from childhood on by *stories*—Coyote stories dramatizing the disastrous consequences of human greed and wastefulness of natural resources; hero stories showing the people the life-or-death importance of living in harmony with nature, participating with knowledge and reverence in its processes, rather than abusing or exploiting them.[1]

Given our ecological predicaments now, and worse ones impending, such stories have much to tell us about our human obligations to the land we have appropriated from the Indians. In particular, the ecological emphasis in Native myths suggests that we need to find ways to reimagine our proper place in the natural order; scientific understandings are indispensable to us, obviously, but it is clear that they are not enough to bring us and our culture back, into alignment, mind and spirit, with the American environment and its ecosystems. Hence the ecological importance of the work now underway to conserve traditional Native American literature; such work is itself a kind of mental ecology, and although we must find our own "postmodern" ways to engage the imagination in the cause of the environment, Native stories point out the need to do so, and the way.

But I want to make my case for an ecology of memory, imagination, and story on an even wider basis. At first glance, John Campbell's tale about how he and his companions didn't find gold one summer doesn't appear to carry with it much environmental significance, but conserving it seems no less important for that—simply because it is a story, after all, something once told, at least in pieces, and still tellable. As the wise man Uchendu declares in Chinua Achebe's novel *Things Fall Apart,* "There is no story that is not true" (Achebe 1969, 130). Uchendu is reflecting in the 1870s on the impending disruption of Nigerian Ibo culture by British colonialists and missionaries, and what he means is that to survive in times of drastic change and upheaval, people need to pay attention to what they tell each other in story form: both traditional narratives and hearsay tales of new wonders and dangers. The Native American novelist Leslie Silko takes the same position at the beginning of her novel *Ceremony*: "You don't have anything if you don't have the stories. / They are all we have, you see, / all we have to fight off / illness and death" (Silko 1977, 2). Silko means, of course, the traditional Pueblo myths that her protagonist Tayo must recover and reimagine if he is to recover from his wartime traumas, but all through Silko's wonderful novel runs the idea, surely relevant to Indians and Anglos alike, that as life itself is an ongoing story, so our human penchant for storying the truth of experience is literally a way of life, a gift of survival not to be trifled with, but cherished and conserved:

> "There is no story that is not true."
> "You don't have anything if you don't have the stories."

Or, to mangle Shakespeare a little: "If all the world is sometimes like a stage, what happens in the world is always like a story."

Now I'm no raconteur, as my children used to remind me when I tried to play like one at bedtime, but I do know some pretty good yarns, from Anglo and Native American repertories, and so the question might be asked, "Why single out a story as incomplete, as full of gaps and shadows as this one, in order to educe the value of an ecology of story?" Well, first of all, precisely because such gaps and shadows are what the kind of literary conservancy I am proposing ought to be able to rectify—so as a story, this one provides a good test case. But the question of why this story? requires other answers, too.

One is simply that I may be the only living inheritor of this story who has any interest in preserving it. My friend John Campbell, who died in Madras in 1978, age ninety, was one of the indispensable pioneers of Central Oregon who in later years thought of himself as a dedicated oral historian rather than as a yarn-spinner; in fact he used to take sly delight in reducing the tall tales of pioneer life as told by some of his contemporaries to plain narratives of documentable fact. I don't know for sure what he would want me to do with the story, now that it is mine, except to keep it firmly anchored in factuality, but, as with most legacies material and spiritual, I am haunted by all the questions I was too incurious and unimaginative to ask him when I could have, and compelled now to try to answer them myself, as best I can.

From an interpretive standpoint, looking at the outline of the story as we have it, I see two possible configurations of meaning and value, one historical and one archetypal. The historical meaning lies in the fact that the narrated events take place in a time, very late in the history of the American West, when, in Central Oregon, Indians and "white-eyes" (as they sometimes call us) were still new to each other, still sorting each other out, still capable of interacting with a directness and unironic openness that would later become virtually impossible. In 1906 there were still people on the Warm Springs Reservation who could remember pre-reservation life, the old Wasco Chinookan and Warm Springs Sahaptin stories and the languages in which they were embedded, which continued to be elements of a still vital traditional Native culture, even though it had been "reservationized" for half a century.[2]

On the other side (literally on the east side of the Deschutes River), in 1906 the sparse white homesteading population of the region looked to their Indian neighbors for seasonal farm help, for horses, for advice on everything from the local climate and trail-finding to Native medicines, for entertainment (as at the grand Warm Springs Fourth of July celebrations), for friendship. One of John Campbell's lifelong *tillikums*, a Wasco elder named Charlie Jackson, told me some years ago about what happened when my grandfather and his family arrived from Missouri in 1900 to take up their homestead on the west rim of "Agency Plains." "Well, your granddad and his people, they came," Charlie told me, "and so my dad crossed the river and rode up there to check them out. He stayed for dinner, and when he came back he told us, 'They seem like decent folks, but they don't know anything, and they're going to need a lot of help from our side.'" Such anecdotes, and John Campbell's tale itself, serve as useful reminders that there have been local moments of relatively easy, coequal interaction between Indians and whites, within the long dismal history of their relations in the West.

The archetypal pattern in the story focuses on John Campbell himself. He was about eighteen that summer, old enough to declare his independence, at least for several weeks after harvest, from working on his father's ranch—old enough to undertake, with something of the savvy and confidence of a man, the perfect boyhood adventure of going into the mountains with an Indian guide in search of gold. Imagine the prospects! Shades of Jim Hawkins and Long John Silver, of Saxton Pope Jr. and Ishi, of C. E. S. Wood Jr. and Chief Joseph—such adventures of initiation and "coming out" appeal to us all with the force of archetype: we've been there ourselves, at least in our dreams. Every time John Campbell told me episodes from his mountain journey, fifty and sixty years later, he did so with a warmth and animation that suggested that he was tapping once again into what he counted to be the great formative adventure of his life.

But, being in his own mind a historian, not a storyteller, he never once told me the whole adventure in one telling, nor did he do so to anyone else that I know of, not even his two sons. And on that problematic note, let's turn again to the story and begin by retelling it, this time including all of its limited baggage of expressive details, as I have collected them piecemeal from John Campbell and his family and friends:

In the last weeks of August in 1906 three men rode west across the Warm Springs Indian Reservation and into the Cascade Mountains south of Mt. Jefferson. No doubt they were leading a packhorse or two laden with their gear and food. They were an oddly assorted trio. The youngest was John Campbell, the eighteen-year-old, red-haired, oldest son of a pioneer rancher, Ed Campbell, who had homesteaded in the 1880s directly across the Deschutes River from the reservation, and for years operated the only ferry on this stretch of the river. The second was a homesteader in his late thirties named Frank Stangland, whose wife had died suddenly on the farm just the year before, in 1903, leaving him with three small children, who were promptly sent back to Indiana to live with their maternal grandparents. The third rider was a very tall Wasco Indian about sixty, named Jim Polk, domestic and occupational status unknown.

The aim of their journey—what they told their families and friends and each other—was to hunt deer as they went and make jerky of the meat, and at the far end of the trip, immediately southwest of the mountain known as the South Sister, to find and mine gold in a glacial stream known as Quartz Creek, where, according to a Wasco story told by Jim Polk, some of his people once found gold nuggets.

Along the way, probably for two weeks or more and into the month of September, Jim Polk held forth as expedition leader, indoctrinating his Anglo companions in the old Wasco ways of mountain travel and hunting. At night, camped along timbered lakes, he told them about the "Stick Indians," mischievous mountain spirits dwelling in certain high gloomy places and capable of reading travelers' minds and luring them off the trail to their grief, unless placated by gifts of matches and bacon. At twilight, Jim Polk drew his friends' attention to what he identified as the soft, plaintive cries of the Stick Indians, and in the morning he pointed out, along the damp sand of the lakeshores, what he said were their small footprints.

Back on the trail and heading south each day, he showed them the traditional Indian system of trail markers—oddly broken and bent branches, twigs stuck in the ground, and so on—and interpreted them: "Three men and two women came this way—good berry patch above the next lake. . . ." And most of all, Jim Polk took pains to show his comrades the intricate network of old-time Indian trails running obscurely, mostly without blazes, all over both sides of the mountains—into hidden coves and lakes, around impenetrable blow-downs, along narrow ridges above rock-slides.

Occasionally they met other travelers, all Indians. None would speak English, but chattered in Wasco or Chinook jargon with Jim Polk, while glancing at Campbell and Stangland as they talked. Once, as the two white men prepared to illegally shoot an elk calf for a little fresh camp meat, Jim Polk suddenly stopped them, saying that he knew somehow that the government ranger at the little settlement of McKenzie Bridge thirty miles to the west would arrest them all if they proceeded. (Later, on their way home, when they detoured to McKenzie Bridge to buy provisions, the ranger praised them for resisting the temptation to kill that elk calf. "I'd have had to send you boys to the pen for that!" How he knew, neither he nor Jim Polk would say.)

At length, leading their horses more often than riding, they followed a steep track running west above timberline, and came out on the high barren saddle between the Middle and the South Sister. Before them, seven or eight miles off to the west-southwest, a series of whitewater streams ran out of the tails of the glaciers and into very deep, steep-sided timbered canyons. One of these, "Quartz Creek," held gold nuggets, or so the story promised.

But that night, a light September snowstorm blew up out of the southwest, and although the snow had mostly melted before breakfast, Jim Polk announced to his friends that he would take them no further. Where they had been going, he said, some Wasco hunters had been trapped in one of the deep canyons many years before by an early blizzard, and those who lived through that awful winter did so, it was said, by eating human flesh. "Bad medicine, *hyas mesachie*," he said. "This little snow was sent to us as a warning, to stay away and go home." So the three turned around, and after detouring to McKenzie Bridge for supplies, and talking to the ranger there, they headed back east over the mountains and into Central Oregon.

As they crossed the divide for the last time and started down into the timber, bound for home, Jim Polk turned in his saddle to look back at the rocks and snow they'd just come through, and murmured, "Good—the old ones didn't want us up there anyway!"

Now I have assembled this version out of all the events and details of the story that I can recollect from John Campbell's partial tellings of it, and in doing so I have tried—perversely, unlike a crafty storyteller!—to maintain a neutral tone. Perhaps we can now say, "The real story might have been something like this," but still, if we liken the idea of narrative form to a bag, it's obvious that this bag can hardly stand upright, it's so underfilled with expressive content. So now we must turn to extranarrative considerations, especially biography, local history, and anthropology, and attempt to eke out inferential connections between such extraneous detail and the story as we have it.

Who were these three men? Remarkably, one of them has been described at length in a recent book. In her memoir of Central Oregon homesteading life, *Some Bright Morning*, Bess Stangland Raber (1983) rather bitterly characterizes her father Frank as insatiably curious, impulsive, cheerfully neglectful of his family, utterly improvident as a homesteader.[3] Her harsh portrait is no doubt colored by the trauma of her mother's sudden illness and death in 1905, when Bess was a small girl, and by the subsequent "rescue" of her and her brothers by their mother's disapproving parents in Indiana, where they remained until adolescence, when they returned to Oregon. So Bess Stangland Raber's judgments of her father as he was around 1905 are probably suspect, but three or four images of him in her book do seem to amplify his role in our story. (1) She reports that he was very friendly with John Campbell's family, and that in fact she and her brothers were taken in by the Campbells, before they were sent back to their grandparents. (Given their friendship with Frank Stangland, one might conjecture that in the eyes of John Campbell's parents, Frank was welcome on the 1906 adventure as a kind of chaperone.) (2) Mrs. Raber characterizes her father as an avid naturalist, a great collector of "specimens" and a student of natural and Indian lore—which is precisely how I remember him in the 1940s, as a kindly old retired farmer, very studious, still living on his tumbledown homestead with his second wife. (3) Mrs. Raber recalls that he was fascinated by stories of "lost" gold deposits, like the legendary Lost Blue Bucket Mine of Eastern Oregon. (4) She indicates how her father was devastated by the death of his young wife, Mabel, in the spring of 1905, and remained distracted by grief and perhaps guilt for years afterward, alone on the farm while his children were growing up in the Midwest and being taught to disapprove of their father.

Now, does the saggy bag of our story stand up a little straighter? I think so. At least a conjectural picture of Frank Stangland and his motives in 1906 has emerged: of someone still burdened by the loss of both wife and children, lonesome, eager to leave his farm and light out for the mountains not only because he temperamentally preferred adventure to homesteading, but because the homestead was, only a year after his wife's death, a place of painful memories. And it's clear that of the three travelers, Frank Stangland would have been the one most captivated by the prospect of gold somewhere over the Cascade Range!

About Jim Polk, I have found very little solid information outside of his role in the story as the expedition's guide, trail boss, and spiritual leader. John Campbell always referred to him fondly and respectfully as *"old* Jim Polk." But according to Indian Service records, there were actually two Jim Polks, father and son, probably both alive in 1906. The elder was born in either 1845 or 1848 and is recorded as having enlisted as a military scout in the Paiute Wars of 1866 and again in the Modoc War of 1872. By both official account and hearsay, he was unusually tall—in fact, a giant by Wasco standards, 6' 4" or even taller. The fact that he is not listed in the 1915 Warm Springs census indicates that he had died before that year. His son James Polk Jr. is listed as having been born in 1869; he was living in the 1920s but not mentioned in a 1934 census and can be assumed to have been dead by then.[4] Which Jim Polk is our man?

All evidence in the story strongly points to the father. The son would have been only about thirty-seven at the time of John Campbell's adventure, no older in fact than Frank Stangland—hardly old enough to merit John's veneration of an "old" Jim Polk. Jim Sr. would, on the other hand, have been around sixty in 1906, "old" to an eighteen-year-old boy, but not necessarily decrepit, although it appears that he did die within a decade. His year of birth, whether 1845 or 1848, has a special historical significance. He would have been a small boy in 1855, the year his people the Wascos were forced by treaty to leave their Columbia River villages and join the Warm Springs Sahaptins and several bands of the Northern Paiutes (enemies of both the Wascos and the Warm Springers!) on the newly created Warm Springs Reservation. According to some Wasco traditions, their hunting and gathering parties had been visiting this region and on south along the Cascades since time immemorial (which seasonal occupation became the U.S. Government's rationale for "giving" them the land), but the elder Jim Polk's generation would have been the first to grow up on the reservation and know its rugged terrain intimately as homeland. And of course it was his generation of young men in the 1860s and 1870s who earned historical recognition and a certain heroic status locally by helping the U.S. Army to quell their old tribal enemies the Northern Paiutes and, later, the Modocs.

So, picture an elderly man, strikingly tall, with a rather romantic past, involving a boyhood in the earliest years of the reservation and military service against Indian "hostiles" in Eastern Oregon and Northern California. The appeal of such a figure for an eighteen-year-old farm boy is obvious; what about Jim Polk's interest in young Johnnie Campbell? It's known that Polk had several sons, his namesake and at least two others, all of them presumably products of agency schooling and other Anglo acculturative influences, all of them grown by 1906. Did Jim Polk Sr. take on young John as a kind of surrogate son or nephew, someone eager and apt, albeit a white-eyes, to whom he could pass on the traditional lore and experience that Wasco men were supposed to pass on to their sons and nephews? The last time I heard John refer to "old Jim Polk," just before his death in 1978, he seemed to affirm some such special relationship: "Jim would always open up with me, but never with my dad or other white folks his own age."

As for John Campbell, when I knew him fifty years and more after his adventure, he was one of nature's aristocrats, a robust, genial, and exceptionally keen-minded old man who was revered by Anglos and Indians alike. His white neighbors recognized him as one of the builders of Central Oregon: he'd had a constructive hand, it seemed, in every public advance in the Madras area, and he carried the region's unwritten history infallibly in his head—a personal history now mostly lost, I must add, except for notations like this one. Amongst the older Indians, his name was like magic—I doubt that any white man was more universally liked and trusted by the traditional people at Warm Springs. Their byword was: "If Johnnie Campbell says it's so, it's *hyas kloshe*, okay." They saw him as one of their own, and I'd like to think that his special identity with the Indians began to take shape in the summer of 1906 under the tutelage of Jim Polk Sr., in the tall timber and foothills of the Cascade Mountains.

Like nearly all American Indian groups, the traditional Wascos followed the custom of the spirit quest, wherein adolescents of both sexes were sent out alone into the mountains to fast and meditate, until they had a visionary encounter with the supernatural animal or natural force that would be their secret guardian and identity sponsor for the rest of their lives (Ramsey 1999, 85–91). Probably John Campbell, who was not a romantic, would blush at the suggestion, but I'll offer it anyway: that his journey with Frank Stangland and Jim Polk amounted to a kind of protracted crosscultural spirit quest and initiation rite, guided on the one hand, perhaps, by an at-loose-ends Anglo widower, and on the other hand by an Indian elder who knew where all the trails went.

Certainly a pattern was established: for the rest of his active life, when work and domestic demands permitted, John delighted in making late summer packtrips into the Central Oregon Cascades, at first over the fading Native trails and then later over the U.S. Forest Service trail systems (built by the Civilian Conservation Corps in the 1930s). On the first trip, back in 1906, the real gold for John Campbell must have been what he found, and was shown, along the way.

Now our attempt to contextualize his story must turn directly to geographical and anthropological considerations. John Campbell never pinpointed the location of "Quartz Creek" on a map, and its location is unknown to me; but a few years after his death I happened to notice on the standard U.S. Forest Service map of the Three Sisters Wilderness Area, southwest of the South Sister, near the glacial head of Separation Creek, and just about where he and his friends expected to find gold, an odd notation: Indian Holes. No one in the local Forest Service offices could tell me what the term meant or where it came from, so in July 1989 my brother Jim and I hiked in to see for ourselves. The country is very rough, and about as remote from roads as any place in Oregon, but it is spectacularly beautiful in late July, with very deep ravines running down from the western flanks of the South Sister, each with its own glacial torrent running through lush meadows waist high in grass and alpine wildflowers—Indian paintbrush, Cascade lilies, shooting stars, spirea, squaw grass—and springs pouring out of every hillside. All of one's glances to the east and north are challenged by the bulk of the South Sister, so much grey rock and glistening ice filling the eye.

Not knowing what "Indian Holes" specified, we aimlessly clambered around all afternoon, up ridges and down into meadows again, wondering if "holes" meant sinkholes or maybe volcanic blowouts or maybe even something the Indians had carved or dug, but we found nothing of the sort. Finally it dawned on us that these small alpine meadows, mostly circular and ringed by tall evergreens, looked from the ridges above very much like holes: holes in the landscape. And confirming the "Indian" part of their identity on the map, we found two telltale signs: an amazing concentration of deer and elk, so heavy that the stench of their fresh manure was overpowering, and, glinting in the sun alongside an elk turd on the freshly-turned earth of a gopher mound, a well-flaked obsidian hide scraper.

With this artifact in view (but sad to tell, no gold nuggets), the puzzle of Indian Holes and its connection with John Campbell's story began to unravel. Clearly, judging from what we found in 1989, the region would have been a paradise for hunting deer and elk. And, on the other hand, looking upslope from the meadows at the bottom of any of the "holes," it was easy to imagine how a sudden heavy snowstorm would make escape virtually impossible. The story about the trapped hunters that spooked Jim Polk now looked entirely plausible.[5]

As my brother and I consulted our map in preparation to return to the trailhead on Foley Ridge to the northwest, we noted that only a few miles northeast of Indian Holes are the Obsidian Cliffs, well known as an ancient Indian source of high-quality volcanic glass for making weapons and tools. And about midway between Obsidian Cliffs and Indian Holes, our map specified another intriguing feature: Racetrack Meadow. There wasn't time on this hike to check it out—as my brother remarked, not impatiently, no wild-goose chase into the mountains should find all its geese at once—but I resolved to come back sooner or later, to see if, as I suspected, Racetrack Meadow in fact marks the site of an old-time Indian racetrack and summer campground, of which several are known in the Oregon and Washington Cascades, invariably located in high alpine settings, rich in game, as here.

The most celebrated of these grounds is located at the southern edge of the so-called Indian Heaven country, south of Mt. Adams, in Washington State. Across a hidden basin, full of jewel-like meadows and streams, a well-marked track runs, surveyor straight, for about a quarter of a mile, the dirt on it so compacted by horse hooves that no vegetation grows on it to this day. At each end, the track loops off the flat and up onto the hillside for a few yards, presumably allowing the Indian jockeys to make a grand turn-around and then race back down the track the other way.

According to documented Indian traditions, the race-grounds at Indian Heaven were in use long before the whites came, serving as a gathering point late each summer for tribes from east and west of the mountains. To stand at one end of the racetrack and survey the scene even now is to know instinctively what such occupations must have been like—racket of dogs and children, lodges and campfires scattered over the basin, preparation of deer and elk meat and huckleberries for the long winter to come, rings of gamblers chanting as the bones passed from hand to hand, much intertribal flirtation and hanky-panky, and everywhere the celebration of good horseflesh—showing it off, trading it, and of course racing it for high stakes and family honor (Hansen 1977).

It must have been life at the brim by Native standards, carefree and joyously sociable. Such happy conjectures were much in my mind, then, in late July 1990, as I hiked in from Foley Ridge to inspect Racetrack Meadow. What I found there, at the intersection of several USFS trails, vividly confirmed the supposition of extensive and long-standing Indian summer occupation: concentrated scatterings of obsidian flakes and shards, along with a few unfinished arrowpoints and hide scrapers, and clearly marked off camping sites in sandy areas around the meadow. The meadow itself, about forty acres in size, is apparently an old meltwater lakebed, very flat and covered with gravel and sparse vegetation—perfect for running horses, whereas most alpine meadows (like those at Indian Holes) are broken up with streambeds, animal burrows, and dense, clumpy vegetation and thus unsatisfactory (in fact downright unsafe) for serious racing. I found no "racetrack" per se, equivalent to the indelible scar at the Indian Heaven site in Washington State, but it appears very likely that the USFS trail running north-south across the meadow (No. 3547B) simply follows the old track.

Overall, the impression of very old, very intensive occupation is strong here, and it is good to note that the Forest Service has lately begun to study its archaeological significance.[6] At Warm Springs, there is very little recollection of summer occupations in this area, suggesting that they must have stopped several generations ago, before the turn of the century—perhaps in part because the huckleberry patches had begun to recede (berries are hard to find now), and of course because, with the advent of firearms and other metal implements, the need for obsidian for weapons and tools ended abruptly, probably soon after the Civil War.[7]

In any event, what we seem to have found is an unexpected piece of Indian ethnohistory embedded in a white pioneer's story, and perhaps in turn illuminating it. One wonders who was more disappointed at not reaching Indian Holes and Quartz Creek—Frank Stangland, with his hopes of finding gold, or Jim Polk, with what must have been a powerful urge to return one more time, even in mixed company, to his people's old summer playground. Somehow I can't believe that young Johnnie Campbell was much disappointed by anything, going or coming.

At this point, further pursuit of the circumstances of what became his story, such as it is, would have to take a purely speculative, fictive slant. What did they eat, those three? Did they really take the time to prepare jerky? What did they talk about around the fire? Was Frank Stangland more and more the odd man out of the trio, with the old Indian and the Anglo boy increasingly paired off as mentor and protégé? Was Jim Polk's authority in calling off the final trek to the supposed gold site challenged by either of his companions? And when they finally got back to the Warm Springs Agency and separated, how did they say goodbye to each other? Given how, as Robert Frost says, "way leads on to way," did the three of them ever meet again, to reminisce about their adventure?

Such speculations are, of course, the irresistible imaginative consequence of all stories, from "The Three Little Pigs" to *War and Peace*, a kind of interpretive residue; and if unaccountable, they are not to be dismissed out of hand, for they do indicate something about the mysterious way a story takes dominion in our minds, one explicit detail evoking or seeming to preclude the possibility of others. "How many children had Lady Macbeth?" "Where did Lear's Fool go?" These used to be questions that New Critics taunted their philological elders with, as examples of fruitless and unwarranted extratextual conjecture, but in years of teaching Shakespeare I've never yet taught a class in which these and similar questions haven't been honestly raised, and now I think they should be heeded, at least on a narratological basis. Shakespeare doesn't tell us the answers about Lady Macbeth's mysterious infants and might even regret that he didn't take better care to preclude our being distracted (mostly in reading) by such queries, but the fact that we do indulge in such extratextual speculation is a healthy and, I would say, honorable confirmation that we are actually engaging a story, sorting it out as it occupies our minds.

Given the very scanty assortment of narrative detail in John Campbell's tale, however, even after contextualization, it would be easy to overwhelm it with speculation—anyway, that way lies the sort of fictive reinvention that I proposed to avoid at the outset. If we must speculate, better to do so about how, according to what storytelling strategies and conventions, the tale might begin in some "full-dress" performance, of the sort it has never received. For example, should we begin:

"It was a dark and stormy night, snowing in fact, and Jim Polk told his friends, 'Boys, we won't go no further. . . .'"

Or: "On August 18, 1906, at about three in the afternoon, a casual observer might have discerned three riders and two packhorses setting off up Shitike Creek in the shimmering heat, for the mountains. Their destination: gold."

Or: "Sing in me, Muse, and through me tell the story nearly forgotten, of those three heroic riders, who wandered. . . ."

Or: "Coyote was going there, and he saw this poor mutilated story limping down the trail, with some people following it, and he thought, 'Aha!'"

In any event, in conclusion I want to briefly turn back to what the tale gives us to know about its elements, my purpose now being directly interpretive—what do these elements add up to in their given order? We've already noted historical and archetypal patterns of meaning—the first having to do with Indian-white relationships at the turn of the century and the second bearing on John Campbell's coming into manhood. That personal focus—it is, after all, now and forever *his* story, not that of his companions—expresses itself in the tonality or "atmosphere" of the narrative. If it's possible to talk about tone without recourse to a fixed verbal text (and I think it is), I'd characterize that tone as spooky, uncanny, *unheimlich*. The terrain is by implication increasingly remote and unfamiliar to John Campbell and Frank Stangland, at least, and their guide through it is an elder not of their own race and culture, who adduces the presence of Stick Indians, mischievous nocturnal spirits affiliated by name and belief with the Wasco Indians, but "other" even to them. Remember that the Stick Indians are said to be telepathic.[8] Later, Jim Polk asserts, in the nick of time as it turns out, a weird telepathic connection with the ranger at McKenzie Bridge—a connection that is subsequently, inexplicably, confirmed by the ranger himself.

Further, the story evokes a special kind of uncanniness in the way it emphasizes alien forms of language. Presumably Jim Polk spoke a form of

English to his companions, but on the trail they meet Indian travelers, who converse with Polk only in Native languages, obviously commenting on the two whites, but unintelligibly. Even more unnerving, perhaps, is the observation that the Stick Indians understand human thoughts without speech, and treacherously try to communicate with people in the language of birds. And Jim Polk's disclosure of a Native language of trail signs opens up a whole new area of foreign, nonverbal discourse, potentially crucial to the safety and well-being of the expedition, but at first, at least, only Jim Polk knows how to read the signs.[9] This pattern and its unsettling effect continues right to the final scene, in which Polk, relieved to be out of the mountains and perhaps still a little spooked by the snowstorm near Indian Holes, appears to render in English a private communication he's had with the spirits of the region, to the effect that the travelers were unwelcome all along: "Good—the old ones didn't want us up there anyway!"

The pattern is striking in a narrative with so few expressive details, and its effect serves, I think, to draw attention to John Campbell's equivocal situation as a sort of initiate into the mysteries of adult life, or more precisely as a young white spirit-quester in an Indian context. The weird and uncanny qualities of his experience seem to correspond to what anthropologist Victor Turner calls the experience of liminality in initiation rituals and rites of passage around the world. Liminality means "at the threshold"; according to Turner, initiation rituals "put the initiand temporarily into close rapport with the primary or primordial generative powers of the cosmos, the acts of which transcend rather than transgress the norms of human secular society." Liminality is "pure potency, where anything can happen, where immoderacy is normal, even normative, and where the elements of culture and society are released from their customary configurations and recombine in bizarre and terrifying imagery" (Turner 1968, 8:577).

If Turner's language here is a little too sweeping and melodramatic for John Campbell's narrative, at least as we have it, the concept of liminality as a phase of initiatory experience does seem to apply, usefully. The particular weirdness of this initiation episode, of course, is colored by the fact that it is a transcultural experience, more Indian, in fact, than Anglo. Even though the ostensible goal of the trip is the thoroughly Anglo one of finding gold, both the goal and the way to it are defined in Indian terms, and—pushing the plot to its symbolic limits, perhaps—the failure of John Campbell to actually reach such a goal may indicate that it was not a real or worthy goal, anyway. The pattern here is a familiar one in tales of youthful adventures and quests in world folklore: the quester comes home with empty pockets but wonderfully, permanently enriched by his experiences along the way. John Campbell doesn't find gold nuggets, nor does he seem to attain an adult Indian identity or spirit guide, but he does acquire, maybe, a lifelong Native perspective, especially on how one belongs to one's homeland. A more fully developed narrative would, I conjecture, play off what John learns against what Frank Stangland is too old and set in Anglo experience (and perhaps too distracted by grief) to learn and against what Jim Polk knows as a Wasco elder, someone who foresees the imminent loss of such knowledge amongst those who live in his homeland, both Indians and Anglos.

Our story presents one other structural pattern, notice of which will bring our "metanarrative" enterprise full circle and to a close. Having labored to compose a kind of secondary story around John Campbell's primary tale, in order to bring out and consolidate its features, I want to point out something that you may have already recognized: that, as embryonic as it is, the primary plot contains and in fact crucially turns on two interior stories, both of them from Indian oral tradition. Campbell's tale begins, remember, with mention of the tale about the Wascos' discovery of gold in the mountains, which provides our travelers with their official purpose to travel; and it reaches its climax and point of reversal with Jim Polk's reference to the disaster of the snowbound hunters, which, used by Polk as a cautionary tale, frustrates the travelers' purpose and sends them home.

It seems strange, though ultimately appropriate, to find that a rudimentary story whose very integrity we have been trying to identify and conserve, contains within itself, egglike, two interior narratives! But this configuration, one of whose effects is always to make us self-conscious that we are in the domain of Story, is of course no more than typical of the magic and power of storytelling. Perhaps we have stories within stories within stories, one level interacting with another, because we need narrative emblems to show that reality is often concentric in meaning, targetlike: worlds within worlds within worlds, John Campbell's boyhood experience within the full completed circle of his long life, and that within the unfinished orbits of your life and mine, and so on. All of which maybe suggests why we have stories in the first place, as moving emblems of life conjoining the local and the universal, the "what is" and the "what might be," and why conserving stories of all sorts and degrees is a necessary kind of ecology and why I've wanted you to have John Campbell's story in the first place, so far as it was ever mine to give.

Notes

This essay began as the "Divisional Lecture" at Reed College in March 1990. I am grateful to Maera Shreiber and Christopher Zinn for inviting me to Reed, and for offering helpful comments on this project.

1. For the text of a Wasco-Wishram environmental-wisdom story in the tragic mode (recorded by Jeremiah Curtin in 1885 at Simnasho on the Warm Springs Reservation), see my *Coyote Was Going There: Indian Literature of the Oregon Country* (Ramsey 1977, 64–65). I have discussed the story in detail in "'The Hunter Who Had an Elk for a Guardian Spirit' and the Ecological Imagination," in *Reading the Fire: Essays in the Traditional Indian Literatures of the America* (Ramsey 1999, 81–95).

2. The culture and oral traditions of the people of Warm Springs (and their Wasco Chinookan and Warm Springs Sahaptin languages) have been recorded and studied for a hundred years now, beginning with Jeremiah Curtin in the 1880s; followed by Edward Curtis, Edward Sapir, and Leslie Spier in the first decades of this century; Walter Dyk in the 1930s; David and Kathrine French, beginning in the forties and fifties; and Dell and Virginia Hymes and others from the fifties to the present. Dell Hymes's monumental study of Chinookan oral literatures, *"In Vain I Tried to Tell You": Essays in Native American Ethnopoetics* (1981) owes much to his work at Warm Springs (and to his awareness of being an Oregonian) and is notable for insisting on the *continuities* of Native American life and culture—on what carries on of the Indian way now, beyond their "classical," pre-contact past. In the case of Warm Springs, those adaptive continuities are finding imaginative expression in the ceramic work of Lillian Pitt, the painting of James Florendo, and the poetry of Elizabeth Woody, among other Warm Springs artists. For an excellent overview of the Warm Springs community, see Cynthia Stowell, *Faces of a Reservation* (1987).

3. See chapters 30 and 34. Mrs. Raber offers a photo (p. 251) of her father with a pack-string in snow, with the caption: "Papa on a combination deer-hunting and gold-finding expedition into the Cascades in 1913"—further evidence of Frank's prospecting impulse. Was he headed back to Indian Holes country, seven years after his journey there with John Campbell and Jim Polk?

4. Personal correspondence with David and Kathrine French, Feb. 18, 1990, from their Warm Springs research files. The help of Professor and Mrs. French has been indispensable to this project.

5. One of John Campbell's surviving sisters, Mrs. Lou Murray of Medford, Oregon, recalls a somewhat different version of this episode. In her account, the three men actually camped at Indian Holes, and Jim Polk inexplicably disappeared from camp for a day and a night, returning, apparently, just before the snowstorm that sent him and his companions on their way home (personal correspondence, 17 April 1990). I have kept to the account given here because it follows John Campbell's own account, as I heard him give it more than once.

6. The McKenzie Ranger District archaeologist, Carole Linderman, has been conducting research in the general area in question east of the Three Sisters and has suggested to me that although there is ample evidence of Indian occupation of various sites for hunting and weapons-making, the terms Indian Holes and Racetrack Meadow are labels given by whites, presumably based on what they had seen or heard about early in this century (personal correspondence, 26 January 1990). It is worth noting here that all Indian sites in the Three Sisters Wilderness area and other federal lands are strictly protected by federal laws.

7. One of David and Kathrine French's Warm Springs acquaintances recalls going up into the Three Sisters country in the 1930s, to an area known at Warm Springs as The Sugar Bowl, to pick huckleberries, but she adds that the berry patches were scattered, and too far from camp (personal correspondence, 18 February 1990).

8. For Warm Springs "Stick Indians" anecdotes, see Ramsey, *Coyote Was Going There* (1977, 85 and 270).

9. This is one of only two references to Northwest Native trail signs known to me. The other appears in Henry L. Abbot's account of his travels through Central Oregon in 1854–55 in search of possible railway routes. In following Indian trails, he noted that "we had occasionally seen blazing, and sometimes twigs broken in the direction of a trail. The blazing generally consists of a single cut, laying bare the wood; but sometimes we found a rude image of a man marked in the bark. This always indicated that much fallen timber was to be expected" (1857, 99).

Raven and the Tide:
A Tlingit Narrative

Told by Emma Marks
Transcribed in Tlingit and translated into English by Nora Marks Dauenhauer
Edited and annotated by Nora Marks Dauenhauer and Richard Dauenhauer

T his story, which we are calling "Raven and the Tide," was recorded by
Nora Marks Dauenhauer from her mother, Emma Marks, in fall 1972 at
the family home in Juneau. Other family members were present, including
Nora's father, Willie Marks, who enters into critical discussion at two points.
Emma Marks, born in 1913, first heard this story growing up on the Italio
River, a remote area between Dry Bay and Yakutat. For a full biography of
Emma, see our *Haa Ḵusteeyí, Our Culture: Tlingit Life Stories* (1994,
378–406).

Like the other texts and translations at the heart of our forthcoming
volume of Tlingit Raven Stories (volume 4 of our series, *Classics of Tlingit
Oral Literature*, with the University of Washington Press), "Raven and the
Tide" has been in progress for many years. The Tlingit-language tape was
first transcribed in 1972–1973 as a project of the Alaska Native Language
Center of the University of Alaska-Fairbanks. It was proofread by colleagues
(including Jeff Leer) and prepared in camera-ready format, but remained
unpublished. Later, under sponsorship of Sealaska Heritage Foundation,
with funding in part from the State of Alaska and the National Endowment
for the Humanities, we were able to resume work on the project. In January
1984 the Tlingit text was entered into the computer, a new technology that
had emerged in the intervening years. In May 1984 the text was translated
into English for the first time, and the story was distributed in a limited,
photocopied, field-test edition of Raven stories used in a summer session at
the University of Alaska Southeast-Juneau.

Our original plan had been to publish our Raven volume first in the
series with the University of Washington Press, but the field-test experience

with students of all ages from Tlingit and Euro-American backgrounds per-
suaded us to hold off and put Raven later in the series. We found that Tlingit
humor (abundant in the Raven stories) was extremely hard for both Euro-
American students and younger to middle-aged students of Tlingit ancestry
to understand and appreciate. Accordingly, in volumes 1 and 2 of the series
(1987, 1990) we instead featured clan crest stories and ceremonial oratory.
These are genres whose tragedy and intricately contextualized ritual are
more obviously complicated at the surface level than the humor of Raven
stories, yet the texts in volumes 1 and 2 ultimately proved far more accessible to readers and easier for them to understand. This puzzling property of
humor suggests that even though tragedy and comedy are experienced universally, even when their literary expressions are equally culturally contextualized, the expression of comedy is somehow more culture specific and
more enigmatic to outsiders than tragedy. During the summer 1984 field test
with Raven we ourselves were laughing until the tears came, but many of
our students just sat, finding the stories more puzzling than amusing. The
more we tried to explain, the more our explanations spoiled the joke. Barre
Toelken has also noted the deep cultural matrix of humor. In a narrative
describing his own long struggle to understand, even incompletely, the intricacies of a Blackfoot joke, Toelken says, "What my Indian friends understood and relished in a few moments took me over four years to understand.
Yet it was only one joke" (1996, 246).

So yet again we set the Raven book aside and did not resume work on
it for another decade. The introduction to volume 4 of our *Classics* series will
address not only issues of humor but also some complex sociolinguistic
dimensions of Raven narratives and their performance. These involve con-
ceptions and misconceptions of what Raven is and is not. (He is a trickster,
transformer, and culture hero; he is not a deity.) With the increasing atmosphere of political correctness, some people are now afraid to laugh, fearing
it will show disrespect. This is surely true for cultural outsiders but is also
true for persons of Tlingit heritage. To the extent that people mistakenly
preconceive Raven as a deity in the Judeo-Christian sense, it becomes
increasingly difficult to appreciate the humor. Others are embarrassed by
Raven's lust, gluttony, and scatological tactics. Our field-test experience in
the mid-1980s encouraged us to look at new ways of translating funny stories into English. These are described below, in the notes following the text
of "Raven and the Tide."

Raven and the Tide	Geesh Daax̱ Woogoodi Yéil
told by	Seigeigée
Emma Marks	x̱'éidáx̱ sh kalneek
translated by Nora Marks Dauenhauer	transcribed by Nora Marks Dauenhauer

Raven went to her first,	A x̱ánt s'é uwagút,

to the Little Elder Who Sits on the Tide.
What was it she said to him?
She didn't think he could do it.
That's why he tried   5
to get a sea urchin.
When he went down along the bull kelp
he'd keep popping back up.
After how many tries
he finally made it.   10
Then he took it
to that place
beside her.
That Little Elder
was sleeping close to the fire.   15
Maybe it was Raven who got
the sea urchin
when he went down along the bull kelp.
After this
he got the sea urchin.   20
That's when he went back
to the Little Elder Who Sits on the Tide.

She's sleeping close to the fire.
The fire
is usually made   25
with a side-piece of wood.
But putting it
on the other side, though,
it's like a white man's
fireplace,   30
there's no shield from the heat.
But on one side
Tlingits put a side-piece of wood there.
She's sleeping beside the barrier log.
So he goes up to her   35
to the Woman Who Sits on the Tide.
Maybe she's the one who orders the low tide.
When he comes in by her he's already eaten
the sea urchin.
Quickly he lifts the barrier log   40
from her side.
He places it on his side of the fire.
"Brrrrr! Droplets of juice from the sea urchin shell
have chilled me!"
is what Raven is saying.   45
He's already needling her.
He already has the sea urchin shell in his hand.

Yax Kis' Shukawdzinugu Shaanák'w xánt.
Wáa sá kwshí ash yawsikaa?
A yeet ash yaawawóok.
Ách áwé akaawa.aakw   5
wé nées' ayawudlaagí.
Wé geesh daax yéi gútji
aax kéi usht'áax'ch.
Wáa yoo kwdayáa sáwé dé
ayaawadlaak.   10
Áwé tle aan woogoot
tle aadé
a xánde.
Wé Shaanák'w
wé gánt uwatáa.   15
Ch'a hóoch gíwé ayaawadlaak
wé nées'
yá geesh daax yéi woogútji.
Átx áwé
ayanadláak wé nées'.   20
Aagáa áwé áa kux wudigút
a xán wé Yax Kis' Shukawdzinugu
    Shaanák'w.
Gánt áwé uwatáa.
Tleikdé áwé yanax yéi yadutánch
awan.ádi   25
yá x'aan.
Yáanáx aa ku.as
tle yú
dleit káa aayí
áx' shóox adu.ak yé yáx   30
tlél a yinaa háadi koostí.
Tleiknáx ku.a áwé
awan.ádi áa yéi ndu.eich.
Áwé yáat áwé át tá.
Wé a xánde nagútch   35
wé Kis' Yax Shuyakawdzinugu.
Du x'akáax' gíwé yéi naléin.

A xáni neil góot áwé de aawaxáa

wé nées'.
Tle a shóotx   40
tle yáadáx áwé kei ayaawatán.
Tle a shóonáx ayaawataan.
"Aaaaa! Nées' gei héenák'u

xat sawli.át!"
yóo áwé yanakéich.   45
De a x'éix áwé aawanóok.
De du jeewú á wé nées'.

While he's doing this
she asks him,
"When was the low tide   50
you ate the raw sea urchin on?"
Maybe that's what it's called.
That's why,
that's why he grabs
that Little Elder.   55
He starts bouncing that sea urchin,
that sea urchin shell all along her butt.
Then he rubs it around on her butt.
"The tide might go down, Raven,"
she's yelling and she's yelling at him.   60
Even then
what did he call him—the one he sent out
   to check?
Maybe it's Xashak'ák'w.
"Run down there   65
to see,
to see if the tide,
is going out."
Then he's satisfied how low the tide is.
Finally, when everything   70
is dried up,
Raven is satisfied.

Then they start rendering grease.
Maybe this Xashak'ák'w
is his nephew.   75
What sort of being was his nephew?
Xashak'ák'w is what he named him.
Maybe he gave names to everything then
because later we'd be giving names to
   people.
He's rendering all sorts of sea life.   80
The tide went out on all kinds of things.
Whatever was at the bottom of the sea
was drained out dry.
Meanwhile Xashak'ák'w
is putting up   85
all kinds of food.
They're rendering
bentwood boxes full, bentwood boxes full.
Meanwhile, Raven
is stringing up the little cods together   90
   through gill and mouth.
He's rendering grease
into their stomachs.
When he's satisfied he's got enough,
he stops.
But his nephew   95
is still putting up food.

Ch'u yéi adaaneiyí áwé de
yéi ash yawsikaa,
"Goot'agáan sá woolaayi   50
léin áwé a kát iyatl'ékw?"
Yéi gíwé duwasáakw wé át.
Ách áwé
ách áwé tle aax aawasháat
wé káa shanák'w.   55
A tóoknáx akawsigóo
wé nées' nées' nóox'oo wé.
A tóogu yoo ayaxítlk.
"De yaa gwaagaalaa, Yéil,"
yóo áwé éex', ash éex'.   60
Ch'a aan áwé
wáa sáwé ayasáakw
wé yóo akuwakéigi káa?
Wé Xashak'ák'w gíwé.
"Aadé neesheex   65
a keekánde
wé kées' keekánde
yánde yaa naléini."
Tle du tóogaa yaa galáa.
Áwé tsá ldakát át xoodé   70
yaa kaklakóox áwé tsá
du tóogaa wootee.

Aatx áwé has aawadákw.
Du kéilk'íx gíwé wusitee
wé Xashak'ák'w.   75
Daa sáwé du kéilk'íx wusitee?
Xashak'ák'w yóo áwé ayasáakw.
Daa sá tle a yáx saa teeyín
yá kaa yáa saa gaxdusáaguch gíwé.
Ldakát át áwé adáakw.   80
Ldakát át xootx kux wudiláa.
Daa sáyá héen taak.ádi
tle a xoot kawlikúx.
Xashak'ák'w ku.a
áwé ldakát yánde   85
yaa akanalgéin.
Lákdíx', lákdíx'
adáakw.
Hú ku.a áwé s'áax' áwé
ax'akla.eesh Yéil.   90
Áwé aawadákw
a yoowú tóode.
Du tóogaa yakunagéi áwé tle
tle ajeewanák.
Wé du kéilk' ku.a áwé   95
kúnáx yánde yaa at kanalgéin.

Raven lies down		A shóox' áwé yan ustáaych	
under each dripping stomach.		wé at yoowú.	
He pokes a hole in the bottom.		A k'óol'náx áwé kunawálch.	
Grease dribbles into his mouth.	100	Du lakaadé áwé koolx'aasch.	100
Eventually		Wáa nanée sáwé	
his own supply		du jeet shoowaxíx	
runs out.		du aayí.	
His own is all gone.		Du aayí du jeet shuxéex áwé.	
He studies the situation.	105	A daat wudzidádi.	105
How's he going to get		Tsu wáa sá a jeetx	
his nephew's supply		ayakgwadlaagí	
away from him?		wé du kéilk' aayí.	
That's when		Aagáa áwé	
Raven comes up with his nightmare	110	ajun nuch.	110
idea.			
He comes up with a bad dream.		Ajun nuch.	
He's talking in his sleep.		Du taayí yoo x'atángi nuch.	
"Waa-waa-waa-waa!!!"		"Waa-waa-waa-waa!!!"	
So his nephew		Áwé kei ash sagitji nuch	
wakes him up.	115	wé du kéilk'.	115
Then Raven tells him		Áwé aan aklanik nuch	
about his dream.		du jóoni.	
"I dreamed		"Yéi áwé axajun nuch	
warriors were attacking us.		xáa áwé haa káa wdinaak.	
That's what I dreamed.	120	Yóo áwé axajóon.	120
Then I was saying to you		Áwé tle yéi iyanaxsakéich.	
'Xashak'ák'w!!!		'Xashak'á-á-á-á-ák'w!!!	
Run outside!!'		Yux neesheex!!!'	
My dreams never lie."		Tlél da.ék ax jóoni."	
That's what he says to him.	125	Yóo áwé yoo x'ayatánk.	125
Maybe this is just to trick his nephew.		A gíwé de ayís.	
Raven's getting ready for something.		Yan uwanéi.	
He's gathering everything		Ldkát át áwé	
for the invasion,		ayís ayawsiháa,	
whatever there is—little pieces of dirt	130	daa sáyá—s'eexx'í sáani	130
and cones,		tle hé s'óos'ani	
the ones from the forest,		yá at gutóodáx	
for warriors		wé xáa yís	
who'll attack them.		has du káa gaxdanaakt.	
So he can steal the grease	135	Dé wé eix agatáawoot áwé	135
he gives him full directions.		tle yan ashukaawajáa.	
"When I begin to talk,		"Tle yóo yaa yanxakéini,	
the way I was imitating them,"		yá aadé x'axatee yé."	
when he starts to talk like that,		yáx yaa yanakéini áwé tle,	
this nephew of his is to run outside.	140	yá du kéilk' yux nagasheexí.	140
He tells Xashak'ák'w		Yá Xashak'ák'w	
to run outside then.		yux nagasheexít ayawuskaayí áwé tle.	
"You're attacking!		"Tle kei gaxyidanáak.	
You're attacking us!"		Haa káa kei gaxyidanáak tle."	
As expected, he's running through his			
dream again.	145	A yáx áwé du jóoni aklaneek tsu.	145
As he's finishing his dream		Tle yánde yaa akanalnígi yáx áwé	

they hear him
telling this nephew of his
to run outside.
Then he slams the door behind him. 150
Meanwhile
he starts gulping from the box.
But his nephew
is fighting with the cones
outside. 155
Raven's gulping down the grease
his nephew had put up,
in the container, the bentwood box.
Is there no end to his drinking?
How much he's drinking! 160
What's that he's saying?
"Wheeeee!!
I'm hitting someone through to the bone
   with my arrow,"
is what he's saying.
What's he talking about? 165
There used to be tongs
to cook with,
for lifting stones.
Is that what he was saying
was somebody's bone cracking? 170
Inside the house
that's what he's slamming together.
That's what's making the noise.
He's crashing around inside.
Here he's already 175
gulped down the grease.
[Nora: He tried to make them believe he
   was shooting arrows?
Willie Marks: That he was breaking
   human bones.
Yes.]
While he's still doing this 180
his nephew comes rushing in and catches
   him on the last container.
"Are you at it again,
you shitty Raven?"
They never called him
anything else. 185
So at this he shoves Raven
into the bentwood box.
Then with him inside
he ties it up.
So Raven asks him, 190
"What are you using to tie me up with,
   nephew?
That's not very strong,"

wuduwa.áx,
wé du kéilk'yéi ayawuskaayí
yux nagashéex.
Tle x'ét aawaxích a ítx'. 150
Ch'a a t'éik áwé
yax yaa ayakanall'úx' wé daneit.
Wé du kéilk' kwá
wé át du een kulagaaw
wé gáanx'. 155
Wé ayawsihayi át
al'úx't áwé wé lákdi kaax eex
wé daneitx'.
Goodé sáyú adanáa noojín?
Tlax yéi adaná! 160
Wáa sáwé yanakéich?
"Aa-aa-aa-aa!!!
Kaa s'aagí tóoli nxaat'óok."

Yú gíwé yanakéich.
Wáa sáwé yanakéich? 165
Ganyal'át'ayi áwé kustée nuch
yá aan at gadus.eeyín,
wé té.
Aa s'aagí tóoli.
Daa sá kwshíwé yéi ayasáakw? 170
Neilx'
áwé x'éix ashaxeech.
Áwé du.áxx.
Ch'a wé neilnáx á áwé át jeewaxeex.
Héix' áwé de wé eix áwé de 175
yax ayakawlil'úx'.
[Keixwnéi: Kaat'óok yóo áwé.

Kéet Yaanaayí: Kaa s'aagí áwé yax yaa
   ayanall'íx'.
Aaá.]
ch'u yéi kunoogú áwé 180
hóoch'i aayí áwé ash káa néil wujixíx.

"Déi yéi gé keeshinóok gé,
Yeil tl'éetl'i?"
Tléil yéi guwanáak
yoo duséixin. 185
Tle a táade kát ash shakaawal'íx'
wé lákt.
Tle aan áwé ash een áwé
adaa wsi.áxw tle.
Aagáa áwé ax'eiwawóos' 190
"Daa sá ách xat keesa.aaxw, kélk'?

Luwat'éex'i át áwé."

Raven advises him.
"But there is something,
there is something, nephew,   195
that our uncles used to tie each other with,
he says.
Then he ties him
like he said,
like Raven told him to do.   200
[Nora: What was that?
What did he call it?
Willie Marks: Maybe old bark. Red cedar bark?
Ferns on a point, isn't that what he called it?
What did he call it?]   205
So just like that,
that's how he did it.
He throws Raven down
from the top of the mountain.
While the box is falling   210
the strings break around him.
Then he flies up out of it.
Caaaaaaw!!!
Maybe that's how it happened. I guess that's all
I know about it.   215

Áa ashukaawajáa,
"Áwu á,
áwu kélk'   195
haa káak hás ách wooch kas.aaxu át,"
yú.á.
Tle áwé ách ash kawsi.áxw
ash x'ayáx
chush x'ayáx.   200
[Keixwnéi: Daa sá wé?
Wáa sáwé aawasáa?
Kéet Yaanaayí: Lyaaní gíwé, laax daayí áwé?
X'aa lukaléet' yóo gíwé aa uwasáa?
Wáa sáwé aawasáa?]   205
De yéi áwé
a yáx áwé.
Shaa shakéetx áwé
daak ash wusigíx'.
Ch'a wéix yei nasxíxi áwé   210
du een a daax yawlik'úts.
Tle a yíkdáx kei wdikín.
Gáaaa!!!
Yéi gíwé. Hóoch'gíwé
aadé xwsikuwu yé.   215

Textual Notes

Title. English titles to this story are variously "Raven and the Tide," "Raven and the Tide Woman," and "Raven and the Tide Controller." The Tlingit title is *Geesh Daax Woogoodi Yéil*, literally "Raven Who Went Down Along the Bull Kelp," referring to the episode that usually triggers the sequence here.

Line 1. *Raven went to her first.* Like most Tlingit Raven stories, this one is highly contextualized—right from the start. Grammatical gender is not indicated in Tlingit, and Tlingit narrative style prefers pronouns over nouns. Literally, the first line is: "he/she/it went to him/her/it first" or "third-singular subject went to third-singular object first." The listener needs to know who's who. The second line confirms who is going to whom: someone is going to the Little Elder Who Sits on the Tide—literally, on the end of the surface of it, according to the series of grammatical prefixes in Tlingit. Although much other information is economically conveyed, still no genders are indicated. Only by context and tradition do we know that the subject is Raven and the object is the Tide-Woman or Tide-Lady. As with other stories in Tlingit oral tradition, you know it's a Raven story because you've heard it before. Because the storyteller knows you've heard it before, he or she can make certain cultural assumptions that are reflected in style. We may predict that a story told by a Tlingit narrator in English to an outside audience would have more explicit references and fewer implicit ones. James Ruppert provides illustration for this idea from Deg Hit'an Athabaskan performance, discussing the concept of the "implied listener" and the relationship of audience to performance and the specific outcome as "text," with examples of performance in Athabaskan and English (1995, 123–35; 227–39).

Barre Toelken discusses this dimension of folklore—a story culturally embedded in a range of connotations that are familiar to insiders but overlooked or bewildering to outsiders. He notes that beliefs and attitudes underlying coyote stories (trickster cousins to the Tlingit Raven stories) "are so strong that the story as a narrative stands only as a tangible marker of cultural details far more complex than any single story itself could possibly show" (1996, 208). In any oral-traditional text, there is more going on than meets the eye. Trickster stories (like tragedies such as Oedipus or Macbeth) are usually violations of social relationships and responsibilities, cultural expectations and ethical standards, but are couched in comedy which, as noted above, is highly contextualized culturally. Traditional stories remain popular and powerful because they operate on different levels of meaning at the same time. One level is more literal and textual, the other more cultural and contextual. Toelken emphasizes that in the folkloric process, structure is but one mechanism for transmitting connotative meaning; the audience supplies the rest. He reminds us that listeners within the tradition are familiar with multiple layers of meaning, and this makes it possible for them to understand and appreciate the stories by supplying contextual information not made explicit in the text. Toelken calls this a "double structure" and notes that it

> is a prominent feature of Northwest Indian myths and that our appreciation of that fact can help us to derive even fuller meaning from the grand myth achievements of the American Indian. . . . I think it is of the utmost importance to recognize that the story would seldom have had an unknowing, naive audience. Not only would the typical listener have heard the particular tale many times, . . . but the listener would have been familiar with the same formulas, attitudes, motifs, numbers, sequences, colors, characters, and other expressive narrative features from innumerable other tales.
>   . . . Thus, while the modern intellectual *reader* of a myth text might certainly register it as a linear story, the native *auditor* could hardly avoid applying the "second half" of the well-known story to the "first half" while the story was being told. . . . (1996, 252)

All of this offers profound implications not only for aesthetics and appreciation, but for theory and practice of editing and translating.

To give readers in translation an even break, we have introduced nouns and gender where they are implied or understood in Tlingit. This is a Raven story, but the explicit noun *Raven* does not appear until line 59. In fact, *Raven* appears only three times in the 215 lines of the story: lines 59 and 183 directly address Raven, and line 90 refers to Raven. This stylistic preference for pronouns over nouns is also characteristic of Koyukon Athabaskan and perhaps other Native American traditions. How do you know it's a Raven story? You just do. We should note that knowledge of this cultural context is very weak among younger generations of ethnic Tlingits. To make the translation more accessible and less alien and bewildering, we have inserted nouns sparingly. There is no intended confusion in the original, so we feel it is legitimate to help out readers in translation.

Line 3. *What was it she said to him?* Two things are noteworthy in this line. First, as noted above, Tlingit pronouns are not marked for gender. They are, however, marked for other indications not marked in English, such as inclusive or exclusive, aforementioned or new character, and the like. Tlingit listeners will know who is talking to whom. Second, line 3 has the first appearance of a feature characteristic of the oral style of Emma Marks and many other Tlingit storytellers. Throughout the story, readers will notice the adverb "maybe" or rhetorical phrases such as "what was" this or that. These translate Tlingit words such as *kwshí* and *gíwé*. Such stylistic distancing from the material is typical of much Native American storytelling and should not be taken as literal uncertainty or a sign of incompetence or lack of knowledge. It is more of a "ritual uncertainty." In Alaska, the Eskimo languages have a bound morpheme that expresses this concept, and Athabaskan languages use words similar to Tlingit, expressing "I guess" or "they say." Such locutions perform a delicate twofold function, simultaneously distancing the storyteller from and bonding him or her to the story and the tradition behind it. Such phrases make it clear that the storyteller is not presenting him or herself as a "know-it-all." He or she is saying, "This is not mine; I didn't just make it up." At the same time, such phrases also establish the storyteller as a receiver of material from a reliable source and as a transmitter of the canonical tradition. Such phrases are at the same time a combination of self-effacement of the individual and reaffirmation of the group tradition, a cultural value.

Barre Toelken explains this well in his introduction to a Navajo Coyote story.

> Phrases like "they say" or "it is said," which may seem redundant in English, are a way for the Navajo narrator to remind his audience constantly that the story and its details derive not from his own cleverness but from the Navajo culture, from the shared heritage of family, neighbors, and friends. Rather than giving the effect of a fresh entertainment by a gifted storyteller, this stylistic element functions as proverbs do for Euro-Americans, producing an aura of cultural authority: I'm not telling you this; the whole culture is

telling you. Moreover, [the storyteller] reduces the potential egotism of his position by making it clear that there are details he does not himself understand. (1994, 592–3)

We think that such phrases may also function to draw listeners and readers deeper into the story by inviting them to use their imagination in considering the events of the story more fully.

Line 4. *She didn't think he could do it.* We join the Raven cycle in progress, with Raven's motives already set in motion, although the storyteller remains vague on the specifics. Raven, always hungry and given to gluttony, is presumably lusting after the culinary goodies that abound on the beaches in Southeast Alaska when the tide goes out. But the woman who controls the tides is not about to let the tide out for him. Typical of other characters in the origin stories in the Raven cycle, she is hoarding a natural resource that Raven will eventually use trickery to obtain for himself—and, coincidentally, for the rest of the animals (and people). We gather that at some point she refused Raven's request and challenged him to get a sea urchin by himself, the hard way, by walking down to the bottom of the sea on kelp.

Lines 6 and 7. *sea urchin . . . bull kelp.* Sea urchin and bull kelp are both commonly found on beaches in Tlingit country, especially on the outer coast. Bull kelp *(Nereocystis luetkeana)*, also called ribbon kelp, is so named because the main stem of the plant, when washed up on the beach, resembles a bullwhip. Kelp are the largest species of seaweed. The long stem, called a stipe, is anchored at the bottom of the sea and with a hollow bulb near the top, from which bunches of blades or ribbons grow upward. This species of kelp grows more than a foot a day in the summer months, and the stem may reach over a hundred feet in length. The Latin name for the plant seems to be in honor of the Russian scientist Fedor (Friedrich) Litke (Luetke), whose reports from his 1826–1829 voyage around the world on the *Seniavin* laid the foundation for oceanographic studies in Russia (Alekseev 1996, 141–42). His assignment was to describe the coasts in detail, and subsequent expedition reports include prolific information on algae. He visited Sitka and commented in his writings on the character of Raven. He also described bull kelp in detail, noting that Postels and Rupricht, naturalists on the expedition, "called it Nereocystis Lutkeana" and that the Russian colonists called it "sea otter cabbage" because of its popularity as a resting spot for sea otters (Litke 1987, 152). Kelp beds are the habitat of sea urchins and sea otters. Bull kelp is the preferred food of the sea urchin, and sea urchins are the preferred food of sea otters.

Sea urchins *(Strongylocentrotus)* are echinodermata, with spines for protection and tube feet for locomotion. They may reach three to five inches across. Three varieties are found in Alaska: red *(franciscanus)*, green *(drobachiensis)*, and purple *(purpuratus)*. The red are the largest and inhabit the deepest pools, downward from the low-tide line. Sea urchin caviar is favored as a delicacy by humans as well as by Raven. The technical, standard reference is Ricketts et al., *Between Pacific Tides* (1994, 98, 238, 286, 446). For a popular habitat-focused study, see O'Clair et al., *The Nature of Southeast Alaska* (1997, 63, 86, 151). A popular booklet with the perspective of eating is Furlong and Pill, *Edible? Incredible!* (1973, 38–39, 54–55).

Line 16. *Maybe it was Raven who got / the sea urchin.* Raven kept bobbing back up. In some accounts, he tricks mink into diving for him. The main point is that he now has a sea urchin, eats it, and keeps the shell to carry out the events of the next episode. The sea urchin is an important image in the story.

Line 23. *She's sleeping close to the fire.* The most difficult problem we face in translating Tlingit texts is that Tlingit has grammatical aspects with no equivalent in English, and the time focus of English is not always equivalent or relevant in Tlingit. Information that is important in Tlingit cannot always be matched in English, and the English choices often enforce categories of thought not present in the Tlingit original. Another feature of English style affects humor. Present tense is often used in English for telling jokes and funny stories. "So he goes up to him and says," and so on. We have caught ourselves and our colleagues telling Raven stories in this way. The question arose: Why not translate Raven stories into the English present, precisely to convey the meta-message that this is a funny story: "He went up to him and said" is more formal or neutral. Likewise, *then* seems a more formal conjunction than *so*.

As an experiment here, we have translated lines 1–22 using English past forms. These lines serve as background or prelude to the central episode in the first part of the narrative. At line 23, Raven is ready for the main action, and we switch to English present, even where Tlingit may have a perfective or other form. In the present story, the Tlingit occasional ("he would say") is common. In English this is awkward, because it implies action over a period of time rather than ongoing action at one moment. We hope that our choice will convey the humor, action, immediacy, and audience involvement that this device creates in colloquial narratives in English. We are still analyzing the range of tense and aspect used in Raven stories when told in Tlingit and English, and we hope to work out a consistent match eventually.

Lines 24–42. Fire images. The imagery in this section of the story relies on Tlingit styles of building a fire. The fire is built up against a log, which is called side-log (*awan.ádi*) in Tlingit. If you want warmth, you can sleep on the side without the log. If you want a heat barrier, you can sleep with the log between you and the fire. Sometimes two logs are employed, a larger and a smaller, with the fire in between. Contrast is implied to the Anglo, "Boy-Scout approved" method of fire building using a tipi-type arrangement of sticks and without a backup log and explicit to a conventional fireplace with the barrier at the back. The grammar of lines 40–42 is ambiguous, but we understand that she is comfortable beyond the heat shield and Raven removes it to increase the heat and force her to move.

Line 36. In Tlingit, the elements of the personal name are reversed here.

Line 46. *He's already needling her.* Raven is trying psychological warfare and minor annoyances to make her angry enough to move, thereby releasing the tide. He starts taunting her and making her uncomfortable. Here he is verbally "rubbing it in."

Lines 56–58. Bouncing and rubbing the sea urchin. Here he is literally rubbing it in. Sea urchins have a spiny shell. First Raven pricks and stabs her, then rubs the spines in. These lines raise a technical problem in translating. English syntax forces the verb into the same line with the repetition of "sea urchin," creating an extra-long line, in contrast to the rhythm of the original. We decided to split the Tlingit repetition over two lines in English.

Line 59. *"The tide might go down, Raven."* This is a danger warning—stop it or else. Tide Woman's language suggests that she doesn't know what Raven is up to, that Raven wants the tide to run out. But this is precisely what Raven has in mind. His plan is to cause her such psychological and physical discomfort that she can no longer bear to sit on the tide. If her bottom is sore, she won't be able to sit on the tide, and if she moves or stands up the tide will go out, exactly what Raven wants and what she doesn't want.

Line 63. *the one he sent out.* In all published versions of the story, Raven sends someone down to the tideline to report on how far out the tide has gone. In Swanton's Sitka version from 1904, told by Deikeenaak'w, he sends Mink to report (Swanton [1909] 1970, 9–10). In Swanton's Wrangell version, told by Katishan, an Eagle checks the tide (120–21). However, variation is to be expected and savored, rather than suspected. Barre Toelken emphasizes that variation is not synonymous with error but is the very life of folklore (1996, 43-44).

Line 72. *Raven is satisfied.* He's satisfied with the low tide. At this point we have inserted a space in the text to separate the next episode into which the narrative flows. In some other versions of the cycle, the two episodes are more widely separated and the second is sometimes called "Raven Tricks his Partner." The two versions collected by Swanton in 1904 differ in their placement of the episodes in relation to each other and to the overall sequence of events in the cycle. Boas suggested that there is no fixed order of episodes in the Raven cycle ([1916] 1970, 571). Sequences of stories tend to cluster together as subgroups or sub-sequences. Along with the classic study by Boas, Goodchild's *Raven Tales: Traditional Stories of Native Peoples* (1991) offers a comprehensive survey of Raven stories. We will have more to say about the Raven canon and the order of episodes in our forthcoming volume. As to content, two kinds of stories—origin stories and trickster stories—overlap in the Tlingit Raven cycle. In the origin stories, Raven's trickery coincidentally benefits others. He doesn't really create much (if anything) new, but he transforms the world from what it was to the form in which we know it today—here, by giving us the changes of the tide. In the trickster episodes, Raven's gluttony benefits no one but himself (as when he steals the grease).

The central cultural point of the story is that when the tide goes out, the intertidal zone is rich in food. There is a Tlingit saying, "When the tide goes out, the table is set." People harvest seafood exposed on rocks or trapped in shallow tide pools. In some versions of this story, the entire ocean is virtually drained and all kinds of fish and whales are explicitly mentioned as being stranded. One popular folk etymology of the ethnonym *Tlingit* is *Lein-git*, Tide People. There are two high and two low tides each day, measured in feet and varying rhythmically in extremes. "Minus-tides" are especially valued because the tide ebbs below the average low tide line, exposing beach not normally accessible.

Line 73. *Then*. The Tlingit is *aatx̱*, meaning "from this time," "from this place," or "from there." We translate it as "then."

Line 73. *rendering grease*. They are turning animal fat into oil, popularly called grease. Today, the most popular kinds are hooligan oil (from the eulachon, a smelt-like fish) and seal oil. The traditional trade route to the interior along which the coastal people traded for inland products was called the grease trail. The most common modern method is frying the fat and straining off the oil.

Line 75. *his nephew*. In Swanton's Wrangell version, Raven is the nephew of X̱ashak'ák'w (Swanton, 120–21).

Line 76. *What sort of being was his nephew?* In the Raven cycle, Raven has different relatives of various species. For example, he steals fresh water from his brother-in-law, Petrel. Regardless of species, Raven is always manipulating the kinship system and always deceiving and betraying those whom he should nurture, protect, and support. Tlingit social structure is matrilineal. A person marries into the opposite moiety, and children follow the mother's line. Children are therefore traditionally not of the same clan and moiety as their father. Accordingly, men receive training and inherit from their mother's brother. In this episode, Raven is violating the traditional channel of tutoring, training, and cultural transmission, which is from maternal uncle to nephew.

Lines 78–79. Naming. We take this as alluding to a covenant on naming.

Lines 85–88. Putting up food. Fat is rendered into oil which is stored in boxes. Bentwood boxes are a prominent feature of northwest coast material culture. Wood is scored and steamed so that three corners can be made from one long piece, and the two ends joined to form a square. In one of the best-known episodes of the Raven cycle, the Rich Man at the Head of the

Nass River is hoarding the sun, moon, stars, and daylight in bentwood boxes in his house.

Line 90. Stringing cod. The sequence of verb prefixes indicates stringing small, roundish objects through the mouth. The line passes through the gills and mouth and on to the next fish. Smaller fish such as hooligan are strung in this manner and hung in the smokehouse.

Lines 91–92. *grease / into their stomachs*. In traditional technology before the introduction of bottles, oil was stored in fish stomachs this way.

Line 105. *studies*. In Tlingit, *wudzidádi*, "he studied." The verb is interesting, because it is a loan word from English. Once borrowed, it was divided according to the rules of Tlingit morphology. *Study* is perceived in Tlingit as s-tudy; the verb stem is *-dádi*, from "-tudy," and the *s* is treated as the Tlingit s-classifier. Classifiers are characteristic of Tlingit, Eyak, and the Athabaskan languages (including Navajo). Tlingit has four basic classifiers, each of which has four predictable grammatical forms, depending on what is being said. The *d* form of the s-classifier is *dzi*. In *wu-dzi-dádi*, *wu-* indicates the perfective, *dzi* is the appropriate form of the classifier, and *-dádi* is the verb stem.

Lines 110–25. The entire dream sequence is Raven's elaborate plot to trick his nephew by creating a plausible scenario for getting him out of the house. His boldfaced lie in line 124, "My dreams never lie," is amusing in light of his true personality. The Tlingit word for "liar" is *k̲'a-li-yéil*, the stem of which is "raven" (*yéil*); literally, "to raven somebody."

Line 127. *getting ready*. Raven is up to something. He's setting his nephew up.

Lines 130–34. Dirt, cones. Raven is arranging the cones and hunks of dirt as if they were warriors attacking. He would be using cones of Sitka spruce and hemlock. Scale and perspective are interesting. In Raven stories, our image is always shifting between that of bird and human. If the nephew is a small bird or animal, the cones would appear as a formidable enemy in terms of size.

Lines 137–45. Through use of dialog and shifting of grammatical subject pronouns, the storyteller is able to begin with Raven's instructions and "fade into" the actual fake attack.

Lines 143–44 are directed at the imaginary enemy.

Line 163. *bone . . . arrow*. The verb in Tlingit is to shoot with bow and arrow, to hit with an arrow. The image is puzzling. Even the storyteller herself asks rhetorically in line 165, "What's he talking about?" In lines 177–78 the fieldworker confirms her understanding of the image, and a listener, Willie Marks, husband of Emma and father of Nora, enters the discussion. Basically, Raven is trying to make it sound as though he's doing heroic battle with the enemy invaders inside the house by shouting and making noise. The Tlingit is literally "bone-hole." We have loosened the translation here.

Lines 166–68. *tongs . . . cooking . . . stones.* Prior to the arrival of metal pots on the Northwest coast, people boiled things in water-tight baskets made of grass, cedar bark, or spruce roots. Rocks were heated on a fire and dropped into the basket using tongs that could be several feet long. Raven is using the tongs for his sound effects, making it sound as though he's hitting or cracking bones with his arrows.

Lines 183–85. *shitty Raven.* The storyteller is a pious, church-going woman. She emphasizes that she's not making this up or saying it on her own, but these are the very same words originally used to insult Raven. Insulting people, animals, and natural features and forces is of course a major breach of protocol in Tlingit. So the storyteller is distancing herself in this regard as well. As for the characters, Raven is always violating the norms of the society, and the nephew does so here, too, through insult and retaliation.

Lines 195–96. *nephew.* As noted above, Raven is exploiting and violating the traditional channels of tutoring and transmission of knowledge and tradition from uncle to nephew. The passage is a parody of tradition. As always, Raven is a negative example. This scene is reminiscent of trickster stories around the world, for example, Br'er Rabbit and the briar patch.

Lines 201–4. Rope discussion. Willie Marks suggests that the rope might have been made of red cedar bark. Emma continues her narrative, suggesting fern or grass. In traditional technology, rope was made of cedar bark, grass or straw, fern, or sinew. The term Emma uses is *x'aa lukaléet'*, "ferns that grow on a point."

Lines 212–13. Raven flies away with his "caw." This ending is typical for an episode in the Raven cycle. Raven always survives the cliff-hanger and flies on or walks further down the beach to his next exploit. The episodes typically begin *in medias res* and are definitely "to be continued."

Lines 214–15. *Maybe that's how it happened. / I guess that's all I know about it.* This is a conventional ending in Tlingit and other Native American storytelling traditions. Such endings should not be taken literally as suggesting incompetence or a lack of knowledge. This usually is, in fact, all there is to the story; the ending is formulaic. Melville Jacobs, an early collector and scholar of Northwest coast oral literature to whom all of us owe an enduring debt, seems to have taken his storyteller, Mrs. Howard, literally. Puzzled, Jacobs notes that her stories are perfect in every other way (1959, 223). Dell Hymes, revisiting the Jacobs texts, has two versions of a story that ends "Now I remember only that far." He discusses at length what he calls "definite indefiniteness" (1981, 303–4, 333–34), especially as a stylistic convention for closing a narrative (1981, 279, 312, 315, 322ff, esp. 325–26). Ron and Suzanne Scollon note this as a closing formula in Chipewyan and Cree. It appears in English, even if the rest of the story is in Chipewyan or Cree, as a regular frame and formula for closing a narrative performance, not the narrative itself, which ends with the Chipewyan or Cree: "Just to there I tell it" (1979, 25–26; Ronald Scollon, personal communication, 3 July 1997). Such endings are also found in Haida stories from Alaska; Charles Natkong and Richard Dauenhauer are at work on a volume of these stories.

Note

We are pleased and honored to contribute to this volume for Barre Toelken. We are just two of the many folklorists who have been influenced by this person and his work, and we are happy for the opportunity to express our gratitude. As friend, colleague, mentor, and advocate, but probably most of all as teacher and inspiration at long distance for over thirty years, Barre has influenced the shape and direction of our work. We especially note his *Dynamics of Folklore* (1979, 2nd ed. 1996) and the ongoing lessons of the Yellowman essays (1969, 1976, 1982b, 1987, 1994). Without Barre's work, ours wouldn't be what it is. In lieu of an essay or article, our contribution here is a selection from our work in progress, a set of Tlingit text, English translation, and annotations for a book of Tlingit Raven stories forthcoming as volume 4 of our University of Washington Press series, *Classics of Tlingit Oral Literature*.

Groups

"Two Moonlight Rides and a Picnic Lunch": Memories of Childhood in a Logging Community

Twilo Scofield

Imagine growing up wild and untamed in a wild and untamed world on the banks of a river in a rural settlement of the great uncut. Picture yourself sitting a moment and smelling the acrid sweetness of the woods, the distinctive odors marking the seasons—dank, damp moss, the spring skunk cabbage, the wildflowers springing up loyal and faithful season after season, rain dripping from fir needles. Stop and listen. You can almost hear the sound of silence broken only by drops of water falling on salal leaves, taking their little bows in turn, gathering courage and girth enough to jump off the end of the leaf, the leaves bouncing back up shaking themselves off and with up-turned face eagerly awaiting the next blessing of rain. Woodland birds titter and gossip in the boughs of fir trees or gather to chat in the vine maples which dominate the underbrush.

Two main gravel roads mark the main streets of town, which wind around the combination mercantile store and post office, the church, and a cluster of houses. Highway 20 skirts the town, where two taverns and a service station are situated, then heads on up the South Santiam Pass to the Cascades. Farms dot the area around the town. Everybody knows everybody. Social life for many is Saturday night at the tavern or the Fir Grove Dance Hall. Sunday is a sermon in our little white church on the hill, where the pastor pulls on a rope to ring the bell calling his flock to worship; his flock—the faithful, those in need of repentance and those who have recovered enough from the hangovers of Saturday night to find comfort in the Lord and His miracles.

Life is simple in Foster, Oregon; work is hard. Forested hills supply the raw material for a living in this small community. The whole town is involved in the lumber industry, perhaps not by choice but by necessity. It is a typical small logging town in Oregon. Everyone is a logger, related to a logger, or in business serving the needs of loggers and their families. Logging is us. Such was the way of the world in the little town of Foster. It was a good place to grow up. During the summer, kids could earn some cash of their own by picking strawberries, raspberries, blackcaps, wild blackberries, and beans. We would get up at the crack of dawn and join our friends to catch the bus to the fields. The mornings had that cool dampness about them in the gray dawn, giving you the feeling you'd be cold all day. We were bundled up for the cold, but by nine o'clock we would have our jackets and sweatshirts tied around our waists because of the heat. At noon we got our lunch boxes from the bus and lunched in the shade provided by two huge maple trees in front of the farmhouse. The older kids would tell jokes and sing and flirt. The younger ones would listen and learn how things were done. There was no sex education in the schools, and your parents certainly weren't going to tell you the facts of life. Your birds-and-bees education was handed down by your berry-field peers. By one o'clock in the afternoon, we'd be home and on our way to the river to swim.

We had a freedom unknown to today's kids. We played games like Cops and Robbers, Kick the Can, and Beckon-My-Base. We learned to roller-skate on the only sidewalk in town—the one right in front of the school. We walked the railroad trestle and dared each other, like a rite of passage, to walk along the top of the guardrail—one slip on the wet wood would plunge you a hundred feet to the creek below. Kids used to hang around the mill and the lumber yard. A favorite thing to do was to ride the conveyor up the burning slash pile and drop off just short of the flames. The mill pond was another source of amusement. It was great fun to walk out onto the floating logs and try your skill at birling. If you fell off, one of your friends would pull you out. Some of the kids couldn't swim, and the water was dirty, but none of us ever thought there was a possibility of drowning. We were invulnerable. Most of us learned to swim in the Santiam River. We spent long summer afternoons at the river without adult supervision. We picked wildflowers in the woods, and on summer days we often found the tallest of vine maple trees, climbed up as high as we could, and rode the branches down to the ground.

Except for self-imposed dangers, we had little to fear in this small town so removed from crime that the biggest prank was the appearance the morning after Halloween of a wagon perched on top of a barn and a number of privies turned over in selected sites around the community where there wasn't an owner/guard sitting inside with a shotgun, which he sometimes fired into the air to scare off potential perpetrators.

Our parents were hardworking and caring people whose goal was to make a decent living, provide for their families, and make sacrifices so their children would have "a better chance than I did." Loggers, or "timber beasts" or "swamp apes," were our heroes. Most of the boys boasted they were going to be log-truck drivers or high climbers. Or they planned to start out as whistlepunks as soon as they were out of high school and work their way up to choker-setters, become hook-tenders, and soon be the "Bull of the Woods," owning their own outfit. Their dream in life was making as many stumps as possible. Others, whose dads were bushlers—fallers and buckers—and were paid according to the number and size of the trees they felled and cut up, thought this work was the hardest and most dangerous and were planning to follow in their dads' footsteps.

My dad worked as a marker and scaler. His job was to measure the fallen trees and mark where the bucker would cut them into logs. The bushlers were paid a percentage based on Dad's figures. The scaler generally had a reputation of being a company man with a "long thumb," scrimping on the measurement to save the company a dime. But Dad was known for his honesty. He had great integrity. He could not be bought by either side. I was proud he was so respected. Dad had work to do at night calculating scale. From about age eleven all through high school, I would sit up with Dad at our chrome-and-gray-masonite (mottled to look like marble) kitchen table and read numbers from a log scale booklet, while he gave me dimensions and then recorded them in his scale book. I formed a mental friendship with these men, seeing their names regularly. I knew these guys by my dad's bookkeeping. They took on personalities as Dad would talk about them. This, I realized, was why I felt so sad about Gunnar Frey.

Gunnar's death hit Dad very hard. Gunnar was a good friend of Dad's, and Dad was among the first to find Gunnar Frey pinned between two logs. Gunnar was a bucker. His last cut had caused a chunk of log to roll, catching him and crushing him up against another log. Dad never talked about accidents in the woods around us kids. He knew we worried, as every kid did, about losing our dad to a falling tree or a widow-maker or a snapped cable. It was dangerous work. There were many accidents. In a logging town, children were not strangers to tragedy. The sound of a siren brought terror to your heart because you knew someone in the woods had been injured or killed. You just waited to find out who—and then were grateful that it wasn't your dad this time. Two of my friends did lose their dad when he was caught in the bight of the line and decapitated. I had lost my Uncle Fred, age twenty, when he got out of his truck to tighten a binder chain. The chain broke, and he was killed instantly when a log fell off his truck and crushed him.

I overheard Dad telling Mom about Gunnar, "I can't get him out of my mind. He was such a helluva nice guy. He was still talking and joking when we were getting the log off him as if when we finally freed him, he'd walk right out of there. As soon as the pressure was off, he turned an awful brown color, not another word, he was gone. That just sticks in my mind. I thought we were going to have to carry out one of the fallers that cut down that tree.

He kept saying over and over, 'I had a feeling about that tree.' We never should have cut it. When you get that feeling, you should know enough to leave it alone. God forgive me, we never should have cut that tree."

Loggers were not a superstitious lot, but they did subscribe to certain beliefs. One of them was that if you had a bad feeling about cutting down a certain tree, you had better leave it and go on to the next. Another belief was if your hands were cold or if you experienced an unexplainable cold feeling, you shouldn't work in the woods that day. It was a warning that something bad was going to happen. My friend's mother related that her husband had complained of feeling cold before he left for work the day he was killed in a logging accident.

Long before you went to school, you had an informal knowledge of how things operated in the woods. You knew that the yarder weighed almost fifty thousand pounds, not including the weight of the log sled. You knew an eleven-by-thirteen special could reel in a log on good ground at about four hundred feet a minute and send the rigging and chokers racing back into the woods at more than a thousand feet a minute. The whistle controlled all log movement and often regulated life or death. A wrong or misinterpreted signal could send tons of rigging hurtling through the air. You took pride in learning the whistlepunk signals. And if you lived close enough to a work site, you could tell what was going on at the landing. A long blast followed by a short one started the crews to work in the morning and announced quitting time at the end of the day. There were two dreaded signals. A repetition of long and short blasts meant fire. Seven long blasts followed by two short blasts repeated over and over meant someone was injured and a stretcher was needed. This signal was often called the dead whistle because injuries serious enough for a stretcher often meant death.

We were all aware of the constant danger and discomfort for those working in the woods. You tried not to think about it and instead used humor to chase away fear. I remember my dad saying, "A logger works with death looking over his shoulder every day. If you stopped to think about it, you'd never go back in the woods." Then he laughed and said, "The only consolation of being killed in the woods is that you'd probably go straight to hell—at last you'd be warm and dry."

Loggers used humor to keep a perspective about the daily dangers inherent in their work. They loved telling stories to kids and greenhorns about the terrible things you might encounter alone in the woods.

Most of us kids had wandered through the woods since we could walk. I guess we decided these creatures wouldn't bother us because we lived here. But we made good use of the stories, adopting them to scare the bejeezus out of city cousins who came to visit. Young college guys who were logging as a summer job were favorite targets for stories and pranks. They were warned about the vicious wizzensnifter and the beavercat. The wizzensnifter is a shy creature. It is short and squat but very fast. Too large to miss but too small to see, it has big buck teeth, so the stumps of the trees it eats have uneven jagged tops. It is named for the sound it makes when it is chewing down a big fir tree, "wizzen-SNIFT." It won't attack unless cornered. If you scare it or threaten it, it can chew off a leg in a matter of minutes. Beavercats are more dangerous than wizzensnifters. They are also known as beaver panthers and are a cross between the flat-tailed beaver and the cougar. They lurk in trees at night waiting for prey to cross their trails. They make a sound that is like a big cat. They have a broad, flat tail like a beaver and are dark colored and virtually invisible at night. If you walk under a beavercat perched in a tree on a dark night, that great big tail will whack you right across the face. Few people survive a beavercat attack.

Run like hell if you come across a highbehind. This creature has a taste for human blood, especially the blood of greenhorns, since they are so innocent and sweet. It runs backwards over its victim so it doesn't leave any tracks. It snatches off the victim's head because that is its favorite morsel.

When a man new to the woods came on the job, there would be the obligatory initiation pranks. One was the axeman's test. A seasoned logger would ask the newcomer if he had ever taken the axeman's test. Of course, he hadn't. The logger would then make a mark in the center of a stump, have somebody blindfold him, and take a whack with his axe, usually hitting the target the first time. Then the new guy was blindfolded and he had to try his luck at hitting the mark on the stump. The others would encourage him by saying how close he was. On the third whack somebody would put the guy's new gloves on the stump where the axe had been falling and the new guy would slice right through them. He would need to be good-humored about this, or he would be the victim of more pranks. On the rigging crew he might be sent for a choker hole or some other nonexistent object. Sometimes they would send a newcomer across the canyon to another work site to get a left-handed marlin spike. The spike is like a huge needle and it is used to separate strands of cable so it can be spliced. Sometimes the other crew would just break up laughing, or they might send him back with the spike so his own crew could have a laugh at his expense.

There were few things that would keep loggers out of the woods. Low humidity, wind, and tinder-dry conditions were among the reasons for shutting down. In a windstorm it was foolish to be where trees were falling down all around you. Loggers left the woods in a hurry. When the humidity was low, fire was a constant danger. Acres of timber could be lost, set off by a single spark. When conditions in the woods were dry, the loggers' working day began around three o'clock in the morning and ended shortly after noon. This "hoot-owling" went on through the hot, dry weather. Mom got up early to get breakfast for Dad and put up his lunch. One night after Dad left for his hoot-owl shift, we were awakened by a scratching noise on the screen of the outside cooler, which was attached to the wall of our house just outside the kitchen. My brother and I huddled with Mom until she was finally brave enough to go peek out the kitchen window. We were following close, hanging on to her skirt. It was a real hoot owl. He had attacked our chickens and was intent on sampling what was in the cooler. I thought he had decided to take up residence in our house. The next day Dad set a trap in the chicken yard using a dead chicken as bait. Sure enough, the owl returned and got his feet caught in the trap. He was flapping his big wings and snapping his beak. Dad killed him and had him stuffed. So the owl did take up residence in our house. He perched on a branch in our living room, wings aloft, like a sentinel, staring with his gold glass eyes throughout my growing-up years.

Dad hated picnics. He said he had a picnic every day in the woods. On rare occasions he would join us down by the river for an afternoon. He couldn't understand why anyone would want to pack food in a basket, carry it up some hill or down to the river, spread a blanket on the ground, balance a dish of food on your lap, compete with bugs and ants, and fight off the bees when you could sit at a table and enjoy a hot meal right in your own kitchen. He joked about the number of days he left for work in the dark and came home in the dark: "In what other job could you have two moonlight rides and a picnic lunch every day with a bunch of fun-lovin' guys?"

We were eager to see our dad home safe from the woods each evening. When we hugged him in welcome, his scent of trees, pitch, and tobacco was like heaven to us. Odors are such strong links to life experiences—tin pants and coat hanging on chairs to dry in front of the wood stove, boot grease drying on cork boots, mingling with the cooking smells from the kitchen in preparation for dinner. To a child it said, All is well with my world.

During the spring and summer, Dad used to surprise Mom with a bouquet of trilliums, babes-in-the-woods, or rhododendrons. When the huckleberries and blackberries ripened, he would pick and bring home enough in his lunch pail for a pie. Other things were carried home in lunch pails (or "nosebags"), too. The owner didn't always realize what he was carrying. Practical jokes were a common source of amusement among the crew, each man trying to outdo the other.

Some of the loggers were single and had their lunches packed for them at White's Cafe. This service was nearly canceled for all time when one of the waitresses opened a lunch box to clean it and prepare a new lunch. She became an unwilling Pandora. A swarm of bees had been captured by some of the logger's crew and put in the lunch pail. The waitress went screaming out of the kitchen, followed by angry bees intent on getting revenge on anyone within their flight pattern. Somebody had the foresight to open the door, and the swarm made for the exit, stinging anyone in their path. Another favorite trick was to fill the lunch pail with ants. It became a habit for some loggers to check their nosebags before they got on the crummy for the ride home.

Uncle Louie owned and operated a gypo logging company—not a high-ball outfit but certainly not a haywire outfit. Uncle spoke fluent cursing. He couldn't utter a sentence without punctuating it with half a dozen expletives. But "he had a heart of gold," as my religious grandmother was fond of saying, and there was nothing he wouldn't do for you. He dressed as all the loggers did, in staggered-off pants, wide suspenders, an old oil-stained red felt hat, and corked boots. The porches and floors of every business in town were pocked and splintered, bearing mute evidence of the years of wear and tear from the comings and goings of loggers. Most loggers kept a couple of thin shingle slats at the door, and when they came home, they stepped onto these slats with their corks and then walked into the house, protecting the floors from cork marks. Some were not so careful. Aunt Eva railed at Uncle Lou for walking into the house with his corks on. He replied, "It's my goddam house, and I'll wear these sons-a-bitches anywhere I want!" His swearing was such a natural thing it never occurred to him, as it did to most loggers, that that kind of language was not to be used around women and children.

George, an absolutely fearless high-climber, worked for Uncle Louie. Dad said if George had a lick of sense he wouldn't climb those spar poles—large trees chosen for their strength and height, usually a hundred-sixty to a hundred-eighty feet tall. After topping, they are rigged with cables and pulleys to ready them for pulling the logs onto the landing. To this day it is a custom for high-climbers like George to show bravado at the conclusion of a successful topping by sitting atop the swaying spar pole and waving their hats to the cheering crew below. They strap on their spurs and gear and start their climb with all sorts of paraphernalia—axes and saws tethered to them—chopping off limbs as they make their way to the top of the tree. Near the top they stop and survey the situation, calculating how many feet from the top they should cut. Then they cut a wedge on one side so the top will fall in a certain direction. They saw the top off and jump quickly down out of the way, catching themselves by digging their spurs into the bark of the tree. It is a dangerous, daring, and exacting feat.

George was an enigma. His general demeanor told you he was neither especially bright nor blessed with exceptional common sense. George did handstands on the top of the pole after he had cut off the top. The reason for George's fearless behavior was that he had only one eye, an injury-induced lack of depth perception. George, as a young boy, had situated himself in the direct line of a rock thrown by a member of an opposing team in a rock fight—one of the ingenious games children of that day devised to entertain themselves. It was a small rock. If it had hit George in the head it would have made only a large painful lump. But it chose instead to damage George's cornea and cause an infection. George, at age twelve, had to have his eye surgically removed. He wore a patch until, as a young man, he could be fitted for a glass eye. This made for a welcome change in George's appearance. It

pleased George, of course, but was disconcerting to others, because that eye
never moved but always looked straight ahead. George's glass eye was the
subject of many conversations at lunch time. One time, it seems, George wore
a patch. It is very uncomfortable to sock a cold eye into your head early in
the morning, he related. So he put his eye in the warming oven of the wood-
stove so it would be nice and warm. This particular morning George's wife
forgot about George's eye sitting there warming up, and as she pulled a plate
from the warming oven, George's eye began to roll. It dropped onto the hot
stove, bounced into the pot of oatmeal, crackled, and shattered.

There were many different jobs in the lumber business. Some men preferred working on water. These were the pond monkeys who used peaveys to
align the logs in a float after they were unloaded into the log pond. After high
school, my brother worked as a pond monkey. His experience as a child playing on the logs served him well. It took agile feet and an alert mind to do this
kind of work. If the logs jammed up, they had to be separated. The logs rolled
in the water. You had to keep your balance or you would get dunked. That
was uncomfortable, but you could also get caught between logs and be
injured, or killed. When things went well, it was like watching dancers as they
leaped gracefully from log to log, gathering them together like they were
sheep in a flock. Pond monkeys had to be "catty on their feet." When there
was a spare moment, the men would practice their birling skills, running in
place on top of a log to get it rolling. There were always friendly competitions
going on. One man would get on either end of a log and begin birling. The
idea was to change directions quickly when your opponent least expected it
and cause him to lose his balance and fall in the water.

Memory takes you back to your childhood, and living helps you interpret it. You can't change it. It is imprinted as strongly as if it were part of
your DNA. Childhoods are like fingerprints—no two are exactly alike. Early
experiences influence your life choices, becoming building blocks for your
future. While embracing the small town, the people, and a way of life that
was disappearing along with the timber, I knew from the time I could reason that I would leave as soon as I was out of high school. I had no intention of marrying a logger and emulating the life of my mother.

This was not because I felt this kind of life was beneath me. On the
contrary, I have great respect for the struggles and joys of raising a family in
this small town. I watched my mother and other mothers like her as they
worked at tending the children, the house, the garden, as they worked at
harvesting, preserving and preparing food, sewing, mending, and always
worrying—always nervous when their husbands were a few minutes late getting home. Each handled her anxiety differently. My mother handed most of
her worry to a higher power. God always knew best. This somehow relieved
her of responsibility and allowed her to get on with day-to-day life.

Perhaps my parents' generation was the last to truly believe that their hard work would ensure a better life for their children. Most parents, like mine, encouraged and expected their kids to go on to college. There was, however, the attitude among many that it was a waste of time and money for a girl to further her education. After all, "What good will it do her? She's just gonna get married and raise her kids." And there were those girls who did graduate from high school, marry their high-school sweethearts, and stay in that small town to raise families. Some are still there.

But the town itself no longer resembles the timber town I knew as I grew up. The mills stand like forgotten skeletons, old tools lying here and there in the dusty remains. An eerie silence replaces the hustle of workers and the productive-but-deafening noise of the saws and machines. Massive trees on thickly wooded hills have been replaced by small firs and under-brush trying valiantly to hide the scars of two new dam projects. Foster is now a recreation area. The sounds of mills and log trucks have given way to those of pleasure craft and jet skis. Instead of loggers birling on logs, you see scores of water skiers, picnickers, swimmers, and fishermen. The change is complete. The little logging town is gone. But to everyone who worked or grew up there one thing will always remain—memories of that unmistakable odor of wood that permeated the air. On cold, foggy nights the air hung like a heavy curtain, a constant reminder that mentally, spiritually, and physically, you were one with the forest.

In Her Own Words: Women's Frontier Friendships in Letters, Diaries, and Reminiscences
Margaret K. Brady

As more and more examples of women's non-traditional literature—letters, diaries, reminiscences—become available in both published and unpublished form, historians, folklorists, and literary scholars alike can begin to understand more fully the nature of the relationships between women on the western frontier, as they have been articulated in these various genres. These previously ignored pieces of writing provide us with an intimate, self-revelatory perspective on the western experience as it was lived by women. Through a comparison of female relationships on the ranching frontiers of Texas and in close-knit Mormon communities in Arizona and Utah, this essay will explore the range of interactions among western women in the nineteenth and early twentieth centuries. Susan Armitage, in discussing the diary of Amelia Buss, has provided a sense of direction for the present study, as she suggests the high degree of importance communication with other women held for those in a sometimes alien, always demanding environment. As Armitage points out, when the impossibility of such direct communication between women became all too obvious, they often turned to their diaries to provide a kind of surrogate support (Armitage 1982).

Such support, whether in the form of letters from a sister "back in the states," infrequent visits from neighbor women living thirty or forty miles away, or the comfort of confiding in one's own diary, was indeed critical for women pioneering in the trans-Mississippi West. As Carroll Smith-Rosenberg has suggested in her research on relations among nineteenth-century American women, a specifically female world developed in eighteenth- and nineteenth-century America that was based both on rigid gender-role differentiation, including severe social restrictions on male-female intimacy, and on the shared experiences and mutual affection of women that eventually became institutionalized in significant female social conventions and rituals: in a "world bounded by home, church, and the institution of visiting—that endless traipsing of women to each other's homes for social purposes[—] . . . women helped each other with domestic chores and in times of sickness, sorrow, or trouble" (Smith-Rosenberg 1986, 233).

A woman's life in nineteenth-century America was, then, a life lived in the presence of other women; womanly friendship was not only casually accepted, but it was the very cornerstone of social relationships within and outside of the family itself. These female friendship networks played significant roles in providing mutual emotional and physical support, in holding communities and kin systems together, and in providing an arena of status and power for women, who were so often denied a place of value in male-dominated society. Whether in intimate discussion of family problems or in letters of support sent across hundreds of miles, women consciously constructed and reconstructed those important female networks. Drawing on the work of Shirley and Edwin Ardener, Cynthia Huff points out that "the knowledge women share with each other when they experience a space reserved for them functions as a wild zone where women can create ideologies and symbol systems they control, where they can inscribe themselves in codes not understood by men" (1996, 124). In East Coast cities and in settlements sprinkled across the western prairies, women in the nineteenth and twentieth centuries continued to do just that.

Women who traveled west had to struggle not only with leaving behind significant others—most of whom were women—but they also had to deal with a reorientation of both sexual roles and social relationships. The initial physical separation itself became a symbol of the dramatic kinds of social and sexual readjustment which followed. As Lodisa Frizell so eloquently questions in her journal:

> Who is there that does not recollect their first night when started on a long journey, the wellknown voices of our friends still ring in our ears, the parting kiss feels still warm upon our lips, and that last separating word Farewell! sinks deeply into the heart. It may be the last we ever hear from some or all of them, and to those who start . . . there can be no more solemn scene of parting only at death. (Jeffrey 1979, 371)

And Agnes Stewart provides us with an even more intimate understanding of the agony these women felt in leaving women friends, an agony it may be hard for some to understand fully in the context of twentieth-century reserve. In her diary, Agnes reveals the depth of her sense of loss: "O Martha my heart yearns for thee my only friend . . . O my friend thou art dear to me yet my heart turns to thee I will never forget thee . . . the earliest friend . . . I know I can never enjoy the blessed privilege of communing with thee yet look for the loss of one I will never see on earth . . . I cannot bear it" (Schlissel 1982, 28-29).

While women back in Pennsylvania or New York might find it a diffi-cult enough task to move from a world almost completely comprised of female relationships to a life with a new husband, apart, at least physically, from former family and friendship networks, the social and psychological impact on the thousands of new brides who moved along the trail to Texas or California or Utah was even more startling. For most of these travelers, not only had all former female relationships been severed, but their sexual identity came under strain from other quarters as well. As women took on tasks ordinarily considered "men's work," thus blurring traditional sex roles, the need to maintain intimate contact with other women in any way possi-ble became even more important to the preservation of a continuity of both personal and social identity in this rapidly changing society. While some his-torians have argued that maintaining outrageously bulky and cumbersome women's fashions was the main way women constantly reaffirmed their womanhood in this role-threatening environment of the frontier (Schlissel 1982, 29), women's insistence on maintaining (through letters) significant relationships with women back home and on forming steadfast new friend-ships in the West were far more important and the primary means through which they adjusted to the reorientation of sex roles. Through these female friendship networks, as tenuous as they sometimes had to be, women cre-atively responded to the new social environment of the West, as well as to the new physical environment.

This essay presents several relevant perspectives for understanding the kinds of relationships women shared with women in the trans-Mississippi West. I focus here on Mormon women in Utah and Arizona and isolated women ranchers of Texas to illustrate the range of intensity and frequency of relationships among women in the West, as well as the underlying simi-larities found in the importance of maintaining meaningful connections with other women at all costs. The different genres in which these women wrote—diaries, letters, reminiscences—provided significantly different opportunities for displays of expressive power. These women recognized the power of words to create and transform their daily experiences, experiences that often involved interacting closely with other women. As Patricia Meyer Spacks has suggested in *The Female Imagination,* "women dominate their own experi-ence by imagining it, giving it form, writing about it" (1975, 322).

Some of the most intense new relationships formed among women on the American frontier were those of Mormon women in Utah and Arizona. Because the Mormon (or LDS) church moved westward *as* a community, its female members more easily maintained the kinds of relationships so impor-tant to them in the days before their westward trek; in many ways Mormon women stand at the far end of the social-relationship spectrum, since the intensity of the interaction between these women was made possible by both geographical proximity and community expectation. Almost all of the Mormon women whose diaries and letters are available lived in close communities with proportionately large numbers of other women. While the practice of polygamy has been cited as at least partially responsible for this female-dominated society (at least in actual numbers), more significantly, the fact that many Mormon men were sent off on proselytizing missions for two years or more created the possibility for the kinds of intense female friendships more often found among unmarried women in the East.

The friendship between Mary Harkin Parker Richards and Jane Snyder Richards, the wife of Mary's husband's brother, is an example of such a relationship. During the two years that Mary Richards stayed at Winter Quarters preparing for the Mormons' journey across the plains, she kept a journal which reveals that much of her time was spent in the company of "Sister Jane." Both of their husbands were away on missions—Mary's husband Samuel in Scotland and Jane's husband Franklin in England. Indeed, the intensity of their friendship seemed somehow foreordained. Mary writes about their meeting: "never was I more rejoiced to meet with a friend than I was to meet with Sister Jane . . . . [W]e talked over many of the scens that had past during our abcance from each other, rejoiced in each others welfare, and sympathized with each other sorrows" (Richards 1996, 89). From that moment on, scarcely a day passed when they were not together—washing ("Friday 25th a beauty full day in the morn went home and getherd together a large washing of clothes and retorned to Jane's to spend Christmass over the wash tub"); writing letters ("Thursday 17th a cold day. was writing in my letter. eve Jane came to stay with me I being a lone. she was writing a letter to Franklin, and I was writing in my Journal. She read me her letter, and I read her most of mine"); or visiting ("Tuesday 19th . . . I accompanied Jane to Maria's were we spent the day very pleasantly"; "Tuesday 26th . . . early in the morn Sister Chester Snyder sent for Jane and my self to come to her house to a quilting"). They also spent almost every night together as the following passages suggest. These are the last lines of five consecutive journal entries (leaving out a Monday entry that implies but does not explicitly state they stayed together), and they are by no means uncharacteristic: "I remained with Jane all night[;] Friday 25th . . . spent the night with Jane[;] Saturday 26th . . . felt very tired staid all night with Jane[;] Sunday 27th . . . went and slept that night with Sister Jane[;] Tuesday 29th . . . Jane Elcy & myself spent about two hours trying to see which could Compose the best Poetry, then retired to bed" (Richards 1996, 102–4, 106–7). The intensity of this relationship cannot be overestimated, I think, and it is certainly not unusual, especially among women who had the advantage of geographical proximity.

Perhaps even more important, these women also operated within a set of community expectations which not only accepted female friendship, but exploited and extolled it as a base of community strength. Mormon women like Mary and Jane lived close enough together to share washday tasks, dressmaking, and child care; they also joined with other women to make quilts for the needy, to "lay on hands" and pray together for the sick, and to provide the direction and energy for enterprises such as the silkworm industry in southern Utah. It was clear to the women *and* to the men in the Mormon West that together women found strength: physical, emotional, spiritual. Lucy Flake, one of the early Mormon pioneers in Arizona, expressed the inter-relationship of those strengths in this diary entry:

> January 1, 1889 Sister Mary J. West and I went to Elsie's to give her a blessing before the birth of her child as was customary in those days. . . . Sister West and I had many wonderful experiences together and we loved each other with a devotion that was closer than that of any earthly ties. Often when I felt despondent I would go up to my dear friends and we would talk and then we would go upstairs and pour out our souls in prayer. We would feel the power resting upon us. I would put my hands on her head and bless her and then she would bless me. I fasted and was greatly blessed and felt so thankful for this wonderful privilege. I always received comfort when we offered up our prayers together. (Flake 1932)[1]

Clearly some of the closest relationships among Mormon women were those of plural wives, although the extent to which polygamy was practiced has been greatly exaggerated. One of the most important points to remember in any discussion of polygamous wives is that every relationship was unique. The relationship between each husband and each of his wives, the way in which new wives were acquired, the personalities of the women involved, whether these wives even lived in the same town—all of these issues, among others, influenced the nature of the relationships which existed between polygamous wives. In many cases, the women found strength and comfort in each other, each wife using her own skills to the advantage of all; in other instances, outright antipathy existed between wives, and any kind of cooperation was marginal at best. Although it is impossible here to examine in detail the range of attitudes expressed by polygamous wives toward one another and toward their husbands, I would like to look briefly at a not-at-all uncommon example of the interesting possibilities of polygamous relationships for women. Eliza Maria Partridge Lyman and her sister Caroline were both married to Amasa Lyman, who in time also married another Partridge sister, Lydia, along with several other women. Eliza and Caroline lived together, and indeed their relationship with their husband seems entirely tangential to their own intimate relationship. The two shared everything from washing to gardening to actually building a house. (Where their husband is during this time is entirely left to conjecture; for, in fact, he is rarely mentioned throughout Eliza's diary). She writes:

> November 1847, Monday 1st . . . My sister Caroline and I have been trying to build a log house for ourselves as we do not feel quite comfortable where we are. We first got possession of an old house which we pulled down and had the logs moved to a spot where we wanted it put up again. As we could not get any one to lay it up for us went at it ourselves, and laid it up five or six logs high, when more brethren came and laid it up the rest of the way. . . . Then I built a fireplace and a chimney. . . . (Lyman 1820–86)

The presence of a man in the family is usually marked only by a terse comment about the birth of a child "daughter of Paulina Lyman and Amasa Lyman" or "son of Caroline Lyman and Amasa Lyman." In polygamous households such as this one, we see most clearly the possibilities and necessities of close female relationships. In many ways, Eliza and Caroline are the family unit.

Such a lack of attention to men in the diaries of women is not restricted to polygamous wives. Elizabeth Hampsten points out in her analysis of nineteenth-century working-class diaries of women in the Midwest that "women's descriptions of men are apt to be blurred, just out of focus or to one side. I had to read a long time in Grace Decor's journal before I realized that T. H. was the man she was married to" (1982, 118). Even though the diaries of women, not only in Utah but all across America, reveal these blurred descriptions of men, the relationships between Mormon women, polygamous or not, often lie at one end of a continuum of intensity of female interaction. Geographical proximity and community expectations contribute to an environment in which female friendships dominate the day-to-day lives of the women involved.

At the other end of that spectrum are the lives of women like those Texas pioneers who settled on ranches far from the hub of community activity. The kind of loneliness that their isolation brought is often revealed in the most understated tones. For example, Ella Bird-Dupont, one of the first settlers in the eastern panhandle of Texas, noted concerning the arrival of several wagons that "this was the first women I had seen in about twelve months" (Bird-Dupont 1935). Other Texas women were more direct in their expression of such loneliness. Margaret Armstrong Bowie confided often to her diary that she could scarcely bear the isolation she experienced as a teenager in the Kekchi Valley of Jack County, Texas. On 28 September 1872 she wrote, "Ma is ready to go back to Waterford and so am I. It is so miserable lonesome here. No church or society nearer than Black Springs six miles away" (Bowie 1872–77). Festive occasions seemed to make Margaret's loneliness all the more acute. On 11 October 1872, she penned

this terse comment: "Oh tomorrow is my 15th birth day and I feel burried
alive in this slow valley." And in January 1873: "This is sister Annie 13th
birth day, but they are all alike in this lonely country place." Even the
events surrounding Christmas (usually special even on the frontier) could
not lift her spirits and she writes: "Dec. 25 We did some extra baking yesterday in case Aunt Rena came or anyone else. But it is too cold and here
we are as usual, down in this Kekchi valley, hid out from the world and
this just the same as all other days, except the children hang up their
stockings and we make believe Santa Claus has not forgotten them entirely" (Bowie 1872–77).

Perhaps Susan E. Newcomb's journal reveals most clearly the intensity of such isolation. On 19 October 1866, from the Stone Ranch in
Throckmorton County, she writes,

> A man that drives cattle cant stay at home with his family
> much. The time passes slow and lonsome with me while he is gone,
> one reason is we live so far from any one eighteen miles from a liv-
> ing being I get very lonsome sometimes when I think about being so
> far from any one in an Indian country, I hope that I will not have to
> live out here always where I can never go to church or go to see a
> friend. It is true that I can see the little birds warbling their sweet
> songs in the branches of the green trees, I can see large herds of cat-
> tle feeding upon the rich green grass that grows upon the Valleys.
> And in the Autumn I can see the big ugly buffalo that fairly black-
> en the valleys and hill sides, I have not said any thing about the
> Antelope the wild Deer and the cunning mule eared Rabbits that
> gallop over the hills of this country. And there is the lofty mountains
> that spread their cool shade across the valleys of the west. and
> besides all these here is my Father and Mother Brothers and Sister
>
> > And my little blue eyed boy
> > A future hope, a present joy.
>
> With all these I cant help being lonsome at times. (Newcomb
> 1865–71)

While many of these settlers simply endured the long days without
female companionship, relying on letters and diary entries to provide them
with a kind of surrogate conversational dialogue, others refused to let geographical space interfere with former interactional patterns. Women traveled thirty, forty, or fifty miles to visit other women, just as they had
traipsed down the block for an afternoon in Boston or New York. Although
the basic visitation pattern was maintained to a surprising extent in Texas,
and the West generally, there were, of necessity, some modifications.
Afternoons of visiting gave way to week-long visits, during which one
woman came to help another do weeks' worth of laundry or put up the

vegetables for the winter. In addition to these day-to-day activities, often women would gather together for special work-related occasions, such as sewing or quilting bees. For many women, the quilt itself became a symbol of the kind of strength provided by the women who helped in its creation. Texan Nancy Jane Logan Teagarden describes such a process quite straightforwardly when she writes in her diary for Tuesday, 1 February, 1870: "Well we have finished our quilt *at last* and I am so proud of it I can hardly—well I don't know how to express my pride. Now I am sure to remember 28 of my friends *a long long* while" (Teagarden 1870–71).

Work-related activities provided women the occasion to visit, exchange information, and accomplish tasks which, undertaken alone, might prove difficult and often monotonous as well. On the ranching frontiers of Texas we find women engaged in a variety of such joint endeavors: Ella Bird-Dupont, for example, writes that shortly after she and her buffalo-hunter husband moved to the panhandle to file claim, "Mrs. Johnes and I also practiced together, as she was learning to use a gun too. Sometimes we would go down on the creek and shoot turkeys" (1935, 32). Although she informs us that "there was but few women on ranches at that time," Bird-Dupont carefully notes the range of possibilities for social interaction that these few women took advantage of (1935, 54). Besides rifle practice, she and the other women she managed to encounter on the plains went berry hunting, rounded up milk cows, and drove miles into town to a dance (leaving all the children with a friend's husband).

In fact, women on early Texas ranches surprisingly often also found occasions for socializing before or after their work. Visiting other women, spending the night or several nights, was carefully noted in diaries and letters. Henrietta Baker Embree's diary, written between 1856 and 1861 in Belton, Texas, reveals her to be an amazingly social young woman. Living in a more populated area than many of her contemporaries in this study, Henrietta delighted in visiting and being visited. Her first diary entry sets the tone for the many pages which follow: "Jan 1 I have been out calling. Spent some hours very pleasantly conversing with my old school mates talking of things that have passed and gone. I too have had visitors this week. It is so pleasant to have friends and associates that you can love and place confidence in as you would a sister" (Embree 1856–61). A less carefully worded but more animated version of the same sentiment reads, "Monday 21st . . . I was this eve, seated flat, on the hearth, my lap full of rags [for making rugs] and dirt—not thinking of companie when, before I was aware of it, Aunt Betsie and Mrs. Kees, were in the back room, they spent the afternoon and dident we dip spit and talk? I think we did" (Embree 1856–61). For Henrietta Embree, and I suspect for many other nineteenth-century western women, a good talk with friends was a kind of cure-all. Of her sister she writes: "Jan 1, 1859 She has the blues tonight but I am hoping she will be over them by

morning—as she is spending the night with a much loved friend." Many
women on nineteenth-century Texas ranches were not as articulate in
describing their visiting patterns as Henrietta; nonetheless it is clear from
page after page of their diaries that female friendship was highly valued in
many different contexts.

Ritual occasions such as births, weddings, and funerals epitomize the
intensity of interaction of these ranch women, for they often confide in journals and reminiscences that it is the strength of other women which supports
them in these rites of passage. When her first husband dies, it is Ella Bird-
Dupont's friend Mrs. Bailey who goes with her to place the tombstone she
had carved on his grave, and when she marries again, she notes that "several of my best old time lady friends made two cakes each for me, two or
three dressed turkeys, and everything else in accordance, a regular oldtime
wedding dinner with Mrs. Campbell as director" (Bird-Dupont 1935, 191).
Later, when her young son dies, Ella writes of her experiences as both the
comforted and the comforter:

> Baby [her daughter] could not be consoled; one of her little girl
> friends Paula Harwell came and spent a week with her which helped
> some to drive away her sorrow. Mrs. Richard came and insisted that
> Baby and I go and spend a few days with her. I did not want to leave
> Mr. Dupont alone, but he insisted so hard I should go. . . . They had
> lost their only little baby about the same age of ours a few months
> before, and they know how to sympathyze with us. She drove with
> us quite a bit while we were there. We called on Mr. and Mrs. Barron.
> They were ranchers on Buck Creek. . . . She looked so young and
> inexperienced for the hard western life that we lived here. She told
> me in after years how lonely she had been at that place and how
> very much she appreciated our visit. (1935, 201)

This is a fine example of the ways in which women relied on each other
to provide the kind of mutual support so necessary in the demanding isolation of the frontier; here both mother and teenage daughter are comforted
by their women friends and, in turn, reach out to support another woman
laboring to make a life in the West. Simple geographical separation was just
not enough to destroy the compelling force which drew women together on
the frontier.

One of the few widely published accounts of women living on isolated
ranches, although not a Texas example, demonstrates probably better than
any other document the resilience of pioneer women, especially in terms of
their ability to maintain and nurture relationships with other women under
the most unlikely circumstances. In *Letters of a Woman Homesteader* (1914),
Elinore Pruitt Stewart not only continues her strong relationship with her former boss, Mrs. Coney, through her letters, but she focuses the bulk of the

content of those letters on her adventures with two other women who live miles and miles away from her Wyoming homestead. With Mrs. Louderer, a strong, seasoned pioneer, Elinore Stewart rides all over the countryside, bringing Christmas dinner to sheep camps, rescuing starving women and children, and simply enjoying the "fresh air." Her other friend, Mrs. O'Shaughnessy, reads her fortune in tea leaves, helps with a sewing bee to provide clothes for an unfortunate family, and shares every holiday celebration. With Mrs. O'Shaughnessy, Elinore participates in an outing in which a group of Wyoming women traveled annually to Utah for fresh fruit; this outing provided nourishment for both the bodies and the spirits of these friendship-hungry women settlers.

Although Elinore's relationship with the brusque and very Scottish Mr. Stewart appears to be a satisfactory one, it is her relationships with these two women which provide focus for her writing and, one would suspect, for her life. Elinore's letters to Mrs. Coney about her friends also direct our attention to the other important consideration of this kind of research: the necessity of examining each genre of women's writing—diaries, letters, reminiscences—to discover the writer's intent in each. One of the most interesting facets of Elinore Stewart's letters is that they are just that, letters, and as such they have a specific rhetorical intent. Through these letters we see Elinore's life not as she lived it but as she wished her friend Mrs. Coney to believe she lived. Just as we select only the choicest, most interesting tidbits to include in our personal narratives shared with friends, so Elinore selected those parts of her life which she believed would most interest Mrs. Coney. The letters also demonstrate quite clearly how, for many women, such correspondence took the place of the kinds of feminine conversation to which they were accustomed. In one letter Elinore says, "I know this is an inexcusably long letter, but it is snowing so hard and you know how I like to talk" (1914, 13); for Elinore, writing to Mrs. Coney is talking, talking to a dear friend so far away.

Through letters, nineteenth-century western women accomplished a number of personal goals. For the all-too-often isolated Texas women ranchers, letters provided a kind of mutual support system, in which problems were aired, advice given, joys shared. Through letters, an important exchange of information took place for these women, who often had no other close female friends in which to confide. When Lizzie Scott Neblett became depressed at finding herself pregnant for the sixth time, she wrote her cousin Jennie, baring her soul and threatening to end her life. Jennie's reply, on 2 January 1860, is a masterpiece of psychological rhetoric. She urges Lizzie to consider how much worse off she could be, comparing Lizzie's plight favorably with her own poverty, ill health, and constant family problems. She employs the strongest combination of gentleness, religious rhetoric, and appeals to motherly sensibilities. But in the end (after more than eight pages), she provides Lizzie with specific information that might allow her some hope for the future:

> I wish I could say something to you, I am unhappy about you, for I understand how you feel, and would fain console you, but I know you are too determined to be miserable, to listen to any reasoning. . . . Lizzie, I know that "The Sponge" *will prevent conception* and tho I deem that a sin, still it is not so bad as killing ones self—So after you are over this trouble remember, if you get so again this will be your own fault. I know the Sponge is a safe and sure preventative. . . . (Neblett 1860)

Such exchange of important information occurs over and over again in the letters of women on the Texas ranching frontier, and other western frontiers as well. Perhaps even more often we find that letters served as significant vehicles for self-expression, wherein women's voices were allowed to be heard. Letters offered the generic possibilities of both immediacy of expression (like diaries, which we will consider later) and of specific epistolary expectations.

Writing in the immediacy of their experiences on the frontier, these women nevertheless were quite familiar with the generic conventions of letter writing in the nineteenth century. In fact, they almost certainly had been exposed to these epistolary conventions through a number of related reading experiences: manuals of letter-writing techniques, popular since the late sixteenth century; epistolary fiction, such as Mary Austin Holley's *Texas*; and perhaps most important, the letters of their own friends and family.[2]

Women's personal letters often included specific instructions for letter writing, such as these words to Bettie Beall from her friend Lucy Bridgewater on 7 June 1869: "When you write, tell me everything new, and do not close until you write me a long letter" (Bridgewater 1869). This urging to tell everything and create lengthy letters is one of the most common meta-epistolary comments in the writing of western women. Every word was held precious, and quite often the arrival of a letter provided the occasion for contact with other women closer by. Henrietta Baker Embree, for example, in reading a letter received from home, reports, "amidst my excitement and joy I just concluded to run over to see Mrs. Arnold and get her to participate with me" (Embree 1856–61). The writings of other Texas women suggest that reading letters aloud was an important form of entertainment, especially in the earliest days on the frontier.

The anticipation of reader expectations surely helped determine the form of these nineteenth-century letters, just as it does in letter writing today. The extent to which rhetorical intent was molded by the urgency to provide needed information, the desire to achieve literary excellence, or even the fatigue of the writer is certainly an important variable in all of this. With respect to generic differences in the expressive forms available to women on western frontiers in the nineteenth century, the presence of an identifiable audience coupled with the specific rhetorical intent of the individual writer contribute significantly to an understanding of the ways in which the expressive power of letters differs from that of diaries.

Many of the journals of women on the frontier also make it abundantly clear that if we are ever to really come to terms with these individual diaries and journals, we must also look more closely at the rhetorical reasons behind journal writing itself. Several contemporary scholars have suggested that women wrote in their journals simply when they didn't have anyone else to talk to. While that may have been the case in some instances, there are a wide variety of other reasons for diary writing: to provide travel notes for future travelers, to satisfy personal literary ambitions, to provide something for one's grandchildren to treasure, to respond to a religious dictum, and the like. And although diaries frequently differ from letters in their solitary, reflective nature, the diaries of some Texas women seem clearly to have been written with a specific audience and purpose in mind. For example, Henrietta Embree's diary for 18 May 1858 suggests that

> I have nothing in my journal interesting to be seen, but then if my friends wanted to see or here it ready why should they not, I have no secrets in it, I expected for it to be seen I intend to take it to Kentucky with me for my Relatives, I thought it would give them some idea of a life in Texas, they could judge for one year of my life, I also thought it would be interesting to read myself in after years. (Embree 1858–61)

Susan Newcomb expands on this last reason in her own diary for 14 June 1867:

> I am writing these things just to keep practice, and perhaps I would be glad to see these scribbling twenty years hence if I should be so fortunate as to live that long. They would call to memory the days of my youth, the days that I spent in my cottage home far in the west, on the frontier of Texas, the only settler of Throckmorton County. (Newcomb 1865–71)

Occasionally the intended audience may change within a single diary. Interestingly, three years after Henrietta Embree suggests that she will send her diary to her "Relatives," she decides that she doesn't "intend to keep the book but send it to Jen." After this statement, the diary frequently addresses Jen until 1 January 1861, when she mysteriously switches back to using the diary as a place to record the most private feelings, oaths, etc., as the following entry attests: "Jan 1, 1861 Mrs. H. Embree promises this, New Years morning that she will lay aside narcotic weed and its *companion*, the pipe excepting at night she must have a few draws" (Embree 1858–61).

This is a particularly interesting journal from the perspective of the analysis of rhetorical intent, since the tone, diction, and other stylistic devices change as the audience changes. In other diaries the writer herself has a nebulous idea of audience as she begins writing but then clarifies both audience and rhetorical intent over a period of weeks, or sometimes years. Susan E. Newcomb began her diary on 1 January 1871 from Waterford, Texas, with an attempt to clarify for herself just who might read this work:

> Sunday Jan 1st:—This is the first day of the week—the first of the month—and the first of the year. The year 1870 is dead, and buried in the past by old time; and a new year has taken its place. It has been very pleasant to day, and I hope it will continue to be pleasant all the year
>
> But it will not be; there will be dark clouds and raging storms ere the year 1871 draws to a close; and there will be many disappointments, and troubles, to encounter during the year, that will look as black—as thunder clouds, and feel as piercing and cold as the wind from the North Pole.
>
> I think it advisable to brace ourselves up and prepare for the worst, but others may look at things in a different light. How ever I have a right to express my opinion any way I choose on this paper, for I dont suppose it will ever be read. It isn't for the public.
>
> Perhaps some one will see it when I am numbered with the dead; but then I will not know it, and as a matter of course I'll not care, and surely no one would ridicule the writings of the dead. I may like to look over this old journal sometime, but it will be of no importance to any one else, until my boy is old enough to read and understand. (Newcomb 1865–71)

We see, then, how Susan Newcomb works out within the first few lines of her diary the fact that her words may well be read by others in years to come, certainly by her son, and that even though she is ostensibly writing for herself and not "for the public," there is an understood silent audience waiting to respond in the future. The attempted eloquence of style further attests to this understanding. Lizzie Scott Neblett opens her diary 16 March 1852, with much the same understanding of audience and purpose eloquently stated; she adds a self-reflective articulation of the power of women's written expression:

> I intend this book as faithful repository of my inmost thoughts, my hopes, my sorrows, my joys. I have ever found relief from sorrow by recording my grief, and in joy have reaped a double harvest—I find in writing, my thoughts assume a tangebility, that I can never arrive at by mere thinking. My heart is now young full of hope, life, and

animation. Reasoning from the regular course of nature, I may have many years yet to live, and as it is insurance to prepare for the wintry season, not only of the year, but of Human Nature, I think it may perhaps afford me some pleasure in those dark hours, when perhaps every earthly tie may be rendered, to read over the thoughts, the feelings of my youth "when life seemed formed of sunny hours. . . ." This book may yet bring me sorrow, for it shall certainly hold my most secret thoughts of everything. Yet I hardly suppose any one will have curiosity sufficient, to prompt them to search into its pages. Yet if anyone should ever read this I hope they will be benefited by my trials and experiences, and that I will not be judged too harshly, if occasionally I err slightly in both precept, and example. (Neblett 1852)

This understanding of the relationship between privacy and the possibility of public perusal is enhanced by Neblett's own sensitivity to the act of writing itself. For she sees in writing a powerful tool for self-examination as well as a benefit to future readers. The recognition of the power of words has rarely been so directly stated. As Cinthia Gannet suggests, such women diarists

> have found ways to inscribe themselves, to make their own modest, but unique and lasting imprint, on texts. They have created texts out of their lives and new lives out of their texts. Texts are marks on the world; they are physical objects, and journals and diaries, while silent, are visible, potentially permanent markers of a life lived, even if just for the diarist herself. (1992, 136)

Examples such as these should make it abundantly clear that to view letter writing as an interactive and diary writing as a solitary endeavor is far too simplistic; diaries, like letters, often were addressed to specific audiences (or to the more general "future reader") and were carefully created with those audiences in mind. Recent scholarship on diaries and their writers suggests that the diary form itself is particularly appropriate for women. Lorna Martens, a critic of the "diary novel," writes that "[a] diary can be written in snatches and with little concentration; it is adaptable to the housewife's interrupted day" (1985, 182). And Suzanne Juhasz reminds us that

> In their form, women's lives tend to be like the stories that they tell: they show less a pattern of linear development towards some clear goal than one of repetitive, cumulative, cyclical structure. One thinks of housework or childcare, of domestic life in general. Dailiness matters to most women; and dailiness is, by definition, never a conclusion, always a process.
>
> The classic verbal articulation of dailiness is, of course, the diary. In form the diary moves in independent units of experience in

an extended present tense. . . . The perspective of the diarist is
immersion, not distance. The diary is finished when the pages run
out, not when some denouement and conclusion are reached.
(Juhasz 1980, 223–24)

For women on the western frontiers, the form of the diary was one that
allowed self-expression within the stringent time constraints imposed by life
in nineteenth-century Texas or Utah or Arizona. For many women the specific forms taken by their journals reflect the exigencies of their lives. While
Susan Newcomb's prose is rich in description and philosophical musing,
other journals are stark, listing only the most significant events in the lives
of women too busy or tired or both to pen more than a few words at odd
intervals. Diaries reflect a whole range of exposure to modes of writing—
from those written by women well-versed in literary techniques, to those by
readers of *Godey's Lady's Book* and other popular periodicals of the day, to
those of other women whose reading experiences consisted primarily of the
Bible and an occasional letter from home. It is this adaptability of the genre
itself that makes it so appropriate for nineteenth-century western women.
Moreover, this adaptable genre by its very existence provided a connection
with other women diary writers. As Gannet also points out, "keeping a journal as part of the social—or domestic—discourse network seems a central
and unique aspect of women's journal traditions" (1992, 133).

Reminiscences differ considerably from diaries and letters, since they
provide the writer with the perspective of time. Written some years after the
immediate frontier experience, these works are often based on diaries, letters, or both. The intervening time allows the writer to shape the narrative
more carefully, to include the most salient features of the frontier experience,
and to edit out any comments or incidents the writer has decided are better
left unsaid. For example, Mary Maverick's 1881 reminiscences, based closely
on her 1850 diary, leave out this sentence from 27 September 1850: "Susan
came and spent the night with me we slept together and held most loving
communion" (Maverick 1850). Although women spending the night with
each other was certainly a common custom, especially before marriage,
apparently this particular entry concerning her friend Susan Hays was left
out rather than have it be misinterpreted by later readers.

Sharon Kaufman has also suggested that reminiscences are often structured in terms of recurring themes that are relevant to the way individuals
envision their lives as meaningful. She writes,

> In the description of their lives, people create themes—cognitive
> areas of meaning with symbolic force—which explain, unify, and give
> substance to their perceptions of who they are and how they see
> themselves participating in social life. As each life is unique, so too

are the themes. But all themes have their sources in the historical, geographical, and social circumstances in which people live, the flow of ordinary daily life, the values of American society, and cultural expectations of how a life should be lived. (Kaufman 1986, 185)

This suggests another way in which the author of a reminiscence may draw on the perspective of time—to re-order significant events and the very evaluation of those events. Similar themes may emerge from diaries or a collection of letters, but they may be more deeply embedded and frequently less self-conscious.

Stylistically, reminiscences are frequently more sophisticated than either journals or letters, since the writer has had more time to fashion the narrative. Those reminiscences that are based closely on diaries include more detailed description, tend to be less romantic, and give a truer picture of nineteenth-century life as it was *lived*; those based solely on recollections are more likely to gloss over details, be more romantic, and provide the reader with a picture of life as it was *remembered*.

Each of these genres of women's writing provides different possibilities for powerful self-expression. While reminiscences are often written by women in the leisure of later years, reflecting on the most important moments of their lives, diaries and letters reveal in the immediacy of the experiences the true contours of what life was like for women, how they dealt with everyday problems, and how they celebrated significant occasions. Within the wide range of individual expressive acts that constitute the basis of this analysis, what becomes increasingly clear is that an understanding of the importance of women's friendships as presented in each of these genres is long overdue. Although women in the West differed considerably from their sisters back East in the kinds of roles they adopted within the family, the kinds of work they engaged in, and the kinds of relationships they had with their male counterparts, these women steadfastly re-created on the western frontier a pattern of intense female friendship that, at its deepest core, was little different from that of women in other parts of America.

Whether women found themselves together in a Mormon community where feminine friendship flourished or alone in Texas, miles from the nearest other woman, these pioneers creatively managed to sustain themselves through the words and works of their friends. Here, I have discussed primarily the everyday activities of women as they gathered together with other women to share the joys and the sorrows of their lives. Such activities organize themselves structurally around work, religion, sickness, health, and a somewhat more nebulous category we might call sociability.[3] It is also important to examine the entire spectrum of interactions among women, ranging from these day-to-day occurrences to the special celebrations of personal rites of passage and annual community-wide festivities. One thing is

clear in all of this: whether we look at one woman reading a letter from a
dear friend or two women huddled over a washtub doing the week's wash or
a group of five or six women with fingers flying over a half-done quilt or an
entire community of women celebrating the birthday of the eldest, in each
case we find a kind of mutual sustenance, a celebration of the ability of
women, through friendship, not only to endure, but to rejoice in the circumstances of their lives because they are lives lived together.

Notes

Part of the research on which this article is based was conducted with assistance
from the University of Utah Research Fund. The article was written during sabbat-
ical leave from the University of Utah.

1. This entry is an interesting example of a mix of diary entry and reminiscence, where
    the events of a particular day call up past memories which are also recorded.
2. Manuals such as Samuel Richardson's *Familiar Letters on Important Occasions*
    ([1781] 1928) and others which followed were popular in America throughout this
    period. Mary Austin Holley's *Texas: Observations, Historical, Geographical and
    Descriptive, in a Series of Letters, Written during a Visit to Austin's Colony, with a
    View to a Permanent Settlement in That Country, in the Autumn of 1831* (1833) was
    especially influential for Texas women writers.
3. The examples I have offered here have been drawn primarily from the writings of
    middle-class Anglo women, but both social class and ethnicity add important
    dimensions to a study of this kind, and future research should broaden the base of
    our understanding of female friendship among women of other classes and ethnici-
    ties as well.

The Concept of the West and Other Hindrances to the Study of Mormon Folklore

William A. Wilson

Although the story of Mormon folklore is considered by many scholars to be inextricably connected with the story of the American West, to read either of these stories as an inevitable part of the other is to read both of them wrong. But associating Mormons with the West is only one of the hindrances to the proper interpretation of Mormon folklore. Over the years such interpretation has been impaired by two separate emphases in folklore and historical studies—first, by a lingering adherence to Robert Redfield's notions of the little (or folk) tradition versus the great (or urban) tradition and, second, by the persistence of the environmental-determinism theories of Frederick Jackson Turner and, especially, of Walter Prescott Webb. Both of these approaches have stopped us from adequately examining what is most important not only in the study of Mormon folklore but in the study of religious folklore in general—that is, the nature of religion itself.

Beginning in the 1930s, Redfield attempted to draw distinctions between what he called "folk" and "urban" societies by viewing folk societies as unsophisticated, homogenous, conservative, agrarian (or rural) enclaves isolated from a surrounding sophisticated, heterogeneous, dynamic, city environment (1930; 1941; 1947; 1955). It would be a mistake to tie Redfield to the nineteenth-century advocates of unilinear cultural evolution. Still, they shared points in common—especially their situating folklore among the rural and unlettered common folk isolated by these circumstances from the more progressive and educated urban world.

These ideas have strongly influenced students of religious folklore in America, particularly those who have focused on what William Clements has called "the folk church." The folk church, says Clements, "constitutes the basic unit in American folk religion" (1983, 139; 1974; 1978). Drawing in part on Don Yoder's well-known distinction between official and unofficial religion (1974), a distinction bearing strong Redfieldian imprints, Clements argues that the folk church is characterized by an "orientation toward the past, scriptural literalism, consciousness of Providence, emphasis on evangelism, informality, emotionalism, moral rigorism, sectarianism, egalitarianism, and relative isolation of physical facilities." More important for our purposes, the folk church, like a Redfieldian or especially a nineteenth-century folk community, exists "outside the main currents of American culture," "often in direct antithesis to the establishment churches" and "mainline religion" and flourishes along this more sophisticated society's "social, economic, political, and even physical margins" among "peripheral social groups," "low-income economic groups," "politically disenfranchised groups," and "people on the wilderness frontier" (Clements 1983, 139).

Others have employed the same distinction between folk and mainline churches. In *Powerhouse for God* (1988), for example, Jeff Todd Titon, citing both Yoder and Clements, defines folk religion "as religion outside of the 'official' or established or normative religion." "So long," he continues, "as the definition of the folk church turns on the 'folk' as a group outside the power structure . . . I am certainly happy with that folk-cultural definition. . . . 'Outside the power structure' is admittedly vague, but it suggests differences in wealth, status, education, and most of all economic and political impact among insiders and outsiders" (1988, 144, 149). In their excellent *Diversities of Gifts: Field Studies in Southern Religion* (1988), Ruel W. Tyson, James L. Peacock, and Daniel W. Patterson bring together a group of essays focusing on what they call "independent Protestants," groups very much like Clements's folk churches. The essays, they tell us in their preface and epilogue, are "studies of Southern religious life, but not of the highly organized and self-publicizing denominations like the Southern Baptists, Episcopalians, Presbyterians, or United Methodists." They are instead groups that "have no national bureaucracies and do not house their faiths in uptown churches" and that "choose not to conform to mainstream models." These churches tend not to attract the wealthy and have no "large-scale hierarchical or associational organization." Members of these churches, who "favor preaching inspired by God directly" and are "suspicious of education in seminaries . . . tend to locate on country roads, mountain ridges, or side streets rather than on the main street or in wealthy suburbs" (1988, xi, xiii, 205).

In *God's Peculiar People: Women's Voices and Folk Tradition in a Pentecostal Church* (1988a), Elaine Lawless eschews some of the above distinguishing features of folk religion but still adheres to what is central in Clements and in Tyson, Peacock, and Patterson—that is, to independent religious enclaves, Redfield's little communities, characterized by the absence of an established hierarchy and of fixed theological and liturgical forms. "Folk religion," Lawless insists, "must be recognized as a traditional

religion that thrives in individual, independent religious groups that owe little allegiance to hierarchical [read 'mainline'] powers" (1988a, 5).

In spite of a certain irreverence that may have crept into what I have
just said, I do not object to the studies I have referred to. These are
admirable treatments of southern fundamentalist and Pentecostal groups.
But I do object to the part being made the standard for the whole—to the
model applied to these investigations of small-scale southern religious
groups becoming the pattern for other studies of American religious folklore.

The main problem with this approach is that it excludes from serious
study the vibrant traditions of those uptown churches. For example, in 1984
Lawless wrote:

> The Mormon religion could never be considered a "folk reli-
> gion"; its standardized, hierarchical make-up prevents the emer-
> gence of the more performative modes and variation typical of folk
> religions. And Mormonism is not a sub-religion or sect, a fringe ele-
> ment of any main-line American denomination; there is no element
> here of little society to larger society of which Robert Redfield
> speaks. (1984, 79)

What do we do, then, with the religious folklore of Mormons, Catholics,
Episcopalians, and other established religions, religions that are not little societies? Clements urges the study of "parallels" to folk religious traits "among
mainline religious groups" (1983, 139). Others follow suit. For example, in the
syllabus of his course in Folklore and Religion given at Utah State University
in 1988, Steve Siporin stated: "We will explore folk religions and parts of
'major' religions that owe their continuity and dynamism more to the practices
and beliefs of their members than to the writings of institutional leaders"—
that is, Siporin's students would study only those parts of official religions that
approximated folk religions. In the syllabus to her course in Folk Religion
given the same year at the University of Missouri, Lawless was unequivocal:
"This course will focus on various religions that have been identified by folklorists as 'folk religions,' that is religions that owe very little, if any, allegiance
to an official, hierarchical governing body. . . . We will also be identifying 'folk'
practices which survive in mainstream, official religions." Lawless then promised to study Mormons for their "'folk' religious qualities."

In recent years, some progress has been made in looking at religious traditions from a broader perspective than that of folk religion. In *Handmaidens
of the Lord: Pentecostal Women Preachers and Traditional Religion* (1988b),
Lawless still referred to folk religion and still cited Redfield, but subsequent
books (1993; 1996) show no evidence of the term or the Redfield citations.
Lawless still teaches a course in folk religion and introduces the course with
readings from Yoder and Clements. To her credit, though, she asks students

in a midterm examination to "develop an argument that outlines the pitfalls of attempting to define a 'folk religion' or a 'folk church.'" The question suggests that she and her students are taking a critical, questioning approach to these concepts. In another course, Religious Expression and Folk Belief, Lawless moves away from folk religions per se and explores phenomena occurring cross-culturally, such as the nature of verbal art, performance, and ritual and belief. Siporin, in his current Folklore and Religion class, still states that he and his students will "explore precisely those dimensions of religion that lie outside organized, formal religious systems." But his selection of course texts like Mircea Eliade's *The Sacred and the Profane: The Nature of Religion* (1959) and Victor Turner's *The Ritual Process: Structure and Anti-Structure* (1969) suggests that this class will also examine religious phenomena cross-culturally. To the extent that other folklore courses across the country follow these models, these are encouraging approaches. But they do not go far enough. There is nothing wrong, of course, in studying independent Protestants, folk religions, or folk churches. But we must not look at all religious traditions in formal vs. informal or institutional vs. noninstitutional terms. We must understand that the formal, hierarchical religious institution may itself be the source of much folklore.

In 1982, Jack Santino, in an intriguing essay entitled "Catholic Folklore and Folk Catholicism," recommended an approach that could, if adopted, produce rich results in the study of organized or mainline religions. In addition to studying "folk Catholicism" (the lore of enclaved groups), Santino argued, researchers should focus on the lore in Catholic communities that results from the circumstance of being Catholic. "I am more interested," he wrote, "in seeing [the St. Francis phenomenon] as an aspect of a larger phenomenon, that of Catholicism, which is itself a cultural force." He continued:

> In addition to popular culture and folk Catholicism, there is another aspect to this corpus of material: the shared, expressive, traditional culture of mainstream American Catholics, members not of Redfield's little, or folk, society, but his great society, people who, although they may be members of an urban ethnic group, share with other Catholics of different backgrounds, not their ethnicity, and more than simply the name of their religion. They also share tales of parochial school education, of nuns and priest, beliefs, legends, and cosmology, perhaps even sharing world views and behaviors which are the result of processes informed by all of the above. . . .
>   . . . perhaps we are better served by the study of Catholic material in ethnic, regional, urban, and familial studies of folklore. It is my experience, however, that Catholics share a body of lore that transcends those categories, that is recognizably based in the experiences

of Catholicism in American and can be most profitably approached as the expression of that experience. (1982, 97, 100)

Reading these lines, one thinks of the lore of Mormon missionaries. They serve in different regions throughout the world and in each region develop a body of lore peculiar to that location, but by the circumstance of being Mormon missionaries and of participating in common experiences, they have developed a body of lore that shapes their identity and binds them together, no matter in which part of the globe they might have served (Wilson 1981).

Santino laments that the kind of lore to which he would direct our attention "has been neither delineated nor studied by folklorists" (1982, 99). I share his lament. We need to move from the narrow concept of *folk religion* to the broader concept of *religious folklore*—that is, to folklore that comes into being simply by virtue of individuals being religious, no matter where they are found. We do not, or should not, talk about folk occupations or folk regions. Rather, we focus on occupational or regional folklore— folklore arising from the circumstance of working at different occupations or of residing in different places. In like manner, we should shift our attention in religious studies to the lore that arises, not just from enclaved groups, but from the circumstances of practicing religion.

In American folklore study in general, we have been able to move from agrarian to urban worlds without neglecting the former, from peripheral to mainline society, discovering in the process that folklore does not just survive in the city but that the city itself generates folklore. It is time to make such a move in religious folklore studies, to see the institutional church, like the city, as a generator of folklore, to recognize what we know to be true in other areas of folklore research—that is, that folklore is common to the species, not just to those living on the margins of modern society. In spite of their churches' hierarchical structures and mainline status, Baptists, Episcopalians, Presbyterians, Methodists, Catholics, and Mormons have generated religious traditions as profoundly significant as those found among independent Protestants. If we can do nothing more than reduce the lore of these established churches to parts of the larger official religion or identify in their lore folk religious elements or parallels to so-called folk religions, then we will have taken a giant step backwards in our attempt to understand the religious behavior of our fellow beings.

In the case of Mormons, the problem of proper interpretation is made more acute by the fact that Mormons are seen not only as a religious group, but also as a regional group. Thus, the Redfieldian notion of the isolated enclave separated from mainline culture once again hinders understanding, this time, paradoxically, because Mormons are seen as belonging to the periphery.

Though Mormon folklorists had been writing about their religious culture for some years, Mormon folklore was brought to the attention of a larger American and international audience by Richard M. Dorson, who in 1959
published his popular *American Folklore* and included "Utah Mormons" in
his chapter on "Regional Folk Cultures," arguing that they were one of the
five richest regional folk cultures in America (1959, 113–21). Identifying these
regional enclaves as "minority cultures," he stated:

> Such nooks and byways resist the relentless forces of change
> and mobility in contemporary American life. In place of mass cul-
> ture, they represent folk cultures, whose roots and traditions contrast
> oddly with the standardized glitter of American urban industrial
> society. In the folk region, people are wedded to the land, and the
> land holds memories. . . . These folk regions become important reser-
> voirs of traditional lore. Much of their folklore will be common to
> other parts of the country and to other countries, but they stand out
> in the density and abundance of their oral tradition. (1959, 75)

In 1964, in *Buying the Wind: Regional Folklore in the United States*,
Dorson reinforced this notion by including Utah Mormons among the major
groups surveyed (497–535). Dorson's view is not quite survivalist, though it
comes perilously close. It defines regional, and therefore Mormon, culture as
agrarian and conservative, in contrast to a dynamic urban society. As a
means of understanding contemporary Mormons the statement is entirely
misleading since the overwhelming majority of Mormons today live in cities.

If Dorson fell short of the mark in characterizing Mormons, John
Greenway missed it completely. In 1964, the same year Dorson published
Buying the Wind, Greenway, then editor of the *Journal of American Folklore*,
added another element to the definition of this regional group—evolutionary
backwardness—and thus harked back not to Redfield, but to Redfield's nineteenth-century predecessors. "Folk to me," he said, "means a phase in the
evolution of culture from primitiveness to civilization, and a folk society is a
homogeneous unsophisticated group living in but isolated from a surrounding sophisticated society by such factors as topography, economics, race, and,
as in the case of the Mormons, religion" (1964, 196). Five years later, in 1969,
Greenway began his *Folklore of the Great West* with a lead essay on the
Mormons, in a section he called "The Good Old Days." In the introduction to
the book, Greenway defined not just Mormons but other western groups as
culturally backward islands, "separated enclaves" surrounded by progressive
mainline American culture. "Since advance lies with numbers in the evolution of culture," he argued, "such dissident groups are condemned to fall
backward, the faster for their coherence"(1969, 3).

Thus in the eyes of at least some leading folklorists, both Mormons
and other western groups have been viewed as somewhat romantic peasant

communities that fit nineteenth-century concepts of folklore. And to a certain degree that idea persists. For example, in 1988 Hector Lee, speaking of the Mormon and western studies of Austin Fife, wrote:

> Because this is a region of spectacular scenic beauty that appeals to tourists, and a milieu that fosters highly advanced educational systems in a modern environment impressively replete with the latest electronic sophistication, it is easy to overlook the fact that there has always been and still is a solid bedrock and thick underlying vein of traditional lore here, which gives a special character to the social structure of the area. (1988, xvi).

That Lee felt constrained to explain that even in an educated, modern, urban society folklore could actually exist suggests that we still have some way to go in our understanding of the nature of folklore in general and of Mormon folklore in particular.

Other sources in historical/cultural studies have also contributed to misleading interpretations of Mormon folklore. In 1893 Frederick Jackson Turner published his famous essay "The Significance of the Frontier in American History." In opposition to the older view that social institutions evolve like germ cells, without reference to environment, he claimed in this and subsequent essays that environment has significantly shaped the course of cultural development. The most important feature of the American environment, he argued, was the presence of an area of free land on the western edge of a constantly advancing frontier. As settlers poured into this free land west of the frontier, they were changed into the ruggedly independent, self-reliant, freedom-loving characters we have liked to call American (Turner 1920).

It would be tempting to see the Mormon migration to the Great Basin in these terms. Consider the following story collected in 1924 from an old pioneer woman whose family had pushed and pulled their meager possessions across the plains in a handcart because they could not afford a team and wagon:

> We were six in family when we started—father, my stepmother, two brothers, a sister sixteen years of age and myself. It seems strange that there were more men and boys died than there were women and girls. My two brothers died on the way, and my father died the day after we arrived in Salt Lake. The night my oldest brother died there were nineteen deaths in camp. In the morning we would find their starved and frozen bodies right beside us, not knowing when they died until daylight revealed the ghastly sight. I remember two women that died sitting by me. My mother was cooking some cakes of bread for one of them. When mother gave her one of them she tossed it into the fire and dropped over dead. I remember distinctly when the

terrible storm came, and how dismayed the people were. My step-mother took my little brother and myself by the hand and helped us along the best she could while sister and father floundered along with the handcart. How we did struggle through that snow, tumbling over sage brush and crying with cold and hunger.

When we camped they had to scrape a place to camp on, and not much wood to make a fire with. The food rations became scarce—there were four ounces daily for an adult and two for a child, and sometimes a little piece of meat. Oh! I'll never forget it, never!

When we arrived in Salt Lake we were taken to the assembly room and the people were asked to take as many of us into their homes as they could take care of. My father and mother were taken to one place and my sister and I each to another. I did not see my father again—he died the next day. . . . I did not stand on my feet until the sixth of March. I lost the first joints of six of my toes. My step-mother then crried me twelve blocks to [a] man's home who had been a friend of father's. Mother would carry me as far as she could, then she would put me down in the snow. Then we would cry a little while and go on again. (Ricks 1924)

It would be easy to see this story as an excellent example of the American character forged by the frontier experience—the resolve to keep struggling forward in the face of desperate odds, to stop and cry for a while but then to get up and go on again, to rub one's bruises after being thrown from a spirited horse but then to get on and ride again, to mourn the loss of the Challenger astronauts but then to put another shuttle into space. And maybe it is. Mormons themselves, who are as susceptible to nationalistic propaganda as anyone, may see the story in that light today.

But for most of them it will carry other messages. It will remind them that their ancestors were on the plains suffering terribly not to fulfill some grand dream of American manifest destiny but because they had been denied their constitutional rights to worship as they pleased, because their prophet Joseph Smith had been murdered, because the Governor of Missouri had issued an order calling for the extermination of all Mormons in the state, and because they had been driven from their homes in Illinois to begin an exodus that would stretch over several decades. Hardly the stuff of patriots' dreams. What's more, the Mormon westward migration and settling of the Great Basin, far from being an exercise in rugged individualism, was one of the most successful communal and communitarian movements since Moses led the children of Israel to the Promised Land.

Turner argued that it was not a specific place but a constantly moving frontier that had shaped American character. In 1931, in *The Great Plains*,

Walter Prescott Webb modified this view by claiming that geography itself (that is, place) was an important determiner of culture. The great plains, said Webb, had three primary characteristics—they were flat, treeless, and arid. Any land west of the Mississippi possessing at least two of these features would significantly determine the life lived there. The Great Plains environment, he said, "constitutes a geographic unity whose influences have been so powerful as to put a characteristic mark upon everything that survives within its borders." And again, "The historical truth that becomes apparent in the end is that the Great Plains have bent and molded Anglo-American life, have destroyed traditions, and have influenced institutions in a most singular manner" (1931, vi, 8). In a similar vein, Richard Dorson, who fixed Mormons in Utah, was to add in *American Folklore*: "Each regional complex contains its own genius . . . depending upon the historical and ethnic and geographical elements that have shaped its character" (1959, 75).

In 1942, eleven years after the appearance of *The Great Plains*, western novelist Wallace Stegner published his influential *Mormon Country*; the same year historian Nels Anderson published *Desert Saints: The Mormon Frontier in Utah*. Both books identified Mormonism not just as a religion but as a place, a western place. Other histories followed, such as Gustive O. Larson's *Prelude to the Kingdom: Mormon Desert Conquest*, in 1947, and Leonard J. Arrington's monumentally important *Great Basin Kingdom: An Economic History of the Latter-day Saints, 1830–1900*, in 1958—not the Mormon Kingdom, nor the Kingdom of God, but the Great Basin Kingdom, a western geographical kingdom.

This notion of geographic determinism sounds clearly in the titles of Austin and Alta Fife's *Saints of Sage and Saddle: Folklore among the Mormons* (1956), and Thomas E. Cheney's *Mormon Songs from the Rocky Mountains* (1968). Fife especially saw himself as a regional folklorist, his Mormon studies being only part of a larger effort to understand the West. The title of Hector Lee's *The Three Nephites: The Substance and Significance of the Legend in Folklore* (1949) is less revealing, but Lee, a friend of Stegner's, clearly saw the legends as part of the pioneer West, useful, he said, as a means of understanding "pioneer concepts, attitudes, and impulses" (1949, 126). And he frequently used Stegner's term, Mormon Country (1949, 9; 1988, 15).

Though all these works at times rise above their titles and tell us things about Mormons having little to do with the West, the public perception of Mormons places them squarely in the center of the West. This is clear from the dust jacket and cover illustrations on the two editions of the Fifes' *Saints of Sage and Saddle*. The 1956 edition, published by Indiana University, shows a bearded westerner—a rifle in one hand, a tablet with mysterious inscriptions in the other—and a rural village in the background. The University of Utah's reprinting of the book in 1980 shows a ragged family trailing a wagon train across a barren western landscape.

Without question, this landscape does play a part in contemporary Mormon lore. For example, Three Nephite stories in which one of the eternal wanderers introduced to us by the Book of Mormon comes to the aid of a family whose car has broken down miles from anywhere are understandable only if one appreciates western distances. But the main function of the landscape is to provide a resonant background. The principal focus is elsewhere, on a God who will intervene to save the lives of the faithful. Consider still one more story:

> A dear L.D.S. [Mormon] lady left her small family in Phoenix to go to the temple in Mesa. While she was in the middle of a session, she got a strong feeling that she should go home—that something was terribly wrong. The feeling wouldn't go away, so she told the temple president and asked him what she should do. He said, "Have no fear. You are doing the right thing by being here. All is well at home." So she continued the session. She hurried home when she was through and found her six-year-old daughter in bed. She asked her daughter if something was wrong. She told her mother that she had left the house while the babysitter was busy with the other children and had gone out by the canal near their house. While she was playing, she slipped on some grass and fell in. She couldn't swim, and the canal is deep. Many people drown this way. But a lady all dressed in white came along just then and got her just before she would have drowned. The lady set her on the bank and made sure she was okay. The little girl asked the lady who she was because she knew that the lady didn't live near by. So, the lady told her what her name was. The lady who saved the little girl was the lady whom the mother had done work for in the temple that day. (Wright 1975)

Barre Toelken, who studies water lore and symbolism in western and Mormon lore, is interested in this story because the themes of water and irrigation make their way into sacred narrative (1991). He is right, of course, but to really comprehend this story one must probe the depths of deeply held Mormon beliefs, beliefs I haven't space to detail fully here. Briefly, Mormons believe that saving gospel ordinances must be performed in the flesh. Since their deceased ancestors have not had this opportunity, Mormons seek out the names of these ancestors through genealogical research and then vicariously perform these ordinances for them in sacred ceremonies in their temples. The session mentioned in the story would be an occasion for performing these ordinances.

To believing Mormons, this story speaks many messages. It encourages them to persist in the search for their ancestral roots; it testifies to the validity of temple ordinances; it suggests that God is a caring God who will protect them in time of need; it stresses the importance of the family and strengthens family ties; it gives them hope that these ties will continue beyond this life. In one narrative situation after another, these messages are brought forcefully home by an artistic performance of the story designed to move listeners to action and are made all the more powerful by the narrative symmetry in which two lives are saved at the same moment—the physical life of the young girl and the eternal life of the rescuer, the mother serving as the link between the two. Surely, no one would argue that the performance of the story is any less powerful because it occurs in a church with a fixed theology and an established hierarchical structure. And one would hope that no one would demean those who tell the story by referring to it as a folk religious element surviving in an established church.

The story has little to do with the West and even less to do with untenable notions of cultural evolution or of isolated cultural enclaves. Anyone who would understand the West must, of course, pay heed to the Mormon role in settling and developing that important part of our country. But the emphasis should probably be more on the impact of the Mormons on the West than of the West on the Mormons. Especially is that true today when most Mormons do not live in the West. Of today's ten million Mormons only ten percent live in Utah, and over half of all Mormons live outside the United States and Canada (Hart 1997). Therefore, any attempt to describe the contemporary Mormon ethos as a result of western landscape will be doomed to failure.

If we are ever to understand Mormons by examining their folklore, we must turn our eyes from the past to the present, from the rural landscape to urban centers, and from the West in general to the faith and commitment that give unity and direction to Mormon life. And we must finally discover behind Mormon folklore typical human beings coming to terms through their lore with enduring life and death questions that know neither temporal nor cultural boundaries.

As folklorists, our aim should be to discover what it means to be human; as folklorists interested in religious behavior, our aim should be to discover what it means to be human and religious. Lawless argues that in our attempts to understand religious folklore we should begin with what is traditional within a particular religion (1988a, 4). I would argue that while we may end with what is traditional, with those expressive religious behaviors we call folklore, we must not start there. We must begin with the religious individual, with *homo religiosus*. Until we work our way back through the cultural overlays of the physical environment, until we discover the generative force that lies behind both highly structured liturgical ritual on the one hand and spontaneous witnessing of the spirit on the other, until we get back to religious individuals in both uptown churches and on mountain ridges, until we comprehend their need for security, their quest for meaning, their desire for the continuance of what they cherish most, until we get there, all our efforts, to quote an old book, may be little more than sounding brass or tinkling cymbals.

And when we get there, when we have worked our way through folk churches, through established churches, through the intricate relationships between canonized dogma and resulting folk expression, through Pentecostal brothers and sisters, through saints of sage and saddle, we will discover at last, standing alone, that splendid and worthy object of our study—*homo religiosus.*

The Coquelle Indians and the Cultural "Black Hole" of the Southern Oregon Coast

George B. Wasson

From my childhood on, I have heard people remark, "Indians never forget. They're always bringing up things from the past." Growing up with one foot in Anglo culture and the other in Southern Oregon coastal Indian culture, I used to wonder about that and felt a little anxious because it seemed to be true. Yet at the same time I knew that the past should not be forgotten but should be carefully told over and over again. Sometimes—as in the telling of stories about Talapus (Old Man Coyote) and about his power (*tamanawis*) that could be used to make his escapades work for good or ill— it seemed that the old people were still living in the olden days and couldn't tell the difference. At other times I'd hear stories or remarks about present-day happenings that brought in the past and wrapped past and present up together. It has taken me decades of experience and reflection to begin to understand that for traditionally minded Indians the past doesn't go away but is present and makes us who and what we are now.

The seeds for my understanding this were planted one day in about 1947 when I was visiting my Aunt Daisy at Empire. She was having some kind of disagreement with people down on South Slough and she was raving about their eternal stupidity or something like that. I made the mistake—as I reflect on it now, a fortunate mistake—of asking her what she meant. Aunt Daisy exclaimed something like, "They don't even know how to cook beans or make coffee. They just boil the coffee beans and pour off the water, then they throw flour on each other's faces and yell, 'Look, now we're white men.'" I asked who, and what flour, and she snapped impatiently about "those soldiers out there" giving the flour to them. I hadn't known about any soldiers down at Charleston, but I knew that World War II had ended not too long before and I wondered whether some of them had stayed hidden down there. I was startled, puzzled, yet I knew when not to ask Aunt Daisy more questions.

Twenty-five years later I read about the Jedediah Smith expedition that came up the Oregon Coast in 1828. My great-grandfather, Kitzn-Jin-Jn-Galada-Lui, head man of the Miluks, of lower Coos Bay, took a delegation of three hundred men to greet the Smith party when they arrived at Cape Arago and lead them to a campsite on South Slough. He prepared a lavish feast for them, provisioned them with fresh meat, and helped them negotiate local estuaries as they left, heading north (George B. Wasson, Sr., unpublished papers in author's possession). It may well have been the Smith party that introduced the Miluks to dried beans and how to cook them—a gift of gratitude in exchange for hospitality. Then in 1851, the military ship *Captain Lincoln* foundered on the North Spit. The South Slough residents helped the soldiers salvage their stores and were rewarded with coffee beans and flour. So, knowing how to boil beans to get them tender enough to eat, they put the coffee beans into pots of water and put in hot stones to cook them. Dark foul water resulted, which they carefully poured off, starting over again. Someone opened a sack of the flour, totally strange to them, and as they saw it turning their hands and arms white, they began covering their faces also, shouting and laughing, "Look, now we're just like white men" (Daisy Wasson Codding, periodic personal communications).

Then it came clear to me. Time had not passed away, leaving the events of the past dim, forgotten. The antics of those South Slough relatives were as vibrant in memory in 1947 as they had been nearly a century before. Aunt Daisy was responding to their foolishness as she had learned it from her mother and grandmother. The present is a compilation of memory of all the events that have ever happened.

For Indians, time is an expansion of experience. Time is spherical. Time is a record of the memory of expenditure of energy. All that has ever happened is memorized and becomes compacted around us just as sound waves emanate from a source and float out all around. Some events are so dynamic in their meaning and effect that they do not dissipate as quickly as other happenings. They might hang nearby as a cloud or fog waiting to be reactivated in the present, where those memories are as current as what's happening right now. If it is worth saying once, it's worth saying over and over: Time is a spherical record of memories of the expenditure of energy. Our past is our present.

Hence, I describe, in the present study, the nineteenth-century events leading to a cultural "black hole" and the devastating effect of this development on today's concerns just as it has been all along for the people of the Southern Oregon coast. For many generations before white contact, the Indian cultures of Oregon's south coast were vigorous and eclectic, yet these cultures were vanquished in a shockingly brief period once continuous contact had become a fact. The devastation was so sudden and so far-reaching that to call the event a holocaust—the Oregon holocaust—is not unreasonable. Mass killings of Indian people and the burning of villages, often with the inhabitants inside their plank houses, swept northward from California in the early 1850s—to Gunther Island, Yontoket, Chetco, Chet-Less-Chun-Dunn, Nasomah, and hundreds more in between.[1]

The genocide left a gaping hole where there had once been cultures. To describe it, I have adopted the concept of the cultural "black hole," under which, as Homer Barnett states, surviving descendants "retained only a few relics of their indigenous culture" (Barnett 1983, 157). Because of the short span between the onset of white contact and the destruction of native cultural, spiritual, and physical integrity, little knowledge has been produced and preserved through scientific research. As observer T. T. Waterman was to sum up the situation in 1931, "A number of ethnologists worked in . . . [the Southern Oregon coast] prior to the writer's advent . . . but relatively little concerning these groups has found its way into print" (Waterman, 6). Because the people and their villages and lifeways were so thoroughly destroyed, only bits and pieces of Indian culture and language have survived.

The Coquilles, or Coquelles—until recently the common spelling was not Coquille but Coquelle (Zenk 1990, 579), pronounced Ko-Kwel' as in tribal use today—are a group from that black hole. (In the present study the spelling "Coquille" is retained in the context of map features and other official names.) I propose to look at the "few relics" of knowledge about the Coquelles in an effort to reconstruct as nearly as possible their lost cultural heritage. My approach will be in part to examine characteristics of neighboring tribes for whom there is fairly adequate information, to draw parallel inferences about the lost information, and in part to draw upon the oral traditions of surviving descendants of the Coquelle black hole, largely my own family.

The antiquity of human occupation in the Coquelle territory has been suggested by archaeological investigations and amateur discoveries at Camas Valley on the Upper Coquille River drainage ranging from 4,500 years before the present (BP) to as much as 11,500 years BP. At the Standley site in Camas Valley, obsidian hydration evidence indicates that occupation may have begun between 4,500 and 5,000 BP. (Additional fragments of clay figurines discovered there date between 1,100 and 400 BP [Connolly 1991, 1]). Archaeological research at the Indian Sands site in Curry County, just south of the Coquelles, has revealed occupation dates as early as 8,200 years BP (Erlandson and Moss 1994). The discovery in Camas Valley of a Clovis-type point made from chert indigenous to that specific area (Wallmann 1994; Erlandson and Moss 1994) dates human occupation of the Upper Coquille territory to as much as 11,500 years BP.

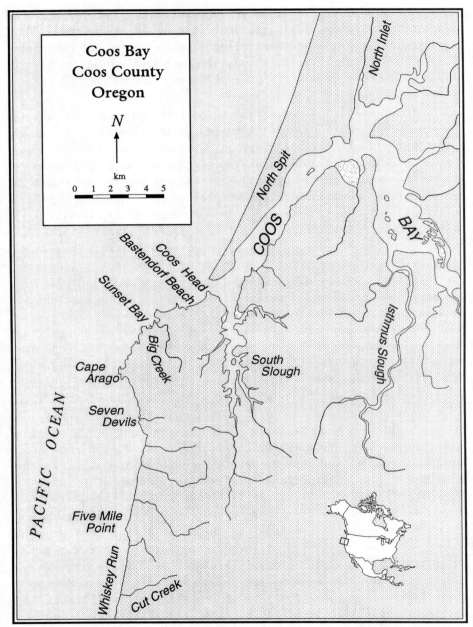

Map by Mark Tveskov

Today's Coquelle Indian tribal members are descended from people who once lived in villages at South Slough and Coos Bay, in villages along the Coquille River, and in coastal villages as far south as the Sixes River (see map). Many are related through intertribal marriage to the Coos, Umpqua, Siuslaw, Tututni, Shasta Costa, Chetco, and Tolowa tribes (though because of a complex series of land claims based upon oral testimony, to be discussed in detail in appendix B, below, the Coquelles and the Coos today are recognized by the federal government as two separate tribes).

Along the coast, the dominant language of the Lower Coquelles (aside from Chinook Jargon, the *lingua franca* of the entire Pacific Northwest) was Miluk, a Kusan (or Coosan) dialect, while that of the inland Upper Coquelles was a dialect of Athabaskan. It is likely that tribal members, whether Lower or Upper Coquelle, also spoke many neighboring languages (Hall 1984, 20; 140–41). Among the Coquelles, for whom village and family life was patrilocal, it was incumbent upon a woman to know or learn the language of her husband's village, to which she moved from her home village. It also seems probable that every young woman had, by the time of her marriage, already learned the several languages her mother spoke. Support for a hypothesis regarding the special multilinguality of women can be noted in the number of multilingual female informants from whom linguists and ethnographers collected language information for the Coos-Coquelle area. My forebears Susan Adulsah Wasson and her mother Gishgiu were each known to have spoken several languages and dialects fluently (George B. Wasson Sr., and Daisy Wasson Codding, periodic personal communications).

Social and political leadership among villages and extended-family bands was acknowledged through group deference to dominant wealthy headmen or to shamans with especially prominent healing powers. (While shamanic medicine was practiced by both men and women, all people sought personal spiritual power through fasting, prayer, and vision quests.) The presence of slavery, not unknown to the Coquelles but less common among them than among the more northerly tribes of the Northwest Coast, along with evidence of wealth accumulation and a form of potlatch suggest that Coquelle culture included elements from farther up the Northwest Coast. On the other hand, Coquelle dance forms, ceremonial clothing, and accouterments of spirituality, including reverence for flicker feathers and redheaded woodpecker scalps, showed relation to their southern neighbors—Tututnis, Chetcos, Tolowas, and Yuroks.

The Coquelle cultural area approximates the drainage of the Coquille River, bounded by Floras Creek on the south, South Slough on the north, and the crest of the Coastal Range on the east, a geography that encompasses all landforms and all soil, plant, and animal types of Western Oregon. There are high prairies and coastal mountain meadows containing lush grasses that once sustained large populations of Roosevelt elk and black-tailed deer.

Valleys were once loaded with roots and bulbs for annual harvests, while the rivers and streams extending to the ocean produced abundant fish, eels, shellfish, and sea mammals. Forests furnished the now-rare Port Orford cedar for canoes and western red cedar for plank houses. The land also yielded the widest variety of basketry materials available anywhere along the West Coast.

Coquelle canoes (carved most desirably from Port Orford white cedar) were basically of "shovel-nose" design, though canoes with special high prows were carved for ocean going (G. B. Wasson, Sr., cited in Harrington 1943). Oral legend tells that one such canoe carried a whole village full of Coquelle people across the Pacific Ocean to escape annihilation by vengeful Chetco-Tolowas. As an indication of the seaworthiness of the Coquelle ocean-going canoe, speakers of Miluk, the dominant Lower Coquelle dialect, have been found living in Japan (Hall 1984, 35). The manufacture of baskets, nets, twine, and other woven materials was among the traditional industries of all Oregon coastal peoples. The Coquelle and their neighbors lived amid abundant resources for those weaving materials. In 1817, trader Peter Corney commented on a friendly encounter with southern coastal people: "They . . . brought some berries, fish, and handsome baskets for sale. These men were tall and well formed, their garment made of dressed deerskins, with a small round hat, in the shape of a basin, that fitted close round the head; none of the women made their appearance" (Beckham 1977, 103). Such hats were reportedly customary for the Coos and Coquelles as well. (It is worth noting that although only men were in the canoes to greet Corney's sailors, his description of the hats they were wearing matches that of the basket hats worn traditionally by Coos, Coquelle, and Yurok women still today.) Though knowledge of gathering, preparation, and weaving has been almost entirely lost due to the cultural annihilation of the black hole, a few weavers in Southern Oregon and Northern California have learned traditional practices from older people, thereby keeping alive those secrets and skills at which Coquelle basketmakers once were counted among the most proficient.

The importance of baskets and other woven materials (twine, rope, mats, and wickerwork) in the cultures of the coastal people is strongly indicated by mention of them in creation myths. Two mythical beings used baskets in creating the world, for example, splitting them open flat and laying them out to protect the newly forming land mass from erosion by ocean waves (Frachtenberg 1913, 5; Jacobs 1940, 239-40). The story implies that basketry, older than humans, comprises the cultural center for coastal tribes. The antiquity of the art is demonstrable in any case. Buried in the mud and silt of the Coquille River, at the Osprey Site near Bullards State Park, archaeologists found openwork woven structures of willow and split cedar, along with numerous fish weir stakes, radiocarbon dated to between 600 and 1,100 years old (Moss and Erlandson 1994). A traditionally woven basket was earlier recovered from the silt just upriver at the Philpott Site, but treatment with linseed oil has rendered it undatable by radiocarbon methods.

Basketry materials such as bear grass and hazel required "burning off" prior to collection and preparation for weaving. Each fall, people would go to the mountains and set fires in the areas where the best grass and sticks were growing. When they returned the following summer, the bear grass would have grown into fresh clumps ready for harvesting. Hazel needed to grow for another season after burning and was harvested the following spring when the sap started flowing again (Thompson [1916] 1991, 331). Burning, a necessary technology for many aspects of tribal life, was applied to control weeds and to produce new shoots for berry production. The Kalapuya seasonally burned the Willamette Valley to enhance the harvest of tarweed seeds *(Lemolo sapolil,* "wild grain" in Chinook Jargon), and by this practice made it a garden-like parkland (Boag 1992). Regular burning not only prevented the growth of brush and cleared out the understory of old-growth forests, it also produced extensive grassy prairies on the ridges and southwestern slopes of the coastal mountains. On these ridges, people dug deep pits, staggered in series along a ridge line; here immense elk herds could be driven and some elk would inevitably fall in. Seasonal burning along the Oregon coast was so regular and noteworthy that the area was known to some sailors as Fire Land. Smoke shrouded the coastal mountains, and fires could be seen burning the entire length of the coast.

Surely there has never existed a more spiritual and ritualized relationship between humans and fish than flourished among the cultural groups of the Northwest Coast and their beloved salmon. So special were salmon to the Coquelles, as to other coastal people, that a highly sacred ceremony was performed upon the arrival of the first salmon. There was an obvious intent to pay honor and tribute to the salmon for returning again to the streams where the people could obtain them for food. A common and primary element of those rituals required that the bones of the honored fish be maintained intact. The flesh was cooked and shared with many people and eaten ritually with great reverence. The whole skeleton was then placed in the water, usually with the head pointed upstream to ensure that the salmon would continue to multiply and return the next season. Salmon fishing was done primarily in the streams, where weirs were constructed to either catch the fish in basket-like traps or contain them in areas where they could be readily speared or dipped out in hand nets.

One of the stories of "Old Man Coyote," collected by John P. Harrington from Coquel Thompson, an Upper Coquelle informant, told of a notable fish dam on the Coquille River and of how the place came to be called *Thet-suh-wuh-let-sluh-dunn* ("place where two large round stones are located on either side of the water"). This place, where there was a riffle, lies on the Upper Coquille River somewhere upstream from the present town of Myrtle Point at a broad stretch of gravel bar. There, in late summer in time for the September salmon run, the Upper Coquelles built a fish weir and a salmon trap, an immense dam of willow stakes driven straight down into the gravel bottom, which spanned the full width of the river. The construction of this dam was a great undertaking and required extensive communal effort to cut, sharpen, and pound the great stakes into place and weave smaller branches between them to form the secure barricade fence. (Such an enormous salmon weir always seemed to be of special importance to all the people along that river. Each coastal stream with a salmon run had reason to have such a structure, and people who were dedicated and accomplished enough to build one that reached from shore to shore had reason to be proud. The larger the dam, the more prestige it bestowed on the builders.)

No one seems to know where Coyote was coming from on the occasion recounted in the following story, or just why, but he was poling his way upstream in his canoe—along with his current wife, the former Mrs. Fishduck—when his progress was halted by the enormous salmon weir. Coyote tried to push his way through, but the structure was too sturdy. True to form, he became angry and vowed to smash through. So he went back down stream and loaded two large round boulders into the bow of his canoe and placed his wife at the stern. Though pushing against the current, Coyote was determined to break through the barricade; but his attempts were too feeble and he failed. At last, in a fit of rage, he poled as fast and hard as he could and broke through. But just as he got to the upstream side, his pole slipped, he lost his balance, and the current threw his canoe back against the weir, flipped it up on end, cata- pulted the boulders out onto either shore, and dumped Coyote and his wife into the water. Using *tamanawis*, the magical powers of his mind, Coyote brought the canoe up from under the swift current and quietly took his wife back down- stream. That's why the place was called *thet* (stones) *suh-wuh-let* (spherical) *sluh-dunn* (on opposite sides of the water-place) (Wasson 1991:86).

Thus was the culture of the south coastal tribes constituted—by inference and analogy and legend—prior to contact with whites. The earliest white visitors found the people of the coast attractive and sociable—"tolerably well limbed" and preferring "cleanliness of body to tattoos." In 1792, Captain George Vancouver, while exploring along the Northwest Coast, anchored his ship somewhere between Cape Blanco and Port Orford. Vancouver's surgeon and botanist, Dr. Archibald Menzies, wrote in his diary about the encounter between the ship's men and the Indians who paddled out to meet them: "[T]hey were of a middling size with mild pleasing features & nowise sullen or distrustful in their behaviour, they were of a copper colour but cleanly, as we observed no vestige of greasy paint or ochre about their faces or among their hair. . . " (Beckham 1977, 102). Twenty-five years later, the fur trader Peter Corney sailed along this same section of the coast. Observing many villages along the shore, he led in close and also met some of the Tututni Indians. He noted: "About noon, several canoes came off within hail of the ship; we waved to them to come closer, which they did, displaying green boughs and bunches of white feathers; they stopped paddling, and one man, whom we took to be the chief, stood up, and made a long speech, which we did not understand. We then waved a white flag, and they immediately pulled for the ship singing all the way. . . ." Corney observed that the Tututni men were "tall and well formed" (Beckham 1977, 102).

Soon enough, white explorers, trappers, and missionaries were streaming to the Pacific Northwest. By the middle of the nineteenth century most of the West Coast was populated with white miners and settlers. Because the rugged Coast Range made the Coquelle-occupied portion of the Oregon coast nearly inaccessible from the east and the rugged coastline did likewise from the west, it was protected from direct white culture contact until the 1850s, long after the rest of the coast had been affected. Even so, the Coquelle were not immune to germ-borne illness brought by whites. Diseases of European origin—gonorrhea, syphilis, measles, and smallpox—had been decimating the native populations along the Northwest coast since the late 1700s. Between 1829 and 1832, "the fevers" swept along the Columbia River, up the Willamette Valley, and on over to the Rogue River Valley and jumped across to the Sacramento Valley, killing up to 90 percent of the village inhabitants in some places (Drucker 1965, 64, 197–98). Archaeological and ethnohistorical findings indicate that the people of the Southern Oregon coast were not spared from these devastations and that an equally high percentage of their populations were wiped out in the same manner at about the same time. An early traveler up the Coquille River reported seeing hundreds of Indians working on fish weirs, while a few years later the same area was described as having only a few workers in those same locations (Chase 1873).

It became inevitable that with the clash of interests and the imbalance of technologies, incoming whites would sooner or later make life difficult for native peoples and would subsequently blame their victims by characterizing them negatively. The writing of Orvil Dodge provides a sample of settlers' attitudes toward the local Indians. In his 1898 book, *Pioneer History of Coos & Curry Counties, Oregon,* Dodge opines,

> No wonder this favoured spot, where food and even luxuries abounded so plentiful, was inhabited with a class of swarthy, indolent Indians who had but little ambition or energy. They were square built and of medium height and those in the northern part of the county, who inhabited Coos bay and its tributaries and the various branches of the Coquille river, were naturally peaceable and friendly to the pioneers, in fact they never became hostile, and it is a fact that is not questioned, that in the early settlement north of Port

Orford there were no massacres so common in the early settlements of the great West, and there were no more tragedies than is common among the Anglo-Saxon or white citizens of this country. (Dodge [1898] 1969)

Setting aside this Anglo-Saxon's inadvertent self-condemnation in the last line quoted, and notwithstanding his characterization of Indians as "indolent," the native people were quite industrious, as indicated by A. W. Chase in his observation (above) of hundreds of Indians working on the fish weirs along the Coquille.

Dodge is moreover silent on a massacre perpetrated by whites against the Coquelles and their neighbors which in one swift move effectively wiped out the native culture of the Central Oregon coast and made way for untrammeled white settlement. Early on the morning of January 28, 1854, the Nasomah village of the Lower Coquille was brutally attacked and destroyed by a mob of forty miners from the nearby diggings at Randolph. Two of the main instigators were named Packwood and Soapy. A week later, an investigative agent named Smith wrote the following report: "A most horrid massacre, or rather an out-and-out barbarous mass murder, was perpetrated upon a portion of the Nasomah Band residing at the mouth of the Coquille River on the morning of January 28th by a party of 40 miners. The reason assigned by the miners, by their own statements, seem trivial. However, on the afternoon preceding the murders, the miners requested the chief to come in for a talk. This he refused to do. . . ." The report goes on to say that a meeting was held and a courier was dispatched to obtain the assistance of twenty more miners from nearby Randolph. Smith further reports,

> At dawn the following day, led by one Abbott, the ferry party and the 20 miners, about 40 in all, formed three detachments, marched upon the Indian ranches and consummated a most inhuman slaughter. . . . The Indians were aroused from sleep to meet their deaths with but a feeble show of resistance; shot down as they were attempting to escape from their houses. Fifteen men and one Squaw were killed, two Squaws badly wounded. On the part of the white men, not even the slightest wound was received. The houses of the Indians, with but one exception, were fired and destroyed. Thus was committed a massacre too inhuman to be readily believed. (Peterson and Powers 1952, 89)

Survivors were herded into temporary concentration camps or dumped onto the reservations of inland tribes, and in less than two years, except for the families of Indian women who were married to white men, the coastal people were gone. The effect on the culture of the Coquelles and their close neighbors was devastating. Yet through the years, bits and pieces of tradition and cultural spirit remained alive among survivors or were placed on record for scientific posterity. A few anthropologists and self-appointed historians recognized the enormity of the obliteration and felt compelled to save or write something of the cultures, however small.

The history taught in Oregon schools is only the official version of Oregon history. There are other truths. For instance, while it is true that the settlers did not have to fight the Kalapuyas, Mollalas, Luckiamutes, or any others to obtain control and possession of the splendid parkland that was the Willamette Valley, those native peoples had already been destroyed by the fevers of 1829–1832, and their villages had become ghost towns whose scattered survivors remained in permanent shock, as though mowed down by a Vietnam War. To the settlers' good fortune, the remaining Indians had been gathered by Jason Lee and his helpers to the Methodist Mission near Salem, "a virtual death camp" (Stephen Dow Beckham, personal communication, 1974), even though the internees were supposedly there as recipients of Christian charity.

It was quite different on the coast in the later 1850s, when the Southern Oregon Indians were herded to a government concentration camp at Yachats. There was no Christian charity here. Yachats was an extermination camp; many interned therein had survived village massacres. Of the more than 2,000 at Yachats, only 260 were covered by the signed treaties of 1855; the rest, from Southwest Oregon (including the Coos and Coquelles), were simply dumped in with them. The provisions supposedly guaranteed by treaty seldom arrived and if they did were too meager to divide among all the starving. In the first decade, fully half died from starvation or from drowning while attempting to obtain mussels for food. These concentration camp facts have never been told in school history books.

With the loss of family and group integrity necessary for appropriate spiritual guidance, many Indians fell victim to moral decay and social chaos. This was especially the plight of younger women, who learned from experience with soldiers and miners how to survive through use of their bodies for sexual purposes. Other examples of social dissolution are recorded. One jealous woman punished a woman from another tribal area who was an "unpurchased wife" of her husband. (According to Miller and Seaburg [1990, 585], "To be respectable a woman had to be purchased in marriage.") The outsider was pounced upon, beaten, and dragged to the fire where her undergarments were ripped off and she was sexually humiliated. In a second, similar incident, the offending woman was chastised with a firebrand. (Jacobs 1939, 116, 117). In a third incident, a young Miluk woman was murdered by a drunken miner. Struggling against his attempts to rape her, she got away and ran down the beach to hide, but he caught up with her and, finding her desperately stuffing sand into her vagina, killed her (Hall 1984, 105).

My own great-grandmother Gishgiu ("Gekka"), as the wife of a local headman, went with the American soldiers in good faith, first to the concentration camp at Reedsport and then on to Yachats, because she believed that the 1851 treaty signed by her husband, Kitzn-Jin-Jn, would eventually be honored (see appendix A, Treaties and Land Claims). However, conditions there continued to be so bad that she lost faith in the word of the American government and ran away. My father and his sisters—Aunt Lolly, Aunt Daisy, and Aunt Mary—often told me, when I was growing up, the story of their grandmother Gekka running away and coming back to South Slough. Diving into the ocean, she swam around the major headlands such as Cape Perpetua and the Sea Lion Caves to evade the soldiers on the trail above. Hiding in brush during the daytime, she walked the long beaches at night, arriving at Coos Bay through the sand dunes. At the turn of high tide, Gishgiu entered the water and swam with the ebb-flow until it carried her across and down to South Slough. There she walked up the slough to near her daughter's home and made herself a comfortable den in a hollow log not far away. At night, Gekka made contact with her daughter, Susan Adulsah, who gave her food. They met secretly that way, until Susan's husband, my grandfather George R. Wasson, became suspicious of his wife talking to someone in her Indian language late at night. He usually thought nothing of her getting up and doing things in the middle of the night, but this became more secretive, and when he discovered that his mother-in-law was living not far away in a hollow cedar log, he insisted that she move into the house with them where she belonged. However, the soldiers from Fort Yamhill had orders to round up runaway Indians, and a detachment was sent out to scour the country where they might be hiding.

One day when grandfather was out in the logging woods with his bull team, word came to the house that two soldiers were headed there to take Gekka back to Yachats. Quickly, the women emptied the storage space behind the living-room staircase and tiny Gishgiu crawled back under the bottom step. Then all the boxes and trunks were shoved into place as though nothing more could possibly be under there. While the soldiers were ransacking the house looking for Gishgiu, some of the younger kids, caught up in the excitement of a game with real soldiers, were running around pointing to the bottom step of the stairs saying "Gekka, Gekka." The soldiers, having no idea what they were hearing, just pushed the kids out of the way as they hurried with their search, pounding the floor with their rifle butts, looking for loose boards under which the old woman could be hidden. One of the older children slipped away and raced through the woods to summon Grandpa for help. They say Grandpa Wasson was a big man, and no two soldiers could stand up to his fury. He marched into his house, grabbed them both by the back of their necks, and threw them out into the yard—or, some say, through the parlor window. He told them to never come back, and they didn't. Gishgiu lived out the remainder of her days with the family, mending clothes, which she could do even though blind by then, doing the things an old grandmother would need to do while sitting in the dark.

In 1853, my grandfather had built the first log cabin at Empire on Coos Bay. By 1856, nearly all of the older Indians had been either killed off or taken away to reservations. My father was born in 1880, the first generation after the coming of the white man. His mother, Susan Adulsah, didn't want to hold him back by hindering him socially with the use of her native languages, so she insisted that he learn English and become educated in the best possible schools. He attended school first at Chemawa. Later he attended the military-style Indian school directed by Captain Richard H. Pratt at Carlisle, Pennsylvania, one of a number of schools founded as part of a massive government program to "kill the Indian and educate the man." Carlisle was free to Indians, so he went there, in 1898, and it changed his life forever. His first choice for a course of study was law, which was acceptable to the school officials. As was the case for students at Carlisle and at all other Indian schools, though, he was also required to learn a trade so he might have a realistic chance at success later on, as it was well understood that Indians could never be successful at professions requiring a college degree. He became a tailor—quite a good one. I am sure he would have liked to practice law, but that was not his destiny. His knowledge of law, though, was beneficial to the Indians back home in Coos Bay. The tailoring never brought much income other than small amounts to cover his meager living expenses. Indians of Western Oregon pledged monthly donations to support his trips to Washington, D.C., but seldom could fulfill their commitments.

My father was destined to spend his adult life as a go-between in the two worlds of Indian and white man, struggling to explain each to the other, never having an opportunity just to be himself in either. That was a common story for many capable and intelligent young Indians just after the turn of the century. The land, hunting and fishing rights, culture, and traditions were all gone with the unratified treaties of 1855. Language was of little use, except for talking with old people or for keeping nosy whites from understanding personal conversations. For most young people, the stigma of being Indians (or "half-breeds") was a major obstacle, and the ability to "talk Indian" was not a quality to show off in public. Moreover, speaking in native languages was a punishable offense in the government schools. Not surprisingly, young Indians all over the country grew up with little or no access to their native languages. Along with loss of language came the loss of cultural and spiritual traditions and tribal identity, as well as anxiety and frustration for young Indians who still knew the major concepts of their ancestral culture—knew how different these were from concepts of the dominant Anglophone culture—and yet were denied self-expression in the home languages so vital to their ancestral heritage.

Some families maintained a steadfast interest and a determined effort to keep ideas and traditions alive, if not in actual practice, then in family memories. So it was in my family. We cared about our history and traditions and never hesitated to let it be known we were Indians. Without our language, though, it was difficult to defend our cultural heritage and pride against the derision of others who mocked Indians in general. Among my siblings, it was my brother Wilfred and I who went on to college and who gathered information on our tribe's culture and history, but there were many times that I realized how limited my knowledge was compared to the vast amount of culture that had been lost to disuse or obliterated by the government policy of "kill the Indian and educate the man." The product of this policy was the cultural black hole. My brother and I had not grown up on a reservation like "real Indians," and we could not prove our tribal background because at that time we were not even from a federally recognized tribe.

At college, I was mortified to realize that I did not know the names and locations of the major tribes in the United States. I did not know the histories of U. S.-Indian relationships. I did not even know the full history of my own tribe's treaty, our language, or our culture, and the more Indians I met the more inadequate I felt. I finally completed my undergraduate degree and immediately entered into a master's program in counseling. At the same time, I was offered and accepted a position as an assistant dean of students at the university. Because I proudly claimed my Indianness, other administrators expected me to be able to answer any questions concerning all Indians and to relate in a "culturally correct" manner to the other Indians on campus, whatever tribe they came from and whatever problem they had for the university to solve. I barely knew my own tribe's culture and history, and my problem was now compounded enormously by not knowing about other Indians as well. One solution was to read and study all I could about all Indians in America. That was a monumental task, and it would lead me into more years of study and research and would demand more skills than I had. It sometimes seemed hopeless.

Through the 1970s and 1980s, there was a major search for self-awareness among concerned Indians all across the country. However, there was no grand plan, no road map or formula, for young Indians to follow in finding themselves in the big picture of the American Indian cultural-historical milieu. All tribes or nations were affected to one degree or another by the black hole, but each was in a different situation—in a different boat (or canoe as it were), adrift, without adequate knowledge of navigation and with no obvious means of propulsion.

Some tribal people were removed from their home areas, relocated into urban settings, and offered education and retraining opportunities at government expense. They were not warned that they would be left to fend for themselves in those urban areas with their newly acculturated skills and training, nor did they receive any help to prepare them for this eventuality.

It seemed as though the ancient flood myth of the Coos Bay area was being lived out again, wherein the People who had rushed to their canoes in advance of the rising waters were set adrift, except for those who had prepared by stashing long ropes in their canoes. They could tie up to the tops of the tallest fir trees on the mountaintops and gradually let themselves back down as the waters receded. Those with shorter ropes either capsized or were forced to cut loose; those with no ropes at all were swept far away into another land.

Perhaps that old story equates to the tribal people who were able to maintain their cultural integrity through the years of acculturation while others ignored their cultural background and drifted into the mainstream or "melting pot" of dominant society. Not all Indians experienced a loss of self-identity, but such was the case for nearly all of those tribal members and descendants from the federally terminated tribes of the 1950s. These terminations, along with federal policies of acculturation, thoroughly undermined the cultural integrity of tribes, including the Coquelles and other small Oregon tribes. The struggle for self-awareness and self-sufficiency has produced extensive social and political schisms among Coquelle tribal members and between the tribe and outside public agencies. Many young tribal members are desperate to understand the overall processes of cultural change and cultural loss experienced by earlier generations. Indications of the extensive variety of lost languages, myths, tales, and cultural traditions in the Pacific Northwest (and most particularly in Southwestern Oregon), now lost, can be noted in the writings of Melville Jacobs, who said that before 1750 the Pacific Northwest

> had sixty to seventy Indian languages, two to three thousand bands, hamlets, or villages, and something under, around, or over two hundred thousand people. This hunting-fishing-gathering population could once have yielded a million or more versions of myths, smaller numbers of tales, and no one can estimate how much of other oral genres. . . . Myths of most variable merit that have been collected over the region total less than a thousand and will never exceed that number. Tales amount to a few hundred, forever so. The bleak harvest is . . . maybe one percent of what could have been obtained if the culture-bound, condescending, and racist invaders had had the slightest capacity to perceive merit in the heritages of non-Europeans. By the time anyone with such capacity went to work, native humiliation and extinction had erased almost everything. Folklore-oriented linguists . . . arrived too late after the pioneers had trampled upon and destroyed the Indians. (Jacobs 1972)

In pondering the analogy of a "cultural black hole" on the Southern Oregon coast, we can note that the black holes of outer space are thought to absorb and condense all available matter within reach but then to be no longer visible or identifiable to the outside observer. Only research from an inside perspective will reveal the lost information so vital to the reculturation of the Coquelles and their neighbors. Meanwhile, the effect of the black hole on the tribes of Southern Oregon was an American holocaust. Just as the holocaust in Germany must be taught and remembered, so must the holocaust in Oregon be taught in our schools, so Oregonians and other Americans will know the true history. That knowledge might better ensure that such a holocaust will never happen again.

Appendix A

Treaties and Land Claims

Coquelle headmen signed the treaty of 1855 with the United States Government (the unratified Port Orford treaty of 1851 also identified several signatories as Coquelle Indians, some of whom were actually Coos), which would have ceded tribal land to the United States in return for a reservation and various tribal rights. Although the treaty was never ratified by Congress, the survivors of the Rogue River Wars of 1856 (survivors also of earlier village massacres by white miners and of U.S. Army retaliations) were marched overland or shipped up the coast by steamers to concentration camps at Reedsport and Yachats. Some were moved later to the Siletz Reservation, while many others died or ran away.

In 1916 George Bundy Wasson began investigating Indian land claims based primarily on broken or unratified treaties and "began a thirty-year campaign for claims settlements in western Oregon" (Beckham 1990, 186). For eleven years he lobbied Congress and finally won permission to go to court in 1929. According to Beckham,

> The concern about injustice, legal rights, and land claims was voiced most clearly by the Coos, lower Umpqua, and Siuslaw. These three tribes—operating as one unit since their treaty agreement with Joel Palmer in 1855—pioneered in using the "system." Their efforts, which set a pattern for other Indian groups throughout the Pacific Northwest, began in 1916. In the summer of that year, George Bundy Wasson, a graduate of Chemawa and Carlisle, went to Washington D. C. to investigate the Indian land claim. Wasson had grown up on his mother's allotment on South Slough on Coos Bay. That trip began eleven lonely and frustrating years of lobbying by these Indians. Like other American Indians they were prohibited by law

from suing the United States government. To bring a suit for their land claims, the Coos, Lower Umpqua, and Siuslaw had to gain a special act of Congress. Not until 1929 did Congress pass the measure which permitted them to go to court.

Case K-345, the lawsuit of the Coos, lower Umpqua, and Siuslaw for settlement of land claims, took nine years to get a judgment in the Court of Claims. During all of the time between 1917 and 1938 these Indians had to pay for their own legal expenses. . . . Each family that could gave $5.00 a month to help pay for George Wasson's trips to Washington, D.C., and to pay for the work of the Attorneys. (Beckham 1977, 37)

In 1931, George Bundy Wasson called upon the most knowledgeable members of the Coos and Coquelle tribes to provide evidence for aboriginal land claims. Court-appointed clerks took Indian testimony in North Bend, Oregon. Seventeen members of the tribes spoke, several of them in their native languages. The aged James Buchanan was one who remembered much of what had happened. In 1875 he had spoken at the Yachats Conference and protested against the closing of the Alsea Reservation. Now in 1931 he spoke again for his people and their land claim. Lottie Evanoff named the villages and fishing places. George, Maggie Sacchi, Annie Peterson, Laura Metcalf, Frances Elliot, and Mrs. William Waters spoke.

On April 2, 1945, the federal Court of Claims decided favorably for the Coquelles and for other coastal groups. The United States Supreme Court overruled an appeal by the Justice Department on November 25, 1946. The case was finally closed in 1950, awarding $1.20 per acre for 722,530 acres. Coquelle descendants were awarded an inheritance of $3,128,000, and after numerous federal deductions, the remainder equaled approximately $2,000 per person. Final settlement was made in per-capita payments, by which the total was divided equally among eligible tribal enrollees—a stratagem that had the unfortunate effect of watering down the payment.

Perhaps the tribal members were glad to get something at last for all they had lost by not having a treaty and giving up all of their land. It seems as though they believed that the end of their status as a legitimate Indian tribe was at hand. It surely seemed impossible to fight the federal government's efforts to destroy their "Indianness" and render them virtually persons without identity, as had already been done to the Coos, Lower Umpqua, and Siuslaw.

The Coos and Coquelles were among those terminated and among those whose cultural losses became most evident during the efforts to obtain federal restoration. Along with restoration as federally recognized tribes, there came a whole new set of problems to compound the cultural turmoil. Restoration required the establishment of a tribal council and adoption of a tribal constitution (upon approval of the BIA and Department of Interior) as well as the acceptance of federal dollars in the form of new-tribes funding.

On August 13, 1954, along with forty-two other Western Oregon Indian tribes, the Coquelles were effectively terminated by President Dwight D. Eisenhower's signing of Public Law 588, making termination effective on August 13, 1956. Termination was not a satisfactory solution to problems of American Indians and did not fulfill the obligations of the federal government to Indian people. Tribal members continued to communicate through a home-printed newsletter. Meanwhile, tribal leaders, spearheaded by Wilfred Wasson, worked with Native American Program Oregon Legal Services (NAPOLS) attorneys Rod Clark and Michael Mason to reverse termination, as other tribes had succeeded in doing. The Coquille Indian Tribe was finally restored to federal recognition by an Act of Congress on June 28, 1989, by passage of the "Coquille Indian Restoration Act" (103 Stat. 91).

When land claims hearings were conducted in the 1930s and 1940s, the Coos (including many Coquelles), Lower Umpqua, and Siuslaw appealed as a confederated group. The Court of Claims denied their appeal due to lack of evidence. The land claims for the "Coos" had been based on the testimonies of the oldest Indians alive at that time. George Bundy Wasson thought there could be no better evidence of aboriginal sovereignty and territorial occupation than the words of the old people themselves. The federal government declared their testimony to be merely hearsay. However, after collecting ethnographic information from the old Indians of that area, John P. Harrington stated that the Coquelles were undoubtedly the true descendants of the aboriginal occupants of their land, hence the land claims settlement for the Coquelles. This decision caused a split between the Coos and Coquelles, which ultimately resulted in separate federally recognized tribes.

Appendix B

Some Notable Coquelle Leaders of the Twentieth Century

Coquel Thompson (1839–1946) was removed as a young man from his Upper Coquelle village to the reservation at Siletz. His vast knowledge of myths and legends, history, traditions, and language diversity made him the most reliable Coquelle informant. He shared information with J. O. Dorsey in the 1880s, with Philip Drucker in 1934, probably with Elizabeth Jacobs in 1935, and with John P. Harrington in the 1940s. It was this information, through Harrington's testimony to the Court of Claims, that firmly established the Coquelles as true descendants of the aboriginal inhabitants of their tribal territory.

Susan Adulsah Wasson (1841–1917) is the most frequently mentioned Coquelle ancestor on the final tribal rolls. She was the daughter of Kitzn-Jin-Jn

Galada-lui, "Man with Heart Too Big for Elk Robe to Meet in the Middle" (also known as Kitchen), headman of the major South Slough village on Coos Bay in 1828, and his wife Gishgiu (also known as Gekka, "Little Old Woman"), daughter of an Upper Coquelle headman. (That marriage was said to have united the Coos and Coquelles.) From her first marriage to Charles Hodgkiss (Hodgkin?), who died at sea, Susan Adulsah had one daughter, Laura. Her second marriage, to Hodgkiss's partner George Richardson Wasson, who in 1849 sailed from New Brunswick around South America to San Francisco and then traveled overland to Jacksonville in 1851 and to Coos Bay in 1853, produced nine more children. Susan spoke several coastal languages and was famed as a historian of the Coos Bay tribal area, having memorized detailed information on family ties, land ownership, myths, and legends.

George Bundy Wasson (1880–1947), my father, was the youngest child of Susan and George R. Wasson to reach adulthood. In his youth, his grandmother Gekka stood with him on a hill above South Slough in Coos Bay. With a slow sweeping gesture of her extended arm, Gekka said, "All this land belongs your *hyas papas* ["grandfathers" in Chinook Jargon]. Someday, *Chawch* ["George" in Chinook Jargon], you get it back." George Bundy Wasson attended both Chemawa and Carlisle Indian Schools, along with his sister *Daisy Wasson Codding* (the first registered nurse in Oregon south of Portland). George spent his adult life as a tailor, timber cruiser, and lobbyist in Congress for Indian land claims. He was the first and most thorough organizer among the Coquelles and an adamant defender of Indian human rights. He married my mother, Bess Finley, in 1923 and they had five children. George died of a heart attack at Cape Blanco in 1947 while assessing tribal mineral rights and land values, before the final Coquelle land claims inheritance was paid.

Charles Edward "Eddy" Ned (1889–1956) was the son of Charles and Susan Ned. He served in World War I, worked many years in the "logging woods," and assisted George B. Wasson in cruising timber. While living with the Wasson family off and on for many years, he served as a "tutor" of Coquelle cultural heritage for the Wasson children. In his elder years he was fondly known as the last full-blooded Coquelle.

Wilfred Carlisle Wasson (1924–90), my brother, the eldest son of Bess Finley and George Bundy Wasson, was known for his wealth of knowledge of Coyote stories, myths, legends, tribal history, and culture. After studying anthropology for several years, he earned in 1974 a Ph.D. in education from the University of Oregon. Wilfred served on the faculties at Oregon State University in Corvallis, Western Washington State University in Bellingham, and the University of Oregon in Eugene, and was a member of the board of directors at D. Q. University in Davis, California. He worked many years on educational and economic development projects for coastal Indians. He served as Coquelle Tribal Chairman and was instrumental in restoring federal recognition to the Coquelle Indian Tribe.

Notes

I wish to acknowledge that the topics and contents of this paper have resulted from many years of conversations with my closest cultural companion, my older brother Wilfred C. Wasson. "Will" inspired me to contemplate life now and long ago. His death in 1990 left me feeling I would never again share the thoughts and memories of Old Man Coyote, family anecdotes, myths, legends, or traditional stories. Now, as I write what I have always known and believed, and report the missing information I have always sought, I find strength and support in remembering how he would have responded to my questions and ideas. I'm grateful that my brother gave me so much to remember and think about. Other members of my family, particularly my mother, Bess Hockema, inspired me to go back to college and write a true history of the Coquelle Indian Tribe. My good friend Barre Toelken expended great amounts of energy listening, exchanging ideas, and encouraging me at times of despair. He's family. I'm honored they think I could do it. I'm humbled by the experience. Finally, I appreciate the support, confidence, and inspiration of the faculty and my fellow students in the graduate program in anthropology at the University of Oregon. Mel Aikens and Madonna Moss have been positive listeners to my creative ideas, and stimulating critics to my academic products. Jon Erlandson, however, is the greatest catalyst in my academic endeavors and accomplishments. His encouragement and advisorial persuasion have helped bring my graduate degree to fruition.

1. Treatments of this period will be found in Jack Norton, *Genocide in Northwestern California* (1979), and in E. A. Schwartz, *The Rogue River Indian War and Its Aftermath, 1850–1980* (1997).

Visible Landscapes/Invisible People: Negotiating the Power of Representation in a Mining Community

Robert McCarl

On 26 May 1996, two demolitions experts from Morrison-Knudsen set charges under the gigantic stacks of the former Bunker Hill smelter in Kellogg, Idaho. A contest was held to determine who would push the button and send the stacks plummeting to the ground. Lining the freeway, front porches, and rooftops of the denuded hillsides were thousands of people who came to watch the spectacle. Among them were two important factions in the community: One faction comprised those who were there to cheer the destruction of a corporate and industrial symbol that to many of the mining and union families of the Coeur d'Alenes, represented a union-busting, corporate form of greed and callousness toward human life that had characterized this valley since the latter part of the nineteenth century. The other group represented at the "Blow the Stacks" rally had lobbied hard to keep the EPA and the state from going through with their plans. This group, made up of chamber of commerce activists, preservationists, and business people who rely heavily upon the tourist trade, wanted to preserve the still-carcinogenic smokestacks so that they could be turned into an interpretive site for tourists. They sought the establishment of a landmark that would portray the positive aspects of the mining industry in the Silver Valley. The button was pushed; the stacks were blown and buried where they fell. A chapter in the history of this contested landscape is closed, while the cultural issues dividing the community continue.

My goal in this discussion is to examine in some detail the origin, development, and current disposition of the opposing cultural perspectives outlined above. To begin, it will be necessary to consider what Eric Wolf suggests is the unrealized challenge of anthropology, and that is to "engage ourselves in the systematic writing of a history of the modern world in which we spell out the processes of power which created the present-day

cultural systems and the linkages between them" (Wolf 1974, 261); accordingly, I start with the premise that any examination of an intellectual
canon must pay attention to the processes of power that engendered it, as
well as to its relationship to other cultural and economic interests. I will
illustrate the development of a laboring subculture in the Coeur d' Alenes
that began with the industrialization of hardrock mining in the late nineteenth century and continues today in the lives and memories of a large
number of valley families. By taking on this task, I also hope to analyze
the development of industrial or occupational ethnography as an important but relatively undeveloped subfield of anthropology and folklore
studies.

Having laid out my goals, I need to quickly frame and define both the
wider and narrower contexts of industrial ethnology—wider in that labor
history, industrial archeology, political economy, occupational folklore,
capitalism, industrialism, post-industrialism, and on and on are germane to
the discussion but take us, perhaps, too wide of our mark; narrower in that
the specific constraints and forms of resistance developed at the point of
production—the epicenter of work culture that extends from the hand and
body of the worker to global networks of production and consumption—
can only be partially illustrated in a short essay. Further (as Paul Willis,
Ken Kusterer, and Martin Meissner have all illustrated), the expression and
form of technique, by its very transformative nature, is not amenable even
to the most sophisticated forms of documentation; it too is placed outside
the scope of this discussion (Willis 1977, 130–36; Kusterer 1978, 163–95;
Meissner 1976).

Centrally, I am addressing the culture of work: knowledge generated in
and around the creation of goods and services that is drawn upon to pattern
and interpret behavior. Yet is this enough? There is something missing, and
it is missing primarily because of the cultural canons and blinders of our
own disciplines. Culture helps us see certain things, but it also occludes
material that is not culturally anticipated. Herbert Gutman in *Work, Culture
and Society*, drawing on the theories of Mintz, Wolf, and Polish sociologist
Zygmunt Bauman, develops a definition of culture as a "kind of resource"
and society as a "kind of arena." He goes on to suggest that

> this approach allows historians to avoid the many pitfalls that fol-
> low implicit or explicit acceptance of . . . the subtle historical
> processes that explain patterns of working class and other behavior
> as no more than what Eric Wolf terms the "expansion of one at the
> expense of the other." An analytical model that distinguishes
> between culture and society reveals that even in periods of radical
> economic and social change, powerful cultural continuities and
> adaptations continue to shape the historical behavior of diverse
> working class populations (Gutman 1976, 18–19).

What is missing from both our definition and our approach to the culture of work is our disregard of labor ideology—that ethos and value system born of collective work experience. We variously refer to such an ideology as class, trade unionism, solidarity, or proletarian consciousness. Yet buried within these concepts, in addition to a resistance or opposition to managerial control, is a different sense of morality, a grounded notion of what is right and wrong based on a body of concrete, shared experiences in the workplace.

This ideology may expand into the political arena during a strike or a job action, but it is primarily a face-to-face, private experience that binds one generation and one worker to the next. Labor ideology is an ineffable and even noble belief in a common good beyond that of the individual; with a few notable exceptions (Pilcher 1972; Nash 1979; Korson 1938, 1943; Green 1978), folklorists have paid little attention to it. The difference between the study of work and the study of labor can be the difference between scientific management (or Taylorism, Human Relations, TQM—it comes under a variety of names) and a clear-headed examination of the workplace as an arena within which power is negotiated daily. Failure—on the part of workers or researchers—to recognize the importance of that power relationship can result in various forms of dismemberment, disease, dislocation, disenfranchisement, rage, blood, and death. Recognition and use of it by workers can result in what June Nash calls "communitas." In *We Eat the Mines and the Mines Eat Us*, Nash describes strategies used by Bolivian tin miners to "resist against alienation that is the essence of the work system in industrial centers:"

> To the extent that the community has these generative bonds of new growth, the people can sustain the most brutal attacks. The mining community has demonstrated the strength of these sentiments that carry it through such periods.
> . . . When the company recognized this, they tried to destroy it by firing or sending into exile the husbands of those women who focused on the sentiments of the communitas, thereby breaking the primary base of solidarity. The rituals in the mine . . . and the offerings to the enchanted spirits are all reminders in normal periods of the root sources of communitas. (Nash 1979, 330)

Nash's trenchant analysis of labor ideology in Bolivia does not completely account for the experience of miners in the United States, but her model provides us with a theoretical seam of concrete cultural experience to which we will return at the end of this discussion. Contemporary miners observe customs, from the initiation of novices to elaborate narratives of legendary miners or union men, that parallel those documented by Nash. The significance of this material lies not only in its demonstration of a response to alienation but perhaps more importantly in its projection of a worldview that is workable above and below ground. Labor ideology is more than simply a response to specific technical and economic conditions of work; it is a value system and a positive ethos that provides the members of these communities with a unique and little-understood way of operating collectively in a world that exerts continual pressure toward individualism and competition.

In order to better understand the culture of labor in the Coeur d'Alenes, we need to go back to the late 1800s. Not long after the boomers and forty-niners moved on to Alaska or decided to try the Boise or the Wood River basins for gold, the discovery of large deposits of lead and silver ore in the Coeur d'Alenes began to attract experienced industrial miners. "Cousin Jacks" from Cornwall, along with Irish, Scandinavian, and Italian workers, began to sign on with the Bunker Hill and Sullivan, the Last Chance, the Polaris, the Badger, and the Nine Mile. Initially these mines required hand skills—single- and doublejacking by hand to place charges, "bardown" solid rock or "muck," and wheel it out on mule cart. By 1890, however, mine owners had begun to find outside investors to assist them in building a railroad, organizing themselves in a mine owners' cartel, and importing steam and later electric mining drills. May Arkwright Hutton, the wife of a labor activist in the region, wrote in her turn-of-the-century autobiography, *The Coeur d'Alenes: A Tale of the Modern Inquisition in Idaho*:

> During the years of 1889 and 1890 the mine owners put machine drills run by compressed air in their mines, with which two men could break down as much rock in one day as ten men could with hand drills.
>
> Old miners who had spent the best part of their lives mining were put back to shoveling, and the shovelers had to perform double the amount of work prior to the advent of the machine drills. (Hutton [1900] 1992, 57–58)

In addition to changes in technology and the resultant destruction of craft, the mine owners decided that they would not support the construction of a miners' hospital in Wallace. (The union had requested that the hospital be supported by diverting a dollar from each miner's paycheck to pay for the construction and staffing of the facility.) This confrontation resulted in a strike, and immediately the mine owners began to implement a prearranged plan to import strikebreakers and non-union miners from around the country. Special trains were loaded in California and at points east with non-union workers, who were shipped into the region. At first, the miners used rhetoric to fight the mine owners' union-busting tactics. Hutton states:

> Jock Hazelton was one of the men stationed by the unions at Tekoa, Washington, the point where the Oregon Railway and Navigation Company takes passengers for the Coeur d'Alene mines,

and when non-union men would arrive from various points, Jock
made it his business to interview them and if he could not persuade
them to return to their homes, he would, with the assistance of the
railroad men, who were in sympathy with the union men in their
cause, manage to get them into trains going in the opposite direction. (Hutton 1900, 61)

With millions of dollars in assets, the mine owners invested heavily in
strikebreaking practices, hiring hundreds of Pinkerton agents, restricting the
passage of union representatives in the region, and challenging the union's
rights at every step of the way. Inevitably, a confrontation between a local
mine guard and a union man erupted in gunfire, the death of three union
miners, and the response of the unionists in the destruction of the Frisco
Mill. Martial law was established; the Army sent troops to "quell the upris-
ing"; union leaders were imprisoned in the bullpen. The events of the strike
culminated in the well-known trial of Big Bill Haywood, following the assassination of Idaho's Governor Steunenberg. The mine "war" of the Coeur
d'Alenes not only brought into sharp relief the ideological conflicts between
miners and mine owners; this period also reflected a political and public
expression of labor ideology born in the stope and maintained to this day.

Using this historical conflict as a starting point for understanding labor
culture, I would like to analyze the implications of the 1892 battle for both
labor history and the development of the industrial paradigm in anthropology. Regarding the former, the miners of the Coeur d'Alenes were not first-
time unionists. Labor struggles in Colorado, Nevada, California, and Utah
added strength to the Western Federation of Miners, who also played an
important role in organizing the region. Many of the leaders and activists in
the WFM were former members of the Knights of Labor. Following the
destruction of the Frisco Mill in 1892 and particularly after the incarceration
of the union men in the bullpen and the killing of Governor Steunenberg,
the preoccupation of more radical WFM leaders like Moyer, Haywood, and
Pettibone opened the Federation to a takeover by the Industrial Workers of
the World. Some commentators, like historian Mark Sullivan in his multi-
volume opus, *Our Times, The United States 1900–1925*, go so far as to claim
that the mine war and the Haywood trial (particularly Haywood's acquittal)
was a turning point in American history:

> [T]hose who had decried American justice, who had alleged the
> impossibility of a fair trial for Haywood, found themselves discredit-
> ed with persons of common sense. Up to that time there had been a
> country-wide trend toward Socialism as a cure for various ills of dem-
> ocratic government; the hysteria and excesses of Debs and the other
> extremists among the Socialists, during and before the Haywood trial,
> had the effect of a brake applied to this trend, indeed almost brought

it to a halt; at a time when in France, Germany and England it was
going forward strongly. (Quoted in Grover 1964, 289)

Though this claim for the impact of the trial is perhaps excessive, there is no
question that the acquittal did mute the effectiveness of some of the more
radical labor activists in the Coeur d'Alenes (Grover 1964; Lingenfelter 1974).

With respect to the formation of the industrial paradigm in anthropology, Eric Wolf links anthropological theory development in the United States
to three distinct phases of American political history: "capitalism triumphant," lasting roughly from the end of the Civil War into the last decade
of the nineteenth century; "intermittent liberal reform," beginning in the
last decade of the nineteenth century and ending with the onset of World
War II; and the America of the "present" (late 1960s). Wolf characterizes this
era in sixties parlance as the age of the military-industrial complex—in
today's parlance, global monopoly capitalism (Wolf 1974, 254). While Wolf's
model of a quarter-century ago cannot of course address more recent critical and interpretive theoretical paradigms, it provides valuable insight on
our subject.

The era of "capitalism triumphant" in which the early Coeur d'Alene
labor struggles took place was, according to Wolf, paralleled in the new discipline of anthropology by Social Darwinism and evolutionary models,
whose theories and methods placed emphasis upon cultural results rather
than cultural processes. Lewis Henry Morgan, John Wesley Powell, and a
multitude of nineteenth-century anthropologists attempted to link existing
human populations in a stage continuum of development (Wolf 1974,
252–253). Industrial and occupational researchers carried this model into the
work environment in an effort to improve the moral and ethical fiber of the
worker, increase his or her allegiance to a capitalist ethos, and increase prof-
its along the way. Yet this attempt to manage labor scientifically (Taylor 1911;
Mayo 1933; Roethlisberger and Dickson 1939) had surprising results.
According to Paul Willis,

> Taylorism . . . [is] aimed at increasing the efficient and rational
> utilization of the forces of production. This involves an objective social-
> ization of production which is likely, in its turn, to bring about what we
> might think of as a socialization in consciousness where interdepend-
> ence is massively recognized and used by workers to control produc-
> tion. Taylor sought to eliminate gold-bricking and systematic soldier-
> ing, but the very rationalization and expansion of production resulting
> from his scientific techniques created the conditions for a greater infor-
> mal control of the work process. Manipulation and control of the forces
> of production therefore bring visible consequences for the social rela-
> tions of production which themselves act back on the forces. (Willis
> 1977, 182)

Retired mineworker Pete Piekarski, who for many years worked in the Bunker Hill smelter, illustrates how shop-floor culture responds to these constraints:

> We had one guy come up there that was a new boss over the blast furnace. He wouldn't listen to reason, that we were supposed to take orders from our shifter. He said, By God, you'll take orders from whoever cause I'm telling you, you have [to] do such and such. So he told us to clean the door on the charge cart. He didn't say how clean or anything, he just said, I want those doors clean. So we parked the motor and the car and started cleaning the door. The reason that he said this was because the door didn't shut tight and it'd scatter muck in between the tracks and they'd have to get a guy from the bullgang to clean in between the tracks. He figured that was extra expense to the blast furnace department, so he's gonna put a stop to that. . . . So we were cleaning the doors; it got to the point where there was nothing left to clean so we took chisels and screwdrivers and we were chipping the doors. . . . In the meantime the furnace go[t] down real low and flames were shooting out everywhere and the smoke was rolling out. So our boss came up the stairs because the tappers were complaining about the furnace being down. He came over to where we were and said, What do you guys think you're doing? So we told him, Your boss Frank Sinclair came along and told us to clean the doors, he didn't say how clean to clean them he just said clean them. We're cleaning them hoping he'll come by and tell it's good enough, otherwise we don't know what to do. He said, You roll those doors up and you fill that furnace up and you leave that man to me. (Piekarski, interview, 1985, BTW-SC-A015, tape 1, ms. 103)

As this interview segment demonstrates, and as Willis points out and I will later discuss, labor has options with regard to its use of the informal knowledge of the workplace that management—in its focus on product rather than process—does not enjoy (Willis 1977, 156–59, 179–83). Chief among these options is access to time and to knowledge of technique, by which workers can adjust the industrial process to fit their needs rather than the strident calibrations of the timekeeper's clock.

Following the turn of the century and up until the late twenties, miners in the Coeur d'Alenes were living in the shadow of the blacklist, the infamous hiring practices and corruption of people like George E. Edmonson. Also known as the "king," Edmonson purportedly needed to hear only a whisper of a miner's association with the Western Federation of Miners, the Industrial Workers of the World, or the labor conflicts of the nineties to send that miner packing (Robert Carroll, interview, 1987, BTW-AD-A004, p. 5).

Increased efficiency in industrial rationalization in the mines, the production of higher-grade ore, and the introduction of smelting on site, however, brought in more miners and above-ground workers and ushered in the fight for the eight-hour day. This fight reawakened the wider solidarity of the nineties and opened the door for the emergent Mine, Mill, and Smelter Workers Union. Mine Mill, comprising many former activists from the old Western Federation of Miners, became one of the most thoughtful and egalitarian unions in the American Federation of Labor, and it dominated the labor scene in the valley from the mid-thirties until it lost membership to a company union and eventually to the steelworkers' union after the disastrous 1960 strike (Rosswurm 1992; Norlen 1992).

To develop our understanding of how Mine Mill built on and extended the community solidarity born at the point of production, we need to look more closely at the tension between corporate goals and the way in which workers redefine those goals and redirect them. Robert Carroll, a retired Mine Mill officer and lifetime miner, recalls mining in the Coeur d'Alenes prior to the Second World War:

> This foreman told me if I didn't do what he told me to do he was going to fire me. Well, I knew I was fired because he had told me it was impossible to do. There was not much muck on the track or in the ditch. So I decided I'd just take an easy shift and go out and get my time. I was walking down the drift and I seen these chutes that come down out of the stopes, and I noticed they had some muck in them. . . . So I just ran my car down there and filled it full of muck, pushed it back from the chute and brought another one down. Then just before quitting time, I dug him a ditch and got a bunch of mud and dirt and water and threw it on top of them. The motorman came out and took the cars out and I was riding the back one. He looked at that and he said, Well, I'll be damned. There won't be any firing today, will there. That's how rotten they were. . . . And then he put me hand-mucking a drift . . . which isn't, usually they put two men mucking, but they put me on a shift by myself and told me to muck out the drift. We had to hand-tram those and dump them and that was eighteen tons—usually a two-man job. I knew I was going to get fired this time. So we had this big general repairman, repairing a drift above. You know, the shift boss only came through once in the morning and once in the afternoon and they don't stay, they run away. As soon as the shift boss went through, this big timberman, he had been a champion mucker in the mines somewhere in Oklahoma, they mucked in big buckets there, Nieberger was his name, bless his heart, he would come down behind the guy, as soon as the boss'd go, and he'd muck seven or

eight cars in nothing flat. Carroll, interview, 1987, BTW-AD-AOO4, pp. 1–2, tape 4)

An informal network of communication and labor solidarity in the mine (as exemplified in Carroll's narrative) not only provides a means of resisting rationalization and alienation through covert strategies shared by workers who control bodies of knowledge outside of management's awareness, this labor culture also embodies a philosophy of mutual responsibility and shared creativity directly parallel to, yet a mirror image of, its managerial counterpart.

Returning to the second part of Wolf's historical framework, the years of "liberal reform" prior to World War II were characterized by a concentration on human flexibility and plasticity. In anthropology, Franz Boas's historical particularism, reacting against Social Darwinism, "called into question the moral and political monopoly of an elite which had justified their rule with the claim that their superior virtue was the outcome of the evolutionary power" (Wolf 1974, 255). Further, "Just as the Social Darwinists had made a moral paradigm of the evolutionary process, so the culture and personality schools of the thirties and the forties made a moral paradigm of each individual culture" (257).

Early investigations of work culture were inspired by the street-corner sociology and participant-observations of Park, Warner, and the Chicago School, which reflected this organic and holistic view of culture (Green 1978). The increasing number of cultural descriptions forced anthropologists into addressing issues of political economy—social structure, community and work. Yet even these efforts (as Wolf states) reflected the investigator's biases: they were "turned inside out, all ideology and morality, and neither power or economy" (257). Industrial anthropologists articulated complex descriptions of parallels between the classical ethnographies of pre-industrial people and the variety of sub-cultures, customs, processes, and forms of corporate organization found in industry (Harding 1955; Hughes 1952; Chapple 1953). Remarkable for their almost total neglect of any critical stance toward class, trade unionism, shop floor culture, or work site resistance, these early accounts of industrial ethnography do not acknowledge hegemony or even the wider constraints of regional or global industrial bureaucracies. We read them today as being implicated in the institutional exploitation of the cultures they aimed to understand; yet we ourselves run the risk of historical ethnocentrism if we fail to acknowledge the specific contexts within which they worked.

If industrial anthropologists erred on the side of decontextualized holism, folklorists studying the expressive culture of the workplace during the same era focused on genres and typologies in micro-contexts that paid little attention to the wider dynamics of industrial or capitalist power.

Folklorists George Korson, Wayland Hand, and (later) Archie Green did, however, seek strategies for returning their research findings to members of the local community. Both Hand and Korson explicitly acknowledged their interest in a neo-Redfieldian notion of the work community as a folk enclave which contained a mixture of earlier craft and verbal traditions that industrial rationalization would eventually destroy. Yet they also (Korson more empirically than Hand) recognized and documented the way in which the songs, stories, and beliefs they were chronicling represented both formal and informal modes of cultural resistance on the shop floor and in the wider community (Korson 1927, 1938; Hand 1942a, 1942b, 1969; Green 1965, 1972).

Archie Green critically exploded earlier paradigms that considered only face-to-face cultural expression as legitimate forms of study and drew the attention of cultural workers to the interplay between popular and mass media in carrying oppositional impulses born in the workplace yet carried in a variety of dynamic forms to wider audiences. More importantly, he identified for American working people themselves the variety of forms which this cultural resistance continues to take in our lives. He led the way in engaging both rank-and-filer and union official in developing a dialogue with cultural workers concerning the important role of cultural and political history that supports the continuing struggle for humane working conditions (Green 1965).

We now come to the last part of Wolf's model—the era of the military industrial complex and the current generation of research in industrial ethnology. First, however, if I am to "engage [myself] in the systematic writing of a history of the modern world in which [I] spell out the processes of power which created the present-day cultural systems and the linkages between them" (Wolf 1974, 261), I must examine my methods and theories as they affect and are responded to by the members of the labor community. Accordingly, I return to Silver Valley to bring us up to date on union and community power struggles leading up to and following the 1960 strike, and attempt to link my research to those processes.

One of the most compelling chapters in the often bloody and inspiring story of miners and their families in the Coeur d'Alenes is their ability to marshal solidarity in the face of implacable odds. By the late 1950s, the leadership of the Mine, Mill, and Smelter Workers was experiencing an aggressive union-busting move on the part of Gulf Resources, the new owners of the Bunker Hill. Cutbacks in the workforce, speed-ups, redbaiting of union leaders, and McCarthy-like witch hunts all came to a head in the sixty strike. Pete Piekarski, recording secretary for the local, describes this period in the following way:

> Before the 'sixty strike . . . it kept getting tougher and tougher to
> get a good contract. When we negotiated with the company, they had

a couple of negotiators on the company's side. One by the name of Ben Mahoney and the other one Pete Nichols. . . . He kept talking all the time about the company's inherent right to manage. A person got the impression that this was the same as the divine right of kings, and was given by God. No matter what you would come up against, they would say that this is our inherent right as the owners. We would point out to them as owners of big property that was a part of society, they had an obligation to society, and it wasn't their inherent right. So one day, we were getting nowhere with them, I believe this was in '59, anyway, I wrote a little thing on a piece of paper, and I told them that as far as I was concerned as a union negotiator, I would conceive that they had inherent rights, if they could reenact the scene where God gave them that right like he did the kings. I says, that was never reenacted, then finally the people threw out the crap about the divine right of kings. There is no divine right to do whatever the hell you damn well please. (Piekarski, BTW-CD-AOll, 1987, Section 13, p. 12)

Once the strike actually began, the membership of the union and their families in the women's auxiliary established a support network of shared resources for striking families. Pete Piekarski relates,

So down in the basement of the strike store, Helen and her crew had a great big crew down there washing and packaging. they had to have a packaging crew, a weighing crew and the store took up an awful lot of people. And at sixteen hours each, unless you could prevail upon some of them to work longer, it was quite a turn over in a matter of one week. Well the assignment desk would send people over to the store, they would send people over to the picketing committee, or the kitchen committee wherever they were needed. (Piekarski, BTW-CD-AOll, 1987, Section 13, p. 37; typescript of Solidarity Committee meeting on August 3, 1990 in Kellogg, Idaho)

Following the failed strike, the company union, Northwest Metal Workers, assisted the new owners in squeezing as much profit as possible out of the Bunker Hill workers in the mine, the smelter, and the zinc plant. This speed-up not only illustrated the changing nature of labor relations in the valley, it also forced Pete and many of the old Mine Millers to realize that in spite of its corporate unionism, a non-mine union contract would be a lot better than anything negotiated by a company union. The steelworkers thus took over representation of the Bunker Hill in 1972, and currently they represent approximately two thirds of the six hundred active miners in the valley. The Bunker Hill shut down in 1982, and the zinc plant and smelter have been almost totally removed or buried as part of the EPA's superfund cleanup effort. This brings us to the current generation of labor culture in the region.

I began working in the Silver Valley in 1986 in an effort to use my skills as an ethnographer to develop community education and action projects that would represent the generations of solidarity that made the Coeur d'Alenes profitable for mine owners but also made Kellogg, Wallace, and Mullan good places to live and raise a family. As a student of labor culture, I had gained experience in developing projects in industrial communities that sought to address labor culture and history on a level that would interest miners and their families (McCarl 1985b). I assumed—since I had worked in a wide variety of union and labor contexts—that these experiences and professional qualifications would hold me in good stead. What I failed to appreciate is that my canonical blinders not only kept me from appreciating some of the more baroque alignments and distributions of power within and outside the labor community, but I also was blithely unaware of how the anthropologists, folklorists, and oral historians who preceded me had left a legacy of cultural exploitation that sat, like the huge tailing piles from the Bunker Hill, as a black shadow of distrust over the entire community.

Ethnohistorians and anthropologists, oral historians and folklorists had periodically swept through the valley collecting material, expounding to outsiders their learned interpretations of local issues and generally reinforcing the view of many valley residents that cultural workers, like the various governmental and educational institutions they represent, are just glib salespeople trying to get old-timers and mining families to part with one more precious possession—their hard-won stories. When I first met Pete Piekarski at a conference I had organized in Kellogg at the Staff House Museum— a Victorian building constructed for mine managers that to this day contains not one example of work culture or union symbolism—he had the following to say:

> You know, one of the things that gets me about all of this here . . . I made three tapes, I've been interviewed three different times. Twice by the University of California at Berkeley and one was a video and one was a plain tape and the Smithsonian sent a woman to interview me. I was so disgusted with interviews I said I won't even put it on tape, but after talking a lot I finally said, OK, let's tape. So we got about three hours after that and when she wrote her story in the Smithsonian she didn't even have the courtesy to send me a copy or tell me where I could buy a copy. And when I finally did get a copy from my sister-in-law, she didn't put in a single word. . . . So when I came here, what I'm interested in finding out is are we actually going to get anything done that is going to benefit the people that I am and where I come from—working people. And if it doesn't benefit them I may as well walk out the door. (Piekarski, in Solidarity Conference Proceedings, August 3, 1990, Kellogg, Idaho, p.79)

Having labored in work sites as a cultural worker since 1975, I have had people like Pete walk out, call me an apologist for corporate interests, and respond to my call for demonstrations of work culture on the National Mall with curses and thrown beer cans; I have been laughed at by fire fighters and miners who consider the study of their work culture at best suspect and at worst an unmanly job for a healthy male. Yet I continue. I am currently working with Tom Carter on a community project in the Coeur d'Alene mining region that has returned to the local Solidarity Committee a brief monograph documenting the historical development of labor culture and a well-organized archive of all of the data they and we collected for the study (McCarl 1997). I do not expect, as I may once have expected, to be lifted on the shoulders of community members to march triumphant down the streets of Kellogg. (I fully expect grousing that, for instance, the pictures we chose cropped off a father's head or were actually taken in Butte, not Mullan.) What I do expect and what I hope to conclude with here is a diversity of opinions, perspectives, concerns, and insights into an appreciation and understanding of specific work cultures in the Coeur d'Alenes. This culture is composed of a variety of what Willis terms the "experiences, relationships and ensembles of systematic types of relationship which not only set particular choices and decisions at particular times, but also structure, really and experientially, how these choices come about and are defined in the first place" (Willis 1977, 1).

These concrete experiences extend out into the community as what Willis calls "penetrations" of labor culture into public discourse. As seen in a final example, Robert Carroll describes an incident from 1937 that epitomizes this process, and he lays the groundwork for some preliminary conclusions about the relationship between ethnography and labor culture and ideology:

> What I was going to tell you, they undertook to fire these teachers. They were good teachers. If they could teach me, they could teach anybody. Just because they said things that somebody didn't like. So, Mr. Graff was the principal of the school, he was a graduate lawyer. He taught business law. Sometimes we would have what we called a bull session. He'd say, Now everybody thinks that State Workmen's Compensation was made to protect the worker. That's the farthest thing from the truth that ever was. It was made to protect the companies. When a man gets killed in the mine now, his family gets a small payoff and that's the end of it. It used to be that they'd sue the company and maybe get twenty-five or fifty thousand dollars. Which was a fortune in those days. He said, So what happens? Mr. Stanley Easton, who was president of Bunker Hill, and his friend William E. Borah, the lone rider senator from

Idaho, get together and Mr. Easton outlined what they would like and Mr. Borah wrote the law and got it passed into law. And there was the Idaho State Compensation law. Stanley Easton was still the president of Bunker Hill at the time and when that got back to the hierarchy, there was trouble. I remember those little company officials' kids would just squirm. . . . They knew where their bread was buttered. They suspended or laid off a bunch of teachers and. . . . We struck em. We shut them down. Surprisingly, there was four hundred thirty-five of us in the school and all but five of us struck. Striking in the mining industry wasn't new. You know what happened in the bullpen in Kellogg. So some of these people were descendants of those people. But we weren't just a bunch of hotheads. We begged the school board to meet with our parents . . . but they refused. We struck for five days and won reinstatement for all of those teachers. (Carroll, interview, 1987, BTW-AD-AOO4, p. 8)

Bob Carroll represents a type of labor activist that we associate with the WFM, Mine Mill, and the syndicalism of an earlier era. Yet his articulation of solidarity—his willingness to put collective action in place of individual security—is still alive in the valley today. Workers' memorials, books by Art Norlen, testimonies by Pete Piekarski, and demonstrations like the memorial service for the 1892 miners killed in the conflict continue to embody this ideology. In a parallel manner, Pete brings to his demands for pension reform and senior citizen rights the zeal and tactics he learned in the smelter and used for years in the union.

The question finally is the relationship between the canons of resistance and solidarity born at the point of production and the role of the cultural worker in representing those cultural experiences to wider audiences. Is it possible to do good ethnography without, as Lila Abu-Lughod asserts, creating "a professional discourse [that] by nature asserts hierarchy" (1991, 151)? How can we (to use Abu-Lughod's phrase in dealing with ethnographic or ethnohistorical issues in labor communities) "write against culture"? A key response to this challenge is, I think, to mirror the concretions of the labor experience. Tangible history, artifacts, buildings, sites of strikes and struggles, photographs, and other primary documents provide insiders with a sense that you are assisting them in developing tangible evidence of their lives. Just as Abu-Lughod and Willis encourage us not to revert to generalities or abstractions in dealing with culture as a multi-faceted, contested, and irreducible terrain, we must also recognize that the forces of power that shape and are shaped by laboring culture themselves are concrete responses to difficult and often life-threatening events.

In answer to the larger question, our implication in the same canonical contradiction as earlier industrial ethnologists—essentially which side you are on—must be individually confronted by researchers within the concrete realities of their work. Although we have moved diachronically beyond Wolf's era of the military-industrial complex, our more interpretive and critical paradigms multiply the complexities of our interaction with people like Pete and Maidell and Robert Carroll. We can certainly agree with E. P. Thompson that there is "no such thing as economic growth which is not, at the same time, growth or change of a culture," but we must also heed his warning that "we should not assume any automatic or over-direct correspondence between the dynamic of economic growth and the dynamic of social or cultural life" (quoted in Gutman 1976, 33). The changes from craft to industrialism, from the WFM to the IWW, Mine Mill, and now the steelworkers reflect, not a total reshaping of labor culture, but only a partial change. There is a cumulative carryover of strategies, legends, experiences, and techniques from one generation of miners to the next, which not only reflects a continuity of experience born of the vicissitudes of the mining experience, but also reflects a conceptualization of self, time, work, place, and community that can only partially be understood through long-term relationships of trust.

Returning to the buried smokestacks in Kellogg, we can see that the cultural and historical contributions of miners and their families also lie, for the most part, beneath the surface: miles of hand-dug drifts and stopes, row upon row of miners' headstones in the graveyards, and page upon page of family pictures commemorating the cradle-to-grave passage of thousands of lives. This material is invisible to outsiders because much of it is private and personal to the miners and their descendants. The public expressions of this culture—union educational and activism campaigns, strikes, opposition to various chamber of commerce and corporate excesses—remain, if only in yellowed strike posters, old newspaper accounts, and the reminiscences of the men and women who participated. International unions today have little use for this information, preferring on the one hand Madison Avenue publicity campaigns of their own or, more commonly, superficial obeisance to the halcyon days of labor struggles in the thirties. This leaves the academic or documenter working in these communities with some dilemmas. How do we distinguish between public and private or personal and oppositional expressive forms? How do we contextualize this material historically, economically, and culturally? And finally, how do we develop the rapport necessary to even begin this discourse?

The answer to all three questions must be based on positioning, on what we might call the angle of engagement between community members and researchers. Our institutional and cultural constraints as documenters differ markedly from those of insiders. A well-told story of sabotage or complicity, no matter how salutary, might have repercussions beyond our knowing. There is a boundary between the levels of insider ethics born at the work-face and my needs as a researcher. This boundary is not only based on different ways of knowing, it is based on class. My relationship to social and economic power depends upon my production of material that balances "objective" analysis with theoretical and formal praxis. The miners' relationship to both narrower and wider economic concerns (the cultural politics of a specific work group and the absentee decisions of multinational corporations) exposes them to a different kind of risk. It is as if we run on parallel tracks extending forever toward the horizon. We have found no way in the United States to jump the track to re-establish ties between academics and members of work communities that draw upon a shared language and a shared ethos. Organized labor plays a role in this divisiveness in its anti-intellectual and conservative ideology, while academia arrogantly assumes that empiricism and/or postmodern critique is a sufficient demand on our intellectual talents.

As I return from the mining areas of north Idaho, they are carefully planting trees and removing years of slag from the heaps surrounding Kellogg. Lead mitigation is still a serious problem, and it will affect the people of the Coeur d'Alenes for generations to come. Recreation tourism is now touted as the new economic balm for this once vibrant, industrial landscape and the people who inhabit it. Unfortunately, the voices, memories, images, and blood of those who created these mountains of silver are for the most part mute. We have raised some of the images, issues and concerns to a level of consciousness. Yet, like those trains chugging along on parallel tracks, we continue to pass each other—catching only a glimpse of passengers moving in the staccato flashes of alternative if not opposite directions.[1]

Note

1.   Readers will gain further knowledge of labor theory, labor history, and Idaho labor history through the following: Burawoy 1979; Cantrell 1995; Fahey 1971; Firth 1948; Gamst 1977; Hand 1946; Kornbluh 1964; Korson 1960; McCarl 1974, 1978, and 1985a; Phipps 1988; Schwantes 1991; Smith 1960; and Wyman 1979.

Personal Essay

Local Character
Kim Stafford

*G*ypsy Slim taught me why each town's outcast eccentric is its patron saint. Until he disappeared, Slim camped by the downtown library in Portland. His plastic tarp stretched between two shopping carts and the stone bench carved with the name of that rebel from the Enlightenment, Laurence Sterne. When citizens would clip along past him, haughty with respectability, Gypsy Slim would jive them with an easy line of talk, until he had them stalled long enough for a real earful: "I don't care if it's family, friend, house, job, creed, ethnic group, country, institution, or sex—they all try to stifle what you can be." Then his saxophone would wrangle their hearts for yes or no.

In every Oregon town where I live or camp, I hear stories about these local saints: Kid Gilnap in Junction City, with his jingling vest of bells; the Eugene man who had his name legally changed to Pro Human so he could flatter and counsel the young; Bottle Mary, west from Otis, who lived on returnable bottles other citizens knew to leave for her behind a particular stump; Wallowa County's own Acy Deucy; Abe Johnson of Redmond; Tubby Beers of Swisshome; and Marge, the gatherer of mushrooms near Florence. As Gypsy Slim explained, these most unorthodox lives become a standard for the rest of us—not a particular way for us all to live, but a sternly individual standard to measure the various lives we lead. The hermit belongs to this ground. Separate from family and career and church and school, this shabby genius becomes the life of the place itself. The tramp passes on; this life stays. A tattered American flag flaps lazily from a branch of cottonwood near Celilo. When the eastbound freight thunders past, a gray hand flickers from the shadows to wave.

The saint dwells alone in a house or camp that defies the surface formalities of the town. Being alone, she or he is uniquely visible to the community, and uniquely free to live out some kind of wishing we cannot. Sweet paradox: the local character is independent of the codes we live by and by this independence is free to honor some deeper code or devotion that we— in our upright ways—believe but cannot express. This may be a devotion to a submerged traditional culture, to the past, to the vulnerable creatures of the natural world, or to the plain dignity of the slow mind.

Friends told me to watch for Acy Deucy, his big black hat sagging over his shoulders, as he walked toward Wallowa from his cabin twenty miles out. He'd come slouching along the country road each Saturday afternoon, with a local river's easy tread. And we traded stories at his expense—about the summer shack where he lived desperate summer and winter high on Promise Ridge, or about the time the harvest cook put two cups of salt into the cake by accident. Acy was a good harvest hand and first to the table. He gobbled up the cake without a flinch. In a word, the man is slow. For this, he is in everyone's care. He is the local character helping the citizens of Wallowa measure their responsibilities.

They say that once at a City Council meeting, Acy Deucy came up on the agenda. As I heard the story several times in Wallowa (where word travels fast and often), Acy's custom was to walk into town Saturday, celebrate until he could barely stand, then sleep it off in the fire station and walk home to Promise on Sunday. For the City Council, this routine became grave.

"When he pulls out those hoses to make a nest for himself," said one, "he jeopardizes the response time of the crew. If they get a call on a Saturday night, they'll have to untangle him before they can jump on the truck and go."

"I've been thinking on that," said another. "When you're talking fire, you're talking life and death. Let's lock the station so he can't get in. I've tried, but you can't reason with that man on a Saturday night."

"If we leave the door open to Acy," a third replied, "we *might* lose a house or even a life to a fire; if we lock the door, we will *surely* lose Acy to the cold. The man will freeze."

They all thought for a time, and then voted to leave the door open as it had been. And there Acy sleeps every Saturday night.

The obvious solution of leaving a mattress or blanket in the fire station for Acy's use never occurred in the several versions of this story I heard. Nor did I ever meet anyone who had actually attended the council meeting where this discussion was supposed to have taken place. Whether the meeting occurred or not, however, the often-repeated account of the meeting serves as a parable for Wallowa residents. In this story the town sees itself playing a gamble of one life—no matter how peripheral and strange—against all the codes and procedures for public safety and efficiency.

One Saturday night I sat by Acy, his big hat hunched over the bar at Baird's Tavern. While the shuffleboard puck slid the length of its table on cornmeal, and two women leaned back to laugh about something one had whispered, while jacked-up cars rumbled slow as autumn down the street outside, Acy began to tell me about his dog, way out at the shack on Promise Ridge, waiting for his return.

"But these schools!" he said suddenly. "They'll be our death!" The bar got quiet for a moment. He swirled the beer in his glass to center the foam, then drained it. "My dog," he said softly, "my dog's a good dog. He just waits inside that cabin no matter how long I'm gone."

I first met Abe Johnson, the bird man of Cline Falls, in the Bend bus station. He had a fifty-pound sack of birdseed slung over his shoulder, a blue stocking cap on his head, and a smashed and greasy cowboy hat on top of that. The pockets on his long canvas coat were torn, and when he took a little jump to shift the load, corn and sunflower seeds scattered from his pockets onto the floor. He set his quart styrofoam cup of coffee onto the end of a crowded bench and began to talk. When everyone else turned away, he turned to me.

"It's the inner-outer!" He raised his dirt-gloved hands in supplication toward me. "It's empathy! That's what makes the birds come in." The woman hiding behind her novel glanced up. The kid in a black T-shirt with sleeves torn away looked over his shoulder from pinball. "Some days they don't want to. They hop around in those trees like they'll never come. But then. . . ." When Abe paused dramatically to straighten up, the sack fell off his shoulder and tipped the cup from its perch. As coffee ran like a gully-washer down the bench, two children, a ski bum, and an old lady leaped from the coffee's path down the trough of polished oak, but Abe never noticed: ". . . then they come right here to my shoulder," he said. "Right here!" He patted his left shoulder, and his face bloomed with joy toward an invisible chickadee. Between his pursed lips was a magic kernel of corn.

Someone appeared from the snack bar with a handful of paper napkins and began with loud sighs to mop coffee from the bench. The old lady picked up Abe's empty cup, turned toward him with a chickadee's deference, then set the cup on top of the newsstand beside him and retreated. The boy's pinball game started to ring and jangle, and Abe brought his eyes into focus on me again.

"One time it was about ten degrees and snowing, but I wanted this magpie to come land on my back." Abe bent down, and let his arms dangle like weeping willow vines. "Magpies are funny. They get it in their mind they won't come, and stubborn!" Abe suddenly flung his arms outward and let out a screeching magpie oath.

"Skeee! Skeeee!" The old woman, twenty feet away across the lobby, backed two paces to the wall. Abe brought his hands up against his heart, and twisted his neck to face me. "That's where the empathy comes. I started to feel it. Sweat dropped off my nose to the snow, I wanted it so bad. And ten degrees!" His fingers snapped into a prayer-clench, and his eyes closed. His lips trembled, then suddenly his eyes smiled open.

"There he came! That magpie didn't want to, but he did. Landed right on my spine and stayed. Hopped around and squalled like he'd hit the

Promised Land." Abe sat down on the sack of birdseed, but immediately
they called the Portland bus and he struggled to his feet, swung the sack to
his shoulder with a fast wheeze of breath, and ambled toward the gate.

As the bus headed north on Highway 97, headlights punching the dark,
most passengers settled in for sleep. Or they pretended to. Abe snorted and
leaned across the aisle toward me. "One time I was down on my belly for
hours watching this beetle—little blue fella with knobby antlers. I followed
him all afternoon and must have covered fifty feet in circles and zags. That
little guy had to work! Watching him, you get to know what it's like to flop
onto your back and wrestle around trying to get up. I wanted to help him,
but I couldn't. Held a twig out once for him to grab, but then I pulled it
away. I wasn't his guardian, I was him! I forgot everything. Got soaked. Got
stiff. Like I dozed, like hypnotized, like born bug! And all of a sudden, this
crow lights on my shoulder, jumps down to snatch that beetle, and goes! I
heard his beak crunch down, felt I was the one to die. Had a hard time getting up, too."

Abe got off in Redmond, and I saw him flop his load into the basket of
a tricycle with a license plate, and pedal west in the dark. He started slow
but had achieved a steady, rambling rhythm by the time he left the pool of
the station's tungsten light.

It was later I read about this man in the news, talked with his neighbors, began to learn the complex relation he has with the human community as a result of his attention to the wild birds. I learned of his confrontation
with the gravel company that wants to scoop rock from under the bird sanc-
tuary he has been informally developing for twenty-five years. A lawyer has
donated time to stall the gravel operation. A local car dealership gave the
three-wheeled cycle I had seen him ride. So far, the dentist Abe approached
has declined to fix his teeth so he can whistle the proper songs to bring in
the birds, but community pressure will be on him to do so.

Abe's work is not ranching or logging or transport or tourists or smoke
jumping or any of the other mainstays of the Redmond community at large.
His work is feeding the wild birds, diverting water from storm run-off to the
trees they nest in, dragging home from the dump old appliances with which
to fashion sculptural feed stations that invite the chickadees but keep the
sparrows clear. For this, no matter how odd, he is a local saint.

One of his neighbors put it this way: When Abe stands like St. Francis—
hands outstretched, a small bird on each palm, and the light of beatitude on
his face, saying, "Here bird, here seed, come you little chatterbox"—anyone
could see why others run interference for his needs in the world.

Several years after our meeting in Bend, I stepped through the juniper
grove that surrounds his shack, calling out to warn him, "Mr. Johnson, are
you there? Mr. Johnson, I met you once in Bend. Do you remember?" I stood
before the shack and heard something fumble around inside. The door

scraped open a few inches and Abe's face appeared sideways. Then his hand reached out toward me holding a kettle of urine. He scowled.

"I don't like the look of that. Way too dark. What do you think?"

"It does look pretty dark," I said. "Hey, you were going to show me the birds."

"Birds?" His face, still sideways, softened to a toothless grin. "Give me a minute to get my boots on."

We carried on a shouted conversation through the door for close to a half hour while he sought the boots inside his box house, then he gave a mighty heave against the debris blocking the door, and got it pulled back far enough to slip through. He wore different hats this time, a short-billed hunter's cap and a tremendous broad-brimmed pilgrim affair on top. His pea-green coat sported six pockets bulging with seed that dribbled out when he twisted or bobbed to peer about. The zipper on his pants had failed, but two belts secured them, and the cuffs were stuffed into a pair of green rubber boots half a dozen sizes too large. Abe's sour fragrance trailed behind him like a river's fog, as he drifted through the tall grass before me from one feed station to the next.

"I came down from The Dalles in '48 to do potato harvest," he told me over his shoulder, "and stayed." He paused to smear a dab of peanut butter on the bark of a juniper tree well-darkened by his custom. "Been on this ground since." He led off again, this time toward a lone apple tree improbably alive among the dry-ground sage. Our path was not a line but a braid. We took the turnings of animals not intent to get somewhere but inquisitive to be everywhere. "There come sunflower." Abe pointed to a clump of dark green in the blond dead grass of July. "That's winterfood for chickadee. I haul it water from the river." We dropped into a ditch that led toward the apple tree. "I dug this ditch to pull the storm-water down off the rim. May lose that tree, though." The trunk stood on a little ring of flat ground Abe had sculpted for it. It had never been pruned or sprayed, living as Abe did by sheer intensity. There were no apples, and the tree didn't cast much shade. He put his hand on the trunk. "Woodpeckers starting to favor it. Bad sign."

The next feed station was an upright, cylindrical water heater laced with rust, with a stack of automobile brake drums on top. He lifted them down one by one, scattered fresh seed from his sack on a pan, then replaced the brake drums.

"These rims keep the sparrows off," he said, tapping the top brake drum with his fingernail. "They can't hang upside down and hop inside like a chickadee can. None of your upright birds can get in here. just chickadees, and snag bird—little wren."

There was a small wind beside my ear, and a chickadee lighted on Abe's left shoulder. Instantly, a sunflower seed appeared between his lips. The chickadee snatched it and was gone. The whole move between them

had the quick grace of something choreographed many chickadee generations back.

We paused at a dead refrigerator in a juniper tree's deep shade. The
door handle was gone, but Abe thrust his thumb through the rusted hole
where the handle had been, and the door popped open. He reached inside
to replenish the seed in his pockets, then shut the door with his knee. We
climbed the slope, which was jumbled with shards of basalt the size of cars
haphazard in a wrecking yard, to the garden. Here Abe had hauled horse
manure in sacks on his back to form a level ribbon of soil winding along
the slope of lichen-brightened rock. He had planted sunflower, tomato,
potato, and corn, and from a cleft behind an old juniper he took a hoe and
began to weed.

I sat in the shade and watched. My camera seemed the toy of another
century. My hands were too clean to coax leaves from rock, as Abe did. In
his hands, a rusted coffee can mended with pitch was Paleolithic. The day
went dumb with calm. As he reached up to handle a flower head, his face
was Inca. His coat was tree bark a wren searched for stray seed. Here at the
place Abe lived, I was like other ungainly citizens of the modern bus ride. In
this garden, we were the strange ones. On this earth, on his home ground, I
was apprentice to Abe.

Over on the wet side, mossy deep in the coast range west from Eugene,
Tubby Beers lived on Indian Creek with his team of Percherons, and his
World War II tank for gypo logging parked in the front yard. The tank's tur-
ret had been removed, and in its place a home-welded boom of steel was
hinged for swivel-work yarding logs. Tubby said with that rig he didn't need
roads. "Long as I'm in second-growth, I go anywhere I want. Course, if I
want to be gentle about it, I use the horses. They don't leave more skid trail
than a short-tailed rainstorm."

Tubby himself had to step sideways through some doors, and it's hard
to believe he ever died. He seemed too vibrant to slip through the frame of
a grave and be gone.

Inside the house that day, when a big laugh closed his eyes and I could
frankly glance around, my gaze swept the world map taped to the ceiling; the
fiddle, mandolin, and guitar hung handy on the wall; the eight stuffed animals crouching hospitably at eye-level on the living room shelf—bear, skunk,
weasel, and related kin. The tribe of the wild lived inside Tubby's mind.

"There were seven men there that day," he began in a rush, "and they're
all dead and my daddy told me and I'm the only one that knows." In the
wake of those words could be the story of Tubby's Uncle Mike riding with
Jesse James. Or Uncle Frank serving as Teddy Roosevelt's personal body-
guard in the battle of San Juan Hill. Or the Beers family fife and drum corps
parting the sea of buffalo as they crossed the plains by wagon. Or a tale of

Tubby's own shenanigans at rodeos and logging shows and other lively celebrations, of Saturday nights riding his horse and roaring wild up-canyon from the Indianola Bar, blasting the sky with his guns for joy.

This time it was none of those. It was the tale of Madera's Grave, the story of a strange and crazy man who was saint in this place before Tubby was born. Lyman Madera built his cabin without a door, as Tubby told it, and had to climb in through a hole in the roof each night to sleep. He lost his son, he prayed, he died with a mountain named for him. That was all. After the story, Tubby plucked his guitar from the wall and prepared to sing.

"Don't write this down," he said, tuning up. "I just want you listening." The song was a terrible fervent thing about the Japs and honor and the flag and our young people today. His tear-filled eyes held mine.

Tubby lived alone, and all his love of things old or musical or wild showed around the house and yard: the five pair of cowboy boots muddy around the stove to dry—all his; the saddle flung over the porch rail; the Percherons sidling eagerly into harnessing position when he stepped toward them. His great hands grabbed the tail of each and pulled. They tensed, but stood unmoved.

Besides his long stories and songs and asides, up a little side canyon Tubby kept a secret for us all. He got quiet and led me out the door and away through the trees to a hidden barn. Inside, he had kept oiled and polished ready for work an entire set of horse-drawn farm machinery. It was a museum in a barn that no one knew but the few he led there. He was historian for the primitive life. He was scholar with no degree or say-so but what he knew was crucial.

"They're all dead and I'm the only one that knows."

Farther west, just over the dunes from the Pacific, Marge Severy kept her home alone. The first time I stopped by, she had mushrooms spread fragrant on the kitchen table to dry—the Japanese pine mushroom that grows only on the slopes of Mount Fuji and on this coast, she said to me.

As one of the last of the local Siuslaw Indian people, she was the original character of the valley. We were the odd ones, the eccentric citizens of this landscape—with our motorized processions and neon fantasies strung out along Highway 101. When a low fog hung over the river and fir trees bowed down with rain, when old swans called from the south dunes and cormorants came winging low over town, I saw her walking. She was a part of those proper customs by fog and bird song. She was with the place, and we were strangers to it. We might one day belong as she had always.

She sat on an overturned boat one Sunday afternoon, watching the university archeologist dig out bones and beads and slender shells, fragile as ash, from a grave at the heart of town. Someone, digging a sewer line, had found the grave. Now it was being removed and labeled for study. The man

worked in the shade of his pit, and Marge, the sun behind her, wore the halo
light of the old and the quiet. There was coherence in the earth. The man
with the trowel and screen laid a ruler in the grave and numbered everything
he took away.

We met again at the Indian cemetery Marge cared for, across from her
house up North Fork. I found her leaning on a hoe among the wooden markers and indistinct plots in the sand. Fog rolled down over a tremendous dune
above us.

"Soon that will be here," she said, gesturing toward the dune. "Pretty
soon I won't be watching over these old graves. That will be kind of a relief,
you know, because then nobody can dig them up to study them, like they do
to our people."

Sometimes before first light, when I stand behind my house in the city to listen, those hermit names come easy to my mouth. I will be one of them. For
I would live their code of poverty and imagination in a doorless patchwork
house guarded by a ferocious goose. I would live by the miracles of the unin-
sured. I would walk only, I would speak for days only with the birds, I would
sing, and tend my village with a hoe.

Maybe it's jail by now for Gypsy Slim. Maybe it's death.

Maybe it's a campsite, somewhere in my life.

References

Aarne, Antti, and Stith Thompson. [1910, 1961] 1987. *The Types of the Folktale*. Rev. ed. Helsinki: Academia Scientiarum Fennica.

Abbott, Henry L. 1857. *Reports of Explorations and Surveys to Ascertain the Most Practical and Economical Route for a Railroad from the Mississippi River to the Pacific Ocean*. Washington, D. C.: War Department.

Abraham, Kitty G., and Evelyn Lieberman. 1985. "Should Barbie Go to Preschool?" *Young Children* (January): 12–14.

Abu-Lughod, Lila. 1991. "Writing Against Culture." In *Recapturing Anthropology*, edited by Richard G. Fox, 137–62. Santa Fe: School of American Research Press.

Achebe, Chinua. 1969. *Things Fall Apart*. New York: Fawcett.

Adler, Thomas A. 1981. "Making Pancakes on Sunday: The Male Cook in the Family Tradition." *Western Folklore* 40, no. 1: 45–54.

Alekseev, A. I. [1970] 1996. *Fedor Petrovich Litke*. Edited by Katherine L. Arndt, translated by Serge LeComte. Fairbanks: University of Alaska Press.

Anderson, Nels. [1942] 1966. *Desert Saints: The Mormon Frontier in Utah*. Chicago: University of Chicago Press.

Armitage, Susan. 1982. "'Aunt Amelia's Diary': The Record of a Reluctant Pioneer." In *Teaching Women's Literature from a Regional Perspective*, edited by Lenore Hoffman and Deborah Rosenfelt, 69–73. New York: Modern Language Association of America.

Arrington, Leonard J. 1958. *Great Basin Kingdom: An Economic History of the Latter-day Saints, 1830–1900*. Cambridge: Harvard University Press.

Art Guide of Forest Lawn with Interpretations. 1941. Glendale: Forest Lawn Memorial Park.

Atwood, Kenneth Ward. 1976. "Dry-Land Farmers" (author unknown). Recorded by Hal Cannon. *New Beehive Songster*. Vol. 2. Salt Lake City: University of Utah Press, Okehdokee Records.

Augustyniak, J. Michael. 1996. *The Barbie Doll Boom*. Paducah, KY: Collector Books.

Barker Texas History Collection. University of Texas, Austin.

Barnett, Homer G. 1983. "Learning about Culture: Reconstruction, Participation, Administration, 1934–1954." In *Observers Observed: Essays on Ethnographic Fieldwork*, edited by George W. Stocking, Jr., 157–74. Madison: University of Wisconsin Press.

Bauman, Richard, Patricia Sawin, and Inta Gale Carpenter, with Richard Anderson et al. 1992. *Reflections on the Folklife Festival: An Ethnography of Participant Experience*. Special Publications Series, no. 2. Bloomington, IN: Folklore Institute.

Beckham, Stephen Dow. 1971. *Requiem for a People: The Rogue Indians and the Frontiersmen*. Norman: University of Oklahoma Press.

———. 1977. *The Indians of Western Oregon: This Land Was Theirs*. Coos Bay: Arago Books.

———. 1990. "History of Western Oregon Since 1846." In *Handbook of North American Indians*, 7:180–96. Washington, D. C.: Smithsonian Institution.

Ben–Amos, Dan. 1976. "Talmudic Tall Tales." In *Folklore Today: A Festschrift for Richard M. Dorson*, edited by Linda Dégh, Henry Glassie, and Felix Oinas, 25–44. Bloomington: Research Center for Language and Semiotic Studies.

Bendix, Regina. 1997. *In Search of Authenticity: The Formation of Folklore Studies*. Madison: University of Wisconsin Press.

Bird-Dupont, Ella. 1935. "True Life Story of Ella Bird-Dupont, Earliest Settler in the East Part of the Panhandle, Texas." Barker Texas History Collection, University of Texas, Austin.

Boag, Peter. 1992. "The Valley of Long Grasses." *Old Oregon* 72, no. 2: 18.

Boas, Franz. [1916] 1970. *Tsimshian Mythology*. New York and London: Johnson Reprint Corporation.

Bode, Carl. 1959. *The Anatomy of American Popular Culture, 1840–1861*. Berkeley and Los Angeles: University of California Press.

Bowie, Margaret Armstrong. 1872–77. Diary. Barker Texas History Collection, University of Texas, Austin.

Boyd, Bill and his Prairie Ramblers. 1936. "Way Out There" (author unknown). San Antonio, TX, Bluebird Records.

Bridgewater, Lucy. 1869. Letter to Bettie Beall, 7 June. Barker Texas History Collection, University of Texas, Austin.

Brunvand, Jan Harold. 1968. "The Taming of the Shrew Tale in the United States." In *The Study of American Folklore: An Introduction*, 304–16. New York: W. W. Norton.

———. 1991. *The Taming of the Shrew: A Comparative Study of Oral and Literary Versions*. New York: Garland.

———. 1998. *The Study of American Folklore: An Introduction*. 4th ed. New York: W. W. Norton.

BTW. 1995. *Building the West*. Compiled by Jody Young. Archive of Kellogg, Idaho Mining. Boise State University.

Burawoy, Michael. 1979. *Manufacturing Consent: Changes in the Labor Process Under Monopoly Capitalism*. Chicago: University of Chicago Press.

Campbell, William. 1853. *An Historical Sketch of Robin Hood and Captain Kidd*. New York: C. Scribner.

Cantrell, John. 1995. "The Controversial Closure of the Bunker Hill Company: Revisiting the Question of Culpability." M. A. Thesis, Boise State University.

Chapman, Ray. 1994. *Uncle Bunker: Memories in Words and Pictures*. Kellogg, Idaho: Chapman Publishing.

Chapple, Eliot. 1953. "Applied Anthropology in Industry." In *Anthropology Today: An Encyclopedic Inventory*, edited by A. L. Kroeber, 819–31. Chicago: University of Chicago Press.

Chase, A. W. 1873. Shell Mounds: Oregon and Notes on Native Tribes. Bureau of American Ethnology, field notes 3230. Washington, D. C: Smithsonian Institution.

Cheney, Thomas E., ed. 1968. *Mormon Songs from the Rocky Mountains: A Compilation of Mormon Folksong*. Publications of the American Folklore Society, Memoir Series, v. 53. Austin: University of Texas Press.

Clements, William M. 1974. "The American Folk Church: A Characterization of American Folk Religion Based on Field Research Among White Protestants in a Community in the South Central United States." Ph.D. diss., Indiana University.

———. 1978. "The American Folk Church in Northern Arkansas." *Journal of the Folklore Institute* 15: 161–80.

———. 1983. "The Folk Church: Institution, Event, Performance." In *Handbook of American Folklore*, edited by Richard M. Dorson, Inta Gale Carpenter, Elizabeth Peterson, and Angela Maniak, 136–44. Chicago: University of Chicago Press.

Coben, Stanley. 1976. "The Assault on Victorianism in the Twentieth Century." In *Victorian America*, edited by Daniel Walker Howe, 160–81. Philadelphia: University of Pennsylvania Press.

Collins, June M. 1974. *Valley of the Spirits: The Upper Skagit Indians of Western Washington*. Seattle: University of Washington Press.

Connolly, Thomas J. 1991. "The Standley Site (35D0182): Investigations into the Prehistory of Camas Valley, Southwest Oregon." *University of Oregon Anthropological Papers*, no. 43. Eugene.

Cordes, Helen. 1992. "What a Doll! Barbie: Materialistic Bimbo or Feminist Trailblazer?" *Utne Reader*, March-April, 46–50.

Croy, Homer. 1949. *Jesse James Was My Neighbor*. New York: Duell, Sloan and Pearce.

Cunningham, Kamy. 1993. "Barbie Doll Culture and the American Waistland." *Symbolic Interaction* 16, no. 1: 79–83.

Dauenhauer, Nora Marks, and Richard Dauenhauer. 1987. *Haa Shuká, Our Ancestors: Tlingit Oral Narratives*. Seattle: University of Washington Press.

———. 1990. *Haa Tuwunáagu Yís, for Healing our Spirit: Tlingit Oratory*. Seattle: University of Washington Press.

———. 1994. *Haa Ḵusteeyí, Our Culture: Tlingit Life Stories*. Seattle: University of Washington Press.

Dégh, Linda. 1972. "Folk Narrative." In *Folklore and Folklife: An Introduction*, edited by Richard M. Dorson, 53–83. Chicago: University of Chicago Press.

Denver, John. "Forest Lawn." *Take Me to Tomorrow*, RCA LSP-4278.

Deutsch, Stefanie. 1996. *Barbie: The First Thirty Years, 1959 through 1989, an Identification and Value Guide*. Paducah, KY: Collector Books.

"Disneyland of Death." 1959. *Time*, 7 December, 107.

Dobie, J. Frank. 1955. "The Robinhooding of Sam Bass." *Montana: The Magazine of Western History* 5: 34-41.

Dodge, Orvil. [1898] 1969. *Pioneer History of Coos and Curry Counties, Oregon: Heroic Deeds and Thrilling Adventures of the Early Settlers.* 2d ed. Bandon: Western World.

Dodson, Ruth. 1951. "Don Pedrito Jaramillo, the Curandero of Los Olmos." In *The Healer of Los Olmos, and other Mexican Lore*, edited by Wilson M. Hudson, 9–70. Publications of the Texas Folklore Society, 24. Dallas: Southern Methodist University Press.

Dorson, Richard M. 1959. *American Folklore.* Chicago: University of Chicago Press.

———. 1964. *Buying the Wind: Regional Folklore in the United States.* Chicago: University of Chicago Press.

———. 1982. *Man and Beast in American Comic Legend.* Bloomington, Indiana University Press.

———. 1983. "Folktale Performers." In *Handbook of American Folklore*, edited by Richard M. Dorson, Inta Gale Carpenter, Elizabeth Peterson, and Angela Maniak, 287–300. Bloomington: Indiana University Press.

Douglas, Ann. 1975. "Heaven Our Home: Consolation Literature in the Northern United States, 1830–1880." In *Death in America*, edited by David E. Stannard, 49–68. Philadelphia: University of Pennsylvania Press.

Duggan, Betty J. 1997. "Tourism, Cultural Authenticity, and the Native Crafts Cooperative: The Eastern Cherokee Experience. In *Tourism and Culture: An Applied Perspective*, edited by Erve Chambers, 31–57. Albany: State University of New York Press.

Dundes, Alan. 1968. "The Number Three in American Culture." In *Every Man His Way: Readings in Cultural Anthropology*, edited by Alan Dundes, 401–24. Englewood Cliffs, N.J.: Prentice-Hall.

———. 1969. "Thinking Ahead: A Folkloristic Reflection on the Future-Orientation in American Worldview." *Anthropological Quarterly* 42:53-72.

———. 1971. "Folk Ideas as Units of World View." *Journal of American Folklore* 84:93–103.

———, and Alessandro Falassi. 1975. *La Terra in Piazza: Interpretation of the Palio of Siena.* Berkeley: University of California Press.

Drucker, Philip. 1965. *Cultures of the North Pacific Coast.* San Francisco: Chandler Publishing.

Ebersole, Lucinda, and Richard Peabody, eds. 1993. *Mondo Barbie.* New York: St. Martin's Press.

Eliade, Mircea. 1959. *The Sacred and the Profane: The Nature of Religion.* Translated by Willard R. Trask. New York: Harvest.

Embree, Henrietta Baker. 1856–61. Diary. Barker Texas History Collection, University of Texas, Austin.

Erlandson, Jon, and Madonna Moss. 1994. "Cultures and Environments of the Pacific Coast of North America from 11,500 to 8,000 Years Ago." In *As the World Warmed: The Archaeology of the Pleistocene-Holocene Transition*, edited by L. Straus, B. Eriksen, J. Erlandson, and D. Yesner. New York: Plenum Press.

Evans-Pritchard, Deirdre. 1987. "The Portal Case: Authenticity, Tourism, Traditions, and the Law." *Journal of American Folklore* 100:287–96.

Faber, Frederick. 1948. "Faith of Our Fathers." *Youthspiration Pocket Hymnal*, edited by Alfred B. Smith. Grand Rapids, MI: Zondervan.

Fahey, John. 1971. *The Ballyhoo Bonanza: Charles Sweeny and the Idaho Mines*. Seattle: University of Washington Press.

Falassi, Alessandro, ed. 1987. *Time out of Time: Essays on the Festival*. Albuquerque: University of New Mexico Press.

Fennick, Janine. 1996. *The Collectible Barbie Doll*. London: Quintet.

Fife, Austin and Alta. 1956. *Saints of Sage and Saddle: Folklore Among the Mormons*. Bloomington: Indiana University Press.

Firth, Raymond. 1948. "Anthropological Backgrounds to Work." *Occupational Psychology* 22:94–102.

Fish, Lydia. 1984. "Father Baker: Legends of a Saint in Buffalo. *New York Folklore* 10:3–4, 23–33.

Flake, Lucy Hannah White. 1932. "To the Last Frontier." Special Collections Department, Marriott Library, University of Utah.

Frachtenberg, Leo J. 1913. *Coos Texts*. New York: Columbia University Press.

Frankfurter, Alexander M. 1988. "A Gathering of Children: Holy Infants and the Cult of el Santo Niño de Atocha." *El Palacio* 94:1.

French, Stanley. 1975. "The Cemetery as Cultural Institution: The Establishment of Mount Auburn and the 'Rural Cemetery' Movement." In *Death in America*, edited by David E. Stannard, 69–91. Philadelphia: University of Pennsylvania Press.

Furlong, Marjorie, and Virginia Pill. 1973. *Edible? Incredible!* Tacoma, WA: Erco, Inc.

Gamst, Frederick. 1977. "An Integrating View of the Underlying Premises of an Industrial Ethnology in the United States and Canada." *Anthropological Quarterly* 50:1–10.

Gannett, Cinthia. 1992. *Gender and the Journal: Diaries and Academic Discourse*. Albany: SUNY Press.

Gardner, Dore. 1992. *Niño Fidencio: A Heart Thrown Open*. Santa Fe: Museum of New Mexico Press.

Gaudet, Marcia. 1994. "Charlene Richard: Folk Veneration Among the Cajuns." *Southern Folklore* 51:154–66.

Geoffrey of Monmouth. 1969. *The History of the Kings of Britain*. London: The Folio Society.

Gillon, Edmund V., Jr. 1972. *Victorian Cemetery Art*. New York: Dover Publications.

Glassie, Henry. 1995. "Tradition." *Journal of American Folklore* 108:395–412.

Goodchild, Peter. 1991. *Raven Tales: Traditional Stories of Native Peoples*. Chicago: Chicago Review Press.

Grant, Richard. 1995. "At the Shrine of the Narcotraficantes." *Esquire*, British edition, July/August.

Green, Archie. 1965. "American Labor Lore: Its Meanings and Uses." *Industrial Relations* 4:189–217.

————. 1972. *Only a Miner: Studies in Recorded Coal Mining Songs*. Urbana: University of Illinois Press.

————. 1978. "Industrial Lore: A Bibliographic-Semantic Inquiry." In *Working Americans: Contemporary Approaches to Occupational Folklife*, edited by Robert H. Byington, 71–103. Smithsonian Folklife Studies 3. Los Angeles: California Folklore Society.

Greenway, John. 1964. Introductory note to "Memories of a Mormon Girlhood," by Juanita Brooks. *Journal of American Folklore* 77:195–219.

————, ed. 1969. *Folklore of the Great West: Selections from Eighty-three Years of the* Journal of American Folklore. Palo Alto: American West Publishing.

Grider, Sylvia Ann. 1996. "Conservatism and Dynamism in the Contemporary Celebration of Halloween: Institutionalization, Commercialization, and Gentrification." *Southern Folklore* 53, no. 1: 3–15

Griffith, James S. 1992. *Beliefs and Holy Places: A Spiritual Geography of the Pimería Alta* Tucson: University of Arizona Press.

————. 1995. *A Shared Space: Folklife in the Arizona/Sonora Borderlands*. Logan: Utah State University Press.

Grover, David H. 1964. *Debaters and Dynamiters: The Story of the Haywood Trial*. Corvallis: Oregon State University Press.

Gutman, Herbert G. 1976. *Work, Culture and Society in Industrializing America: Essays in American Working-Class and Social History*. New York: Knopf.

Hall, Roberta L. 1984. *The Coquille Indians: Yesterday, Today, and Tomorrow*. Lake Oswego: Smith, Smith, and Smith.

Halpert, Herbert. 1990. "Mosquitoes on the Runway." *Western Folklore* 49:145–61.

Halpert, Herbert, and Emma Robinson. 1942. "'Oregon' Smith, an Indiana Folk Hero." *Southern Folklore Quarterly* 6: 163–68. Cited in Dorson 1982: 110–11.

Hammond, Joyce D. 1995. "The Tourist Folklore of Pele: Encounters with the Other." In *Out of the Ordinary: Folklore and the Supernatural*, edited by Barbara Walker, 159–79. Logan: Utah State University Press.

Hampsten, Elizabeth. 1982. *"Read This Only to Yourself": The Private Writings of Midwestern Women, 1880–1910*. Bloomington: Indiana University Press.

Hand, Wayland D. 1942a. "California Miner's Folklore: Above Ground." *California Folklore Quarterly* 1:24–46.

————. 1942b. "California Miner's Folklore: Below Ground." *California Folklore Quarterly* 1:127–55.

————. 1946. "The Folklore, Customs and Traditions of the Butte Miner." *California Folklore Quarterly* 5:1–27, 153–78.

————. 1969. "American Occupational and Industrial Folklore: The Miner." In *Kontakte und Grenzen*, edited by Hans Foltin, 453–60. Göttingen: Verlag Otto Schwartz.

Hansen, Mel. 1977. *Indian Heaven Back Country: Southwest Washington Cascades: Trails, Lakes, and Indian Lore*. Beaverton, Ore.: Touchstone Press.

Harding, Charles F. 1955. "The Social Antropology of American Industry." *American Anthropologist* 57: 1218–31.

Harrington, John P. 1943. Notes of Interviews with Some Coquille People at Siletz in 1943. Anthropological Archives. Washington, D. C.: Smithsonian Institution.

Harris, Neil. 1966. *The Artist in American Society*. New York: George Braziller.

Hart, John L. 1997. "Ten Million Members Worldwide." *LDS Church News*, 1 November, 3, 5.

Henningsen, Gustav. 1965. "The Art of Perpendicular Lying." *Journal of the Folklore Institute* 2:180–219.

Henry, Lyell D., Jr. 1995. *Was This Heaven? A Self-Portrait of Iowa on Early Postcards*. Iowa City: University of Iowa Press.

Hilbert, Vi, ed. and trans. 1985. *Haboo: Native American Stories from Puget Sound*. Seattle: University of Washington Press.

Hohmann-Delf, Maria. 1985. "Jennifer and Her Barbies: A Contextual Analysis of the Child Playing Barbie Dolls." *Canadian Folklore Canadien* 7, no. 1–2: 111–20.

Holden, William Curry. 1978. *Teresita*. Owings Mills, Md.: Stemmer House Publishers.

Holley, Mary Austin. 1833. *Texas: Observations, Historical, Geographical and Descriptive, in a Series of Letters, Written During a Visit to Austin's Colony, With a View to a Permanent Settlement in That Country in the Autumn of 1831*. Baltimore: Armstrong and Plaskett.

Holt, James Clarke. 1982. *Robin Hood*. London: Thames and Hudson.

Howe, Daniel Walker. 1976a. "Victorian Culture in America." In *Victorian America*, edited by Daniel Walker Howe, 3–28. Philadelphia: University of Pennsylvania Press.

———. 1976b. *Victorian America*. Philadelphia: University of Pennsylvania Press.

Huff, Cynthia A. 1996. "Textual Boundaries: Space in Nineteenth-Century Manuscript Diaries." In *Inscribing the Daily: Critical Essays on Women's Diaries*, edited by Suzanne L. Bunkers and Cynthia A. Huff, 123–38. Amherst: University of Massachusetts Press.

Hughes, Everett C. 1952. "The Sociological Study of Work: An Editorial Foreword." *American Journal of Sociology* 57:423–26.

Hutton, May Arkwright. [1900] 1992. *The Coeur d'Alenes, or, A Tale of the Modern Inquisition in Idaho*. Ann Arbor: UMI Out-of-Print Books.

Hyde, Douglas. [1899] 1967. *A Literary History of Ireland from Earliest Times to the Present Day*. New York: Barnes and Noble.

Hymes, Dell. 1981. *"In Vain I Tried to Tell You": Essays in Native American Ethnopoetics*. Philadelphia: University of Pennsylvania Press.

Jackman, E. R. and Reub A. Long. 1977. *The Oregon Desert*. Caldwell, Idaho: Caxton Press. Cited in *The Stories We Tell: An Anthology of Oregon Folk Literature*, edited by Suzi Jones and Jarold Ramsey. Corvallis: Oregon State University Press, 1994.

Jacobs, Laura. 1998. *Barbie: Four Decades in Fashion*. Rev. ed. New York: Abbeville Publishing.

Jacobs, Melville. 1939. *Coos Narrative and Ethnologic Texts*. Seattle: University of Washington Press.

———. 1940. *Coos Myth Texts*. Seattle: University of Washington Press.

———. 1959. *The Content and Style of an Oral Literature: Clackamas Chinook Myths and Tales*. Chicago: University of Chicago Press.

———. 1972. "Areal Spread of Indian Oral Genre Features in the Northwest States." *Journal of the Folklore Institute* 9:10.

Jacobus de Voragine. 1969. *The Golden Legend*. New York: Arno Press.

Jeffrey, Julie Roy. 1979. *Frontier Women: The Trans-Mississippi West, 1840–1880*. New York: Hill and Wang.

Jones, Gwyn, 1968. *A History of the Vikings*. London: Oxford University Press.

———. trans. [1961] 1988. *Eirik the Red and Other Icelandic Sagas*. London: Oxford University Press.

Jones, Suzi. 1976. "Regionalization: A Rhetorical Strategy." *Journal of the Folklore Institute* 13:105–20.

Juhasz, Suzanne. 1980. "Towards a Theory of Form in Feminist Autobiography." In *Women's Autobiography: Essays in Criticism*, edited by Estelle C. Jelinek, 221–37. Bloomington: Indiana University Press.

Kaufman, Sharon. 1986. *The Ageless Self: Sources of Meaning in Late Life*. Madison: University of Wisconsin Press.

Keller, F. W. 1947. "Blue Mountain," by F. W. Keller. Recorded by Austin and Alta Fife. 336.68 Fife MCI, 608.

Kirshenblatt-Gimblett, Barbara. 1998. *Destination Culture: Tourism, Museums, and Heritage*. Berkeley and Los Angeles: University of California Press.

Kiskaddon, Bruce. 1987. *Rhymes of the Ranges: A New Collection of the Poems of Bruce Kiskaddon*. Edited by Hal Cannon. Salt Lake City: Gibbs M. Smith.

Kornbluh, Joyce. 1964. *Rebel Voices: An I. W. W. Anthology*. Ann Arbor: University of Michigan Press.

Korson, George. 1927. *Songs and Ballads of the Anthracite Miner*. New York: Hitchcock.

———. 1938. *Minstrels of the Mine Patch: Songs and Stories of the Anthracite Industry*. Philadelphia: University of Pennsylvania Press.

———. 1943. *Coal Dust on the Fiddle: Songs and Stories of the Bituminous Industry*. Philadelphia: University of Pennsylvania Press.

———. 1960. *Black Rock: Mining Folklore of the Pennsylvania Dutch*. Baltimore: Johns Hopkins University Press.

Kusterer, Ken C. 1978. *Know-How on the Job: The Important Working Knowledge of "Unskilled" Workers*. Boulder: Westview Press.

Lange, Yvonne. 1978. "Santo Niño de Atocha: A Mexican Cult is Transplanted to Spain." *El Palacio* 84:4.

Larson, Gustive O. 1947. *Prelude to the Kingdom: Mormon Desert Conquest, a Chapter in American Cooperative Experience*. Francestown, N. H.: M. Jones Company.

Lawless, Elaine J. 1984. "'I Know If I Don't Bear My Testimony I'll Lose It': Why Mormon Women Bother to Speak at All. *Kentucky Folklore Record* 30:79–96.

————. 1988a. *God's Peculiar People: Women's Voices and Folk Tradition in a Pentecostal Church*. Lexington: University Press of Kentucky.

————. 1988b. *Handmaidens of the Lord: Pentecostal Women Preachers and Traditional Religion*. Philadelphia: University of Pennsylvania Press.

————. 1993. *Holy Women, Wholly Women: Sharing Ministries of Wholeness Through Life Stories and Reciprocal Ethnography*. Philadelphia: University of Pennsylvania Press.

————. 1996. *Women Preaching Revolution: Calling for Connection in a Disconnected Time*. Philadelphia: University of Pennsylvania Press.

Lee, Hector H. 1949. *The Three Nephites: The Substance and Significance of the Legend in Folklore*. University of New Mexico Publications in Language and Literature, no. 2. Albuquerque: University of New Mexico Press.

————. 1988. Introduction to *Exploring Western Americana*, edited by Alta Fife. Ann Arbor: UMI Research Press.

Lévi-Strauss, Claude. 1967. *Structural Anthropology*. Translated by Claire Jacobsen and Brooke G. Schoepf. Garden City: Doubleday.

Lincoln, Kenneth. 1993. *Indi'n Humor: Bicultural Play in Native America*. New York: Oxford University Press.

Lingenfelter, Richard E. 1974. *The Hardrock Miners: A History of the Mining Labor Movement in the American West, 1863–1893*. Berkeley: University of California Press.

Litke, Frederic. 1987. *A Voyage Around the World, 1826–1829*. Translated by Renée Marshall. Kingston, Ont.: Limestone Press.

López Sanchez, Sergio. 1995. "Malverde, un bandido generoso." *Fronteras* 1, no. 2: 32–40.

Lord, M. G. 1994. *Forever Barbie: The Unauthorized Biography of a Real Doll*. New York: Morrow and Company.

Lyman, Eliza Maria Partridge Smith. 1820–86. Journal. Special Collections Department, Marriott Library, University of Utah.

Macklin, Barbara June, and N. Ross Crumrine. 1973. "Three North Mexican Folk Saint Movements." *Comparative Studies in Society and History* 15:89–105.

MacNaughton, Glenda. 1996. "Is Barbie to Blame?: Reconsidering How Children Learn Gender." *Australian Journal of Early Childhood* 21, no. 4: 18–24.

Malory, Sir Thomas. 1971. *Works*. Edited by Eugene Vinaver. London: Oxford University Press.

Margo, Albert M. 1997. "Why Barbie is Perceived as Beautiful." *Perceptual and Motor Skills* 85:363–374.

Martens, Lorna. 1985. *The Diary Novel*. Cambridge: Cambridge University Press.

Mattel Toy Company. http://www.barbie.com, 1999.

Maverick, Mary. 1850. Diary. Barker Texas History Collection, University of Texas, Austin.

Mayo, Elton. 1933. *The Human Problems of an Industrial Civilization*. New York: Macmillan.

McCarl, Robert. 1974. "The Production Welder: Product, Process and the Industrial Craftsman." *New York Folklore Quarterly* 30:243–53.

———. 1978. "Occupational Folklife: A Theoretical Hypothesis." *Western Folklore* 37:3–18.

———. 1985a. *The District of Columbia Fire Fighters' Project: A Case Study in Occupational Folklife*. Smithsonian Folklife Studies, no. 4. Washington, D. C.: Smithsonian Institution Press.

———. 1985b. "Fire and Dust: Ethnography at Work in Communities." *Practicing Anthropology* 1 and 2:21–22.

———. 1997. *Contested Landscapes: The Above and Below Ground Landscape of Idaho's Coeur d'Alene Mining District*. Salt Lake City: University of Utah, Graduate School of Architecture, 1997.

McCorkle, Jill. 1994. Introduction to *The Art of Barbie*, edited by Craig Yoe. New York: Workman Publishing.

McCracken, Grant David. 1996. *Big Hair: A Journey into the Transformation of Self*. Woodstock, NY: Overlook Press.

Mechling, Jay. 1986. "Children's Folklore." In *Folk Groups and Folklore Genres: An Introduction*, edited by Elliott Oring, 91–120. Logan: Utah State University Press.

Meissner, Martin. 1976. "The Language of Work." In *Handbook of Work, Organization and Society*, edited by Robert Dubin, 257–69. Chicago: Rand McNally.

Mendelson, E. M. 1968. "Worldview." In *International Encyclopedia of the Social Sciences*, edited by David L. Sills. New York: Macmillan.

Miller, Jay, and William R. Seaburg. 1990. "Athapaskans of Southwestern Oregon." In *Handbook of North American Indians*, 7:580–88. Washington, D. C.: Smithsonian Institution.

Mitchell, Claudia, and Jacquelin Reid-Walsh. 1995. "And I Want to Thank You, Barbie: Barbie as a Site for Cultural Interrogation." Review of *Mondo Barbie* (Ebersole and Peabody). *Review of Education/Pedagogy/Cultural Studies* 17, no. 2: 143–55.

Moss, Madonna, and Jon Erlandson. 1994. *An Evaluation Survey and Dating Program for Archaeological Sites on State Lands of the Southern Oregon Coast*. Department of Anthropology, University of Oregon.

Motz, Marilyn Ferris. 1983. "'I Want to Be a Barbie Doll When I Grow Up': The Cultural Significance of the Barbie Doll." In *Popular Culture Reader*, edited by Christopher O. Geise and John G. Nachbar. 3d ed. Bowling Green, Ohio: Bowling Green University Press.

Mullen, Patrick B. [1978] 1988. *I Heard the Old Fishermen Say: Folklore of the Texas Gulf Coast*. Logan: Utah State University Press.

Nash, June. 1979. *We Eat the Mines and the Mines Eat Us: Dependency and Exploitation in Bolivian Tin Mines*. New York: Columbia University Press.

Neblett, Jennie. 1860. Letter to Lizzie Scott Neblett. 2 January. Barker Texas History Collection, University of Texas, Austin.

Neblett, Lizzie Scott. 1852. Diary. Barker Texas History Collection, University of Texas, Austin.

New Catholic Encyclopedia. 1967 ed., s.v. "Saints."

Newcomb, Susan E. 1865–71. Diary. Barker Texas History Collection, University of Texas, Austin.

Nolan, Bob. 1934. "Tumblin' Tumbleweeds." Los Angeles: Williamson Music Company.

Norlen, Art. 1992. *Death of a Proud Union: The 1960 Bunker Hill Strike.* Cataldo, Idaho: Tamarack Publishing.

Norskog, Howard L. 1990. "The Black Lady Mare." In *New Cowboy Poetry: A Contemporary Gathering,* edited by Hal Cannon, 82–83. Salt Lake City: Gibbs M. Smith.

Norton, Jack. 1979. *Genocide in Northwestern California.* San Francisco: Indian Historian Press.

Norton, Kevin I., Timothy S. Olds, Scott Olive, and Stephen Dank. 1996. "Ken and Barbie at Life Size." *Sex Roles* 34: 287–94.

O'Clair, Rita M., Robert H. Armstrong, and Richard Carstensen. 1997. *The Nature of Southeast Alaska: A Guide to Plants, Animals, and Habitats.* Anchorage, Seattle, and Portland: Alaska Northwest Books.

Olds, Patrick C., and Myrazona R. Harris. 1997. *The Barbie Doll Years, 1959–1996: A Comprehensive Listing and Value Guide of Dolls and Accessories.* Paducah, Ky.: Collector Books.

Parton, James. 1864. *The Life and Times of Benjamin Franklin.* New York: Mason. Cited in David M. Larson, "Eighteenth-Century Tales of Sheep's Tails and One of Benjamin Franklin's 'American Jokes.'" *Philological Quarterly* 58 (1980): 242–47.

Paton, Lucy Allen, ed. 1912. *Arthurian Chronicles.* London: Dent.

Peterson, Emil R., and Alfred Powers. 1952. *A Century of Coos and Curry: A History of Southwest Oregon.* Portland: Binfords and Mort.

Petzoldt, Leander. [1990] 1995. *Kleines Lexikon der Dämonen und Elementargeister.* Munich: Verlag C. H. Beck.

Phipps, Stanley S. 1988. *From Bull Pen to Bargaining Table: The Tumultuous Struggle of the Coeur d'Alenes Miners for the Right to Organize, 1887–1942.* New York: Garland.

Pictorial Forest Lawn. 1953. Glendale: Forest Lawn Memorial Park.

Pilcher, William W. 1972. *The Portland Longshoremen: A Dispersed Urban Community.* New York: Holt, Rinehart and Winston.

Posen, Sheldon I. 1993. "On Folk Festivals and Kitchens: Questions of Authenticity in the Folksong Revival." In *Transforming Tradition: Folk Music Revivals Examined,* edited by Neil V. Rosenberg, 128–36. Urbana: University of Illinois Press.

Postman, Neil. 1985. *Amusing Ourselves to Death: Public Discourse in the Age of Show Business.* New York: Viking.

Raber, Bess Stangland. 1983. *Some Bright Morning.* Bend, Ore.: Maverick Press.

Ramsey, Jarold. 1977. *Coyote Was Going There: Indian Literature of the Oregon Country.* Seattle: University of Washington Press.

———. [1983] 1999. *Reading the Fire: Essays in the Traditional Indian Literatures of the Far West.* Lincoln: University of Nebraska Press. Rev. ed. University of Washington Press.

Rand, Erica. 1994. "We Girls Can Do Anything, Right, Barbie?: Lesbian Consumption in Postmodern Circulation." In *The Lesbian Postmodern,* edited by Laura Doan and Robyn Wiegman, 189–209. New York: Columbia University Press.

Raspe, Rudolph Erich. [1786] 1987. *Singular Travels, Campaigns, and Adventures of Baron Münchausen*. London: Methuen.

Redfield, Robert. 1930. *Tepoztlan, a Mexican Village: A Study of Folk Life*. Chicago: University of Chicago Press.

———. 1941. *The Folk Culture of Yucatan*. Chicago: University of Chicago Press.

———. 1947. *The Folk Society*. Indianapolis: Bobbs-Merrill.

———. 1955. *The Little Community: Viewpoints for the Study of a Human Whole*. Chicago: University of Chicago Press.

Richards, Mary Harkin Parker. 1996. *Winter Quarters: The 1846–1848 Life Writings of Mary Harkin Parker Richards*. Edited by Maurine Carr Ward. Logan: Utah State University Press.

Richardson, Samuel. [1741] 1928. *Familiar Letters on Important Occasions*. New York: Dodd, Mead & Company.

Ricketts, Edward F., Jack Calvin, and Joel W. Hedgpeth. 1994. *Between Pacific Tides*. 5th ed. Revised by David W. Phillips. Palo Alto: Stanford University Press.

Ricks, Joel. 1924. Pioneer Narratives Collection. File MS 389. Special Collections Library, Utah State University, Logan.

Ritson, Joseph. 1823. *Robin Hood: A Collection of All the Ancient Poems, Songs, and Ballads*. Vol. 1. London: William Pickering.

Robins, Cynthia. 1989. *Barbie: Thirty Years of America's Doll*. Chicago: Contemporary Books.

Rodriguez, Lourdes, ed. 1994. *La Ruta de los Santuarios en México*. México: CVS Publicaciones, S. A.. de C. V.

Roethlisberger, F. J., and William J. Dickson. 1939. *Management and the Worker: An Account of a Research Program Conducted by the Western Electric Company, Hawthorne Works, Chicago*. Cambridge: Harvard University Press.

Rossie, Jean-Pierre. 1994. "Symbols and Communication Through Children's Dolls: Examples from North Africa and the Sahara." *Communication and Cognition* 27:301–20.

Rosswurm, Steve, ed. 1992. *The CIO's Left-Led Unions*. New Brunswick, N.J.: Rutgers University Press.

Rubin, Barbara, Robert Carlton, and Arnold Rubin. 1979. *Forest Lawn*. Santa Monica: Westside Publications.

Rubin, Cynthia Elyce, and Morgan Williams. 1990. *Larger Than Life: The American Tall-Tale Postcard, 1905–1915*. New York: Abbeville Press.

Ruppert, James. 1995. "'A Bright Light Ahead of Us': Belle Deacon's Stories in English and Deg'Hitan." In *When Our Words Return: Writing, Hearing, and Remembering Oral Traditions of Alaska and the Yukon*, edited by Phyllis Morrow and William Schneider, 123–35, 227–39. Logan: Utah State University Press.

The Saga of the Jómsvikings. [1955] 1990. Translated by Lee M. Hollander. Austin: University of Texas Press.

Sampson, Martin J. 1972. *Indians of Skagit County*. Mt. Vernon, WA: Skagit County Historical Society.

Sandburg, Carl. 1927. *The American Songbag*. New York: Harcourt, Brace.

Santino, Jack. 1982. "Catholic Folklore and Folk Catholicism." *New York Folklore* 8:93–106.

Sarasohn-Kahn, Jane. 1998. *Contemporary Barbie Dolls: 1980 and Beyond*. Norfolk, Va.: Antique Trader Books.

Schlissel, Lillian. 1982. *Women's Diaries of the Westward Journey*. New York: Schocken Books.

Schmitt, Jean-Claude. 1983. *The Holy Greyhound: Guinefort, Healer of Children Since the Thirteenth Century*. Cambridge: Cambridge University Press.

Schwantes, Carlos A. 1991. *In Mountain Shadows: A History of Idaho*. Lincoln: University of Nebraska Press.

Schwartz, E. A. 1997. *The Rogue River Indian War and Its Aftermath, 1850–1980*. Norman: University of Oklahoma Press.

Scollon, Ronald, and Suzanne B.K. Scollon. 1979. *Linguistic Convergence: An Ethnography of Speaking at Fort Chipewyan, Alberta*. New York: Academic Press.

Settle, William A., Jr. 1966. *Jesse James Was His Name: Or, Fact and Fiction Concerning the Career of the Notorious James Brothers of Missouri*. Columbia: University of Missouri Press.

Shibano, Keiko Kimura. 1994. *Barbie in Japan*. Kenosha, Wis.: Murat Caviale.

Silko, Leslie Marmon. 1977. *Ceremony*. New York: New American Library.

Smith, Helena H. 1970. "Sam Bass and the Myth Machine." *The American West* 7:31-35.

Smith, Robert W. 1960. *The Coeur d'Alene Mining War of 1892: A Case Study of an Industrial Dispute*. Corvallis: Oregon State University Press.

Smith-Rosenberg, Carroll. [1975] 1986. "The Female World of Love and Ritual: Relations Between Women in Nineteenth-Century America." *Signs* 1, no. 1: 1–29. Rpt. in *Feminist Frontiers II: Rethinking Sex, Gender, and Society*, edited by Laurel Richardson and Verta A. Taylor, 229–49. New York: Random House.

Snyder, Gary. 1974. *Turtle Island*. New York: New Directions.

———. 1990. *The Practice of the Wild*. San Francisco: North Point Press.

Snyder, Sally. 1964. Skagit Society and its Existential Basis: An Ethnofolkoristic Reconstruction. Ph.D. diss., University of Washington.

Spacks, Patricia Meyer. 1975. *The Female Imagination*. New York: Knopf.

Steckmesser, Kent L. 1965. *The Western Hero in History and Legend*. Norman: University of Oklahoma Press.

———. 1966. "Robin Hood and the American Outlaw: A Note on History and Folklore." *Journal of American Folklore* 79:348-55.

———. 1970. "The Oklahoma Robin Hood." *The American West* 7:38-41.

Steele, Valerie. 1995. *Art, Design, and Barbie: The Evolution of a Cultural Icon*. New York: Exhibitions International.

Stegner, Wallace. 1942. *Mormon Country*. New York: Bonanza Books.

———. *A Sense of Place*. Audio cassette. Louisville, Colo.: Audio Press, 1989.

Stern, Susan. 1998. *Barbie Nation: An Unauthorized Tour*. 54 min. New Day Films. Videocassette.

Stern, Sydney Ladensohn, and Ted Schoenhaus. 1990. *Toyland: The High-Stakes Game of the Toy Industry*. Chicago: Contemporary Books.

Stewart, Elinore Pruitt. [1914] 1961. *Letters of a Woman Homesteader*. Lincoln: University of Nebraska Press.

Stout, Daniel A., Jr., and Russell H. Mouritsen. 1988. "Prosocial Behavior in Advertising Aimed at Children: A Content Analysis." *Southern Speech Communication Journal* 53: 159–74.

Stowell, Cynthia. 1987. *Faces of a Reservation*. Portland: Oregon Historical Society.

Stromberg, Peter. 1996. "Elvis Alive?: The Ideology of American Consumerism." In *Contemporary Legend: A Reader*, edited by Gillian Bennett and Paul Smith, 289–98. New York: Garland Publishing.

Strong, Arturo Carillo. 1990. *Corrido del Cocaine: Inside Stories of Hard Drugs, Big Money, and Short Lives*. Tucson: Harbinger House.

Summers, Beth. 1996. *A Decade of Barbie Dolls and Collectibles, 1981–1991: Identification and Values*. Paducah, Ky: Collector Books.

Sutton, Horace. 1958. "Ever-Ever Land." *Saturday Review*, 5 April, 23–25.

Sutton-Smith, Brian. 1986. *Toys as Culture*. New York: Gardner Press.

Swanton, John R. [1909] 1970. *Tlingit Myths and Texts*. New York and London: Johnson Reprint Corporation.

Taft, Michael. 1983. *Tall Tales of British Columbia*. Victoria: Sound and Moving Image Division, Province of British Columbia.

Taylor, Frederick Winslow. [1911] 1967. *Principles of Scientific Management*. New York: W. W. Norton.

Teagarden, Nancy Jane Logan. 1870–71. Diary. Barker Texas History Collection, University of Texas, Austin.

Theriault, Florence. 1992. *Barbie Rarities: The Dolls, the Costumes, Miscellany: An Identification and Value Guide*. Annapolis, Md: Gold Horse Publishing.

Thomas, Jeannie. 1995. "Pickup Trucks, Horses, Women, and Foreplay: The Fluidity of Folklore." *Western Folklore* 54:213–28.

Thompson, John. 1994. "Santo Niño de Atocha." *Journal of the Southwest* 36, no. 1 (spring): 1–18.

Thompson, Lucy. [1916] 1991. *To the American Indian: Reminiscences of a Yurok Woman*. Berkeley: Heyday Books.

Titon, Jeff Todd. 1988. *Powerhouse for God: Speech, Chant, and Song in an Appalachian Baptist Church*. Austin: University of Texas Press.

Toelken, Barre. 1969. "The 'Pretty Languages' of Yellowman: Genre, Mode, and Texture in Navajo Coyote Narratives." *Genre* 2:211–35. Rpt. in *Folklore Genres*, edited by Dan Ben–Amos, 145–70. Austin: University of Texas Press.

———. 1971. "Cultural Bilingualism and Composition." *English for American Indians* (spring): 29–32.

———. 1976. "A Circular World: The Vision of Navajo Crafts." *Parabola* 1:1, 30–37.

———. 1982a. "Native Arts and Public Policy." In *Native Arts Issues 81/82*, edited by Suzi Jones, 41–47. Anchorage: Alaska State Council on the Arts.

———. 1982b. "Seeing with Both Eyes." In *Native Arts Issues 81/82*, edited by Suzi Jones, 8–13. Anchorage: Alaska State Council on the Arts.

————. 1983. "The Basket Imperative." In *Pacific Basket Makers: A Living Tradition*, edited by Suzi Jones, 25–36. Fairbanks: Consortium for Pacific Arts and Cultures and University of Alaska Museum.

————. 1987. "Life and Death in the Navajo Coyote Tales." In *Recovering the Word: Essays on Native American Literature*, edited by Arnold Krupat and Brian Swann, 388–401. Berkeley: University of California Press.

————. 1991. "Traditional Water Narratives in Utah." *Western Folklore* 50:191–200.

————: 1994 "Coyote, Skunk and the Prairie Dogs." In *Coming to Light: Contemporary Translations of the Native Literatures of North America*, edited by Brian Swann, 590–600. New York: Random House.

————. 1995. *Morning Dew and Roses: Nuance, Metaphor, and Meaning in Folksongs*. Urbana: University of Illinois Press

————. [1979] 1996a. *The Dynamics of Folklore*. Rev. ed. Logan: Utah State University Press.

————. 1996b. "From Entertainment to Realization in Navajo Fieldwork." In *The World Observed: Reflections on the Fieldwork Process*, edited by Bruce Jackson and Edward D. Ives, 1–17. Urbana: University of Illinois Press.

————, and Tacheeni Scott. 1981. "Poetic Retranslation and the 'Pretty Languages' of Yellowman." In *Traditional American Indian Literatures: Texts and Interpretations*, edited by Karl Kroeber, 65–116. Lincoln: University of Nebraska Press.

Toor, Frances. 1947. *A Treasury of Mexican Folkways*. New York: Crown Publishers.

Tosa, Marco. 1998. *Barbie: Four Decades of Fashion, Fantasy, and Fun*. New York: Harry N. Abrams.

Turkel, Ann Ruth. 1998. "All About Barbie: Distortions of a Transitional Object." *Journal of the American Academy of Psychoanalysis* 26:165–77.

Turner, Frederick Jackson. 1920. *The Frontier in American History*. New York: Henry Holt.

Turner, Victor W. 1968. "Myth and Symbol." *International Encyclopedia of Social Science*.

————. 1969. *The Ritual Process: Structure and Anti-Structure*. Chicago: Aldine Press.

————., ed. 1982. *Celebration: Studies in Festivity and Ritual*. Washington, D.C.: Smithsonian Institution Press.

"Twin Fates (and Dates) for Barbie and Kato." 1999. *Time*, 22 March, 121.

Tyson, Ruel W., Jr., James L. Peacock, and Daniel W. Patterson, eds. 1988. *Diversities of Gifts: Field Studies in Southern Religion*. Urbana: University of Illinois Press.

Urry, John. 1990. *The Tourist Gaze: Leisure and Travel in Contemporary Societies*. London: Sage Publications.

Wallmann, Steve. 1994. "Camas Valley Clovis Projectile Fragment." *Screenings*.

Wason-Ellam, Linda. 1997. "If Only I was Like Barbie." *Language Arts* 74:430–37.

Wasson, George B., Jr. 1991. "The Memory of a People: The Coquilles of the Southwest Coast." In *The First Oregonians*. Portland: Oregon Council for the Humanities.

Waterman, T. T. 1931. The Athapascan Indians of Southwestern Oregon and Northwestern California. Bureau of American Ethnology 3183, field notes. Washington, D. C. Smithsonian Institution.

Waugh, Evelyn. 1947. "Death in Hollywood." *Life*, 29 September, 77–84.

———. [1948] 1965. *The Loved One*. New York: Dell.

Webb, Walter Prescott. 1931. *The Great Plains*. Boston: Ginn and Company.

Welsch, Roger. 1976. *Tall Tale Postcards: A Pictorial History*. South Brunswick: A. S. Barnes.

Westenhouser, Kitturah B. 1994. *The Story of Barbie*. Paducah, Ky: Collector Books.

Whipple, Lucky. 1985. "Chookaloski Mare." In *Cowboy Poetry: A Gathering*, edited by Hal Cannon, 134–36. Salt Lake City: Gibbs M. Smith.

Willis, Paul E. 1977. *Learning to Labour: How Working-Class Kids Get Working-Class Jobs*. New York: Columbia University Press.

Wilson, William A. 1981. *On Being Human: The Folklore of Mormon Missionaries*. Sixty-Fourth Faculty Honor Lecture. Logan: Utah State University Press.

Wolf, Eric R. 1974. "American Anthropologists and American Society." In *Reinventing Anthropology*, edited by Dell Hymes, 251–63. New York: Vintage Press.

Wright, Kathryn. 1975. Manuscript. Brigham Young University Folklore Archives.

Wroth, William. n.d. "Miracles, Miraculous Images and Living Saints in Mexican Folk Catholicism." Manuscript in possession of James S. Griffith.

Wyman, Mark. 1979. *Hard Rock Epic: Western Miners and the Industrial Revolution, 1860–1910*. Berkeley: University of California Press.

Yocom, Margaret R. 1993. "'Awful Real': Dolls and Development in Rangeley, Maine." In *Feminist Messages: Coding in Women's Folk Culture*, edited by Joan Newlon Radner, 126–54. Urbana: University of Illinois Press.

Yoder, Don. 1974. "Toward a Definition of Folk Religion." *Western Folklore* 33:2–15.

Zelinsky, Wilbur. 1992. *The Cultural Geography of the United States*. Rev. ed. Englewood Cliffs, N. J.: Prentice-Hall.

Zenk, Henry B. 1990. "Siuslawans and Coosans." *Handbook of North American Indians*, 7:572–79. Washington, D. C.: Smithsonian Institution.

Notes on Contributors and Editors

MARGARET K. BRADY is a professor of English and American Indian studies at the University of Utah. Her first book, *"Some Kind of Power": Navajo Children's Skinwalker Narratives* (with an introduction by Barre Toelken), received the American Folklore Society's Benjamin Botkin Prize. *"Unselfish Usefulness": Mary Susannah Fowler, Mormon Poet and Folk Healer* (Utah State University Press) is scheduled for release late in 2000. Brady has also published articles on women's narrative traditions, the development of narrative competence, and ethnic folklore; she is a past editor of the journal *Western Folklore*.

HAL CANNON, founding director of the Western Folklore Center (1980) and the Cowboy Poetry Gathering in Elko, Nevada; founding folk arts coordinator for the Utah Arts Council (1976-85); and founding leader (1972) of the Deseret String Band/Bunkhouse Orchestra, has published a dozen books, exhibit catalogues, and recordings on the culture and folk arts of the West. He produces public-radio features such as the award-winning "Voices of the West," as well as "Folk Economy," and, with his wife, Teresa Jordan, "The Open Road." Cannon's achievements in public folklore have earned him awards from the Cowboy Hall of Fame, the governor of Utah, and the University of Utah. He also received the Will Rogers Lifetime Achievement Award.

RICHARD DAUENHAUER, a poet, writer, and translator, has lived in Alaska for over three decades, since his late twenties. He served as Alaska's poet laureate from 1981 to 1988 and won an American Book Award in 1991. Holding degrees in Slavic languages, German, and comparative literature, he has published several hundred poems from the German, Russian, classical Greek, Swedish, Finnish, and other languages. He is devoted to applied folklore, linguistics, and teacher training with regard to Alaska Native languages and oral literature, serving for several years as director of language and cultural studies at Sealaska Heritage Foundation, Juneau. He has taught at Alaska Methodist and Alaska Pacific Universities and the University of Alaska-Southeast.

Writer-scholar NORA MARKS DAUENHAUER was raised in Juneau and Hoonah, as well as on the family fishing boat and in seasonal subsistence sites around Icy Straits, Glacier Bay, and Cape Spencer. Her first language is Tlingit and she is widely recognized for her research and publication in Tlingit oral literature (she earned a degree in anthropology in 1976) in addition to creative writing (her Tlingit Raven plays have been staged in several venues internationally, including the Kennedy Center in Washington, D.C.). In 1991 she won an American Book Award from the Before Columbus Foundation. For several years she served as principal researcher in language and cultural studies at Sealaska Heritage Foundation in Juneau. She has four children, thirteen grandchildren, and three great-grandchildren. Together, Richard and Nora Marks Dauenhauer have coauthored and coedited several editions of Tlingit language and oral literature.

JAMES S. GRIFFITH retired in 1998 from the University of Arizona Library's Southwest Folklore Center, which he had run since 1979. He is currently a research associate at the University of Arizona's Southwest Center. A folklorist with a primary commitment to public-sector work, he also taught at the university and has published widely on the folklore, folk arts, and folklife of the Arizona-Sonora borderlands. His current projects include a survey of the religious art of Sonora, Mexico, and a book based on the material introduced in this article. Never a student of Barre Toelken's, Griffith has enjoyed the man and his work for almost thirty years.

SUZI JONES first met Barre Toelken when he gave a lecture on ballads to her junior English class at Ontario (Oregon) High School in 1963, and again when he spoke to Professor Attebery's English classes at the College of Idaho, where she received a B.A. in philosophy in 1968. Later, she became a graduate student of Toelken's, earning her Ph.D. from the University of Oregon in 1978. With Toelken as a mentor, she learned how to write and to teach and discovered that the distance between research and the real world needn't be great. She never has understood the dichotomy between "academic" and "public-sector" folklore. Author, editor, field researcher, festival organizer, curator, and administrator, she has worked as a folklorist for the Smithsonian Institution, the American Folklife Center, the Oregon Arts Commission (1977-80), and the Alaska State Council on the Arts (1980-86); as a senior program officer at the National Endowment for the Humanities (1986-97), and, since 1997, as deputy director at the Anchorage Museum of History and Art.

BARRY LOPEZ's books include a novella-length, illustrated fable called *Crow and Weasel*; *Arctic Dreams*, for which he received the National Book Award; and several collections of essays and short stories, among them *Field Notes*, *About This Life*, and *The Rediscovery of North America*. He lives in western Oregon.

ROBERT McCARL is an associate professor of anthropology at Boise State University. He has published in a variety of journals and anthologies on the subject of occupational culture. He is currently editing a collection of essays devoted to the study of work and completing a manuscript documenting several of the community-oriented projects he has conducted over the past fifteen years.

ELLIOTT ORING received his Ph.D. in folklore from Indiana University and is currently professor of anthropology at California State University, Los Angeles. He has written extensively about folklore, humor, and cultural symbolism. His books include *Israeli Humor: The Content and Structure of the Chizbat of the Palmah* (1981); *The Jokes of Sigmund Freud: A Study in Humor and Jewish Identity* (1984); *Humor and the Individual* (1984); and *Jokes and their Relations* (1992). He also edited *Folk Groups and Folklore Genres: An Introduction* (1986) and *Folk Groups and Folklore Genres: A Reader* (1989). He served as editor of *Western Folklore* and is currently on the editorial board of *Humor: International Journal of Humor Research*. Dr. Oring is a fellow of the American Folklore Society and a folklore fellow of the Finnish Academy of Science and Letters.

JAROLD RAMSEY grew up on a ranch near Madras, Oregon, and took degrees in English from the universities of Oregon and Washington. For many years he has been a member of the English faculty at the University of Rochester, in New York. His writings include four books of poetry, a collection of Oregon folk literature (*The Stories We Tell*, coedited with Suzi Jones), and several books on American Indian oral/traditional literature, including *Coyote Was Going There: Indian Literature of the Oregon Country*, and *Reading the Fire: Essays in the Traditional Indian Literatures of the Far West* (1983; revised and republished in 1999). All of his work on Indian narratives owes much, he says, to the writings and example of Barre Toelken.

TWILO SCOFIELD, of Eugene, Oregon, brought folklore and folk music into the public-school social-studies classroom, and over two decades taught many other teachers how to do the same. She has produced or participated in the production of many educational books, pamphlets, and videos on traditional arts and the integration of these into the curriculum, and has served on the arts and folk arts panels of the arts commissions of Idaho and Oregon. A singer and performer of traditional music, as well as composer and performer of songs, she has played and sung at conferences, workshops, concerts, benefits, and classrooms and on records, sound tracks, and television throughout the Pacific Northwest and elsewhere in the United States. She took coursework with Barre Toelken and performed folk music with him in various venues.

STEVE SIPORIN is associate professor of English and history at Utah State University. Barre Toelken introduced him to the study of folklore at the

University of Oregon in the early 1970s. Now he teaches a wide variety of folklore courses and writes on oral narrative, western folk art, and Italian-Jewish culture. His book, *American Folk Masters: The National Heritage Fellows*, celebrates a gifted group of American folk artists.

KIM STAFFORD studied Chaucer and folkore with Barre Toelken at the University of Oregon, and so charged, completed a Ph.D. in medieval literature there in 1979. He is an essayist and poet and directs the Northwest Writing Institute at Lewis & Clark College, where he teaches writing. His books include *Having Everything Right: Essays of Place*; *Lochsa Road: A Pilgrim in the West*; *A Thousand Friends of Rain: New & Selected Poems*; and *Wheel Made of Wind*, a CD of local songs.

POLLY STEWART was Barre Toelken's student at both the undergraduate and graduate levels. A professor of English at Salisbury (Maryland) University, she has conducted research in and taught subjects ranging from folklore and folklife through comparative mythology, Chaucer, Norse literature, Arthurian literature, and lesbian/gay literatures and cultures. She has written on women's folklore, traditional singing in Northern Idaho, the influence of folk regionalism in the shaping of historical events, coding in the Child Ballads, and a number of related folkloric, cultural, and literary topics.

C. W. SULLIVAN III is professor of English at East Carolina University and a member of the Welsh Academy. He is author of *Welsh Celtic Myth in Modern Fantasy*; editor of *The Mabinogi: A Book of Essays*; *The Dark Fantastic: Selected Essays from the Ninth International Conference on the Fantastic in the Arts*; *Science Fiction for Young Readers*; and *As Tomorrow Becomes Today*; and coeditor of *Herbal and Magical Medicine: Traditional Healing Today*. He is immediate past president of the International Association for the Fantastic in the Arts, editor of *Children's Folklore Review*, and editorial board member of *Para*doxa: Studies in World Literary Genres*. His articles on folklore, mythology, fantasy, and science fiction have appeared in a variety of anthologies and journals.

JEANNIE THOMAS does *not* have a room full of unboxed Barbies, nor does she have 236 Barbies lined up in her closet, roasting in her oven, or tied to the fence in her backyard. She did, however, have the good fortune to study with Barre Toelken, who as it turns out, has much in common with Barbie: he too has German roots, lives in the West, and plays western ballads on a guitar. Also, depending upon her incarnation, Barbie is Native American, Japanese, or Japanese-American—all cultures Toelken has written about with eloquence. A former editor of *Midwestern Folklore*, Jeannie Thomas is an associate professor of English and teaches in the folklore program at Utah State University with Toelken. Thomas's research interests include gender and folklore, legend, humor, and laughter. She is the author of *Featherless Chickens, Laughing*

Women, and Serious Stories, which received the Elli Köngäs-Maranda Prize of the American Folklore Society Women's Section in recognition of its contributions to feminist and gender studies.

GEORGE VENN, who holds a B.A. from Albertson College of Idaho and an M.F.A. from the University of Montana, has lived, studied, and taught in Ecuador, Spain, England, and China. He is the author of four books—*West of Paradise* (1999), *Marking the Magic Circle* (1987), *Off the Main Road* (1976), and *Sunday Afternoon: Grande Ronde* (1975). Venn's writing has been recognized regionally by the Northwest Writers' Andres Berger Award for Poetry (1995) and his editing distinguished by the Stewart Holbrook Award (1994) for the six-volume *Oregon Literature Series*. Nationally, he has been awarded a Pushcart Prize for Poetry (1980) and a Multicultural Publishing Award from the National Council of Teachers of English (1994). In 1987, Oregon State University Press described him as "an Oregon writer of uncommon sensitivity and skill and one of the most prominent regionalists of the Pacific Northwest." In 1970, he was appointed director of the Creative Writing Program at Eastern Oregon University, La Grande, where he is now writer-in-residence and professor of English.

GEORGE B. WASSON is an enrolled one-quarter Coos-Coquelle member of the Coquille Indian Tribe. Great-grandson of Kitzn-Jin-Jn-Galada-Lui ("Kitchen"), a Coos village headman, and Tcitc'kiu (Gishgiu), an upper Coquelle woman, grandson of their daughter Susan Adulsah and George R. Wasson, a Scottish immigrant, he grew up on the southern Oregon coast learning cultural and oral traditions from older relatives. After early retirement from a twenty-year career in academic administration at the University of Oregon, Wasson entered the graduate program in cultural anthropology there and is presently a Ph.D. candidate. His primary interest is in building and enriching the University of Oregon's Knight Library Special Collections archive of "lost" cultural information—historical, ethnographic, linguistic— on the Native peoples of the cultural "black hole"of southwest Oregon and northern California.

WILLIAM A. WILSON earned his Ph.D. in folklore from Indiana University. He has authored the prize-winning *Folklore and Nationalism in Modern Finland* (1976); *On Being Human: The Folklore of Mormon Missionaries* (1981); and numerous articles on folk religious narrative. He has served as editor of *Western Folklore* and as president of the Utah Folklore Society, as a member of the Utah Arts Council, as chair of the Folk Arts Panel of the National Endowment for the Arts, and as a member of the executive board of the American Folklore Society (AFS). A fellow of the AFS, Wilson is retired from Brigham Young University, where he was director of the Charles Redd Center for Western Studies.